PS Atiyah

EDINBURGH STUDIES IN LAW

Volumes in the series:

James Goudkamp (ed), *PS Atiyah: An Academic Autobiography* (2026)

Andrew R C Simpson and Jørn Øyrehagen Sunde (eds), *Comparative Perspectives in Scottish and Norwegian Legal History, Trade and Seafaring, 1200–1800* (2023)

Jonathan Hardman and Alisdair D J MacPherson (eds), *The Floating Charge in Scotland: New Perspectives and Current Issues* (2022)

Hector L MacQueen (ed), *Continuity, Influences and Integration in Scottish Legal History: Select Essays of David Sellar* (2022)

Guido Rossi (ed), *Authorities in Early Modern Law Courts* (2021)

John W Cairns, *Enlightenment, Legal Education, and Critique: Selected Essays on the History of Scots Law, Volume 2* (2015)

John W Cairns, *Law, Lawyers, and Humanism: Selected Essays on the History of Scots Law, Volume 1* (2015)

Paul J du Plessis and John W Cairns (eds), *Reassessing Legal Humanism and its Claims: Petere Fontes?* (2015)

Remus Valsan (ed), *Trusts and Patrimonies* (2015)

Eric Descheemaeker (ed), *The Consequences of Possession* (2014)

Neil Walker (ed), *MacCormick's Scotland* (2012)

Elaine E Sutherland, Kay E Goodall, Gavin F M Little and Fraser P Davidson (eds), *Law Making and the Scottish Parliament* (2011)

J W Cairns and Paul du Plessis (eds), *The Creation of the* Ius Commune*: From* Casus *to* Regula (2010)

James Chalmers, Lindsay Farmer and Fiona Leverick (eds), *Essays in Criminal Law in Honour of Sir Gerald Gordon* (2010)

Vernon Valentine Palmer and Elspeth Christie Reid (eds), *Mixed Jurisdictions Compared: Private Law in Louisiana and Scotland* (2009)

John W Cairns and Paul du Plessis (eds), *Beyond Dogmatics: Law and Society in the Roman World* (2007)

William M Gordon, *Roman Law, Scots Law and Legal History* (2007)

Kenneth G C Reid, Marius J de Waal and Reinhard Zimmermann (eds), *Exploring the Law of Succession: Studies National, Historical and Comparative* (2007)

Hector MacQueen and Reinhard Zimmermann (eds), *European Contract Law: Scots and South African Perspectives* (2006)

Elspeth Reid and David L Carey Miller (eds), *A Mixed Legal System in Transition: T B Smith and the Progress of Scots Law* (2005)

https://edinburghuniversitypress.com/series/esil

EDINBURGH STUDIES IN LAW
VOLUME 20

PS Atiyah

An Academic Autobiography

Edited by James Goudkamp

EDINBURGH
University Press

Edinburgh University Press is one of the leading university presses in the UK. Publishing new research in the arts and humanities, EUP connects people and ideas to inspire creative thinking, open new perspectives and shape the world we live in. For more information, visit www.edinburghuniversitypress.com.

Edinburgh University Press Ltd
13 Infirmary Street, Edinburgh EH1 1LT

Typeset in New Caledonia by
by Cheshire Typesetting Ltd, Cuddington, Cheshire, and
Printed and bound in the UK using 100% renewable electricity by
CPI Group (UK) Ltd

A CIP record for this book is available from the British Library

ISBN 978 1 3995 4984 4 (hardback)
ISBN 978 1 3995 4986 8 (webready PDF)
ISBN 978 1 3995 4985 1 (epub)

EU Authorised Representative:
Easy Access System Europe
Mustamäe tee 50, 10621 Tallinn, Estonia
gpsr.requests@easproject.com

MIX
Paper | Supporting responsible forestry
FSC www.fsc.org FSC® C013604

This book is printed using paper from well-managed forests, recycling and other controlled sources

Contents

Foreword

What can I say about this remarkable autobiography that Patrick Atyah wrote and set aside? I could note the many coincidental similarities in our backgrounds. Like him I was an outsider in my adopted country (America in my case, the UK in his) who came to be viewed as very much an insider. Like him I had a brilliant, scientist, older brother whom I spent my life trying to live up to. Like him I was at Magdalen College, Oxford in the early 1950's. And, while I did not read law, like him, I had interesting interchanges with Rupert Cross, John Morris and Guenter Treitel. And, most important, like him I focused my attention in law on Torts – on Civil Liability more generally – and took what was at the time an unusual, some would say paradigm breaking view of the subject. And these similarities, especially described so well in the picture that he draws of himself in this book, are worth a few words. But it is also worth noting how differently in the end our lives turned out.

Patrick wrote about Torts in the early 1960s in a way that was completely different from most English or European lawyers. He saw it as a public law area as much as a traditional private law discipline. This, as he writes, brought him to the attention of my then colleague and longtime friend Robert Stevens[1] and the *Law in Context* series. This led to Patrick's invitation to Yale Law School in 1968. Yale Law School, then as now, overly self-important, was not especially inclusive. But it did provide a base from which he could become immersed in the new approaches to civil liability that were bubbling here and in Canada. He met Al Conard at Michigan, Bob Keeton at Harvard, Allen Linden in Canada and of course me, who was already a very young full professor at Yale. All of us had had a significant influence on Geoffrey Palmer and the Right Honorable Sir Owen Woodhouse whose total reconstruction of accident law in New Zealand influenced Patrick greatly.

All his led him to write one of the three important reviews[2] of my first book, *The Costs of Accidents*. This book, which, published in 1970, pulled

1 At the time Professor at Yale Law School, subsequently President of Haverford College, and Master of Pembroke College, Oxford.

2 PS Atiyah, "Book review: *The Costs of Accidents* by G Calabresi" (1970) 44 *Australian Law Journal* 297.

together my writings from 1961 to 1970, became, as he notes in his autobiography, the foundation of an Economic Approach to Law. That approach, as he further says, was taken up by free marketeers (unfortunately perhaps) as the basis of some very "right-wing" (his word) views of appropriate legal structures. The three reviews are worth describing.

One by Frank Michelman of Harvard[3] took my work into the field of Property Law and ultimately led to my most cited article, "The Cathedral."[4] Another, by Richard Posner, liked the Welfare Economics side of my book, but was troubled by the more general social welfare, spreading and wealth distribution concerns in it.[5] Patrick's, in contrast, liked the latter discussions but was dubious about the more traditional economic, incentive-based parts of it. In time, however, Posner (especially as a Judge), came to accept some of my broader discussions. And, more germane, Patrick came to understand and use parts of the more traditional economic analysis. And this, I believe, led to some of his most productive and influential writings. As this book points out, he became, correctly, a dominant scholar and teacher in the UK In Civil Law, I would say, the dominant scholar.

But it is after this that his career and mine went in very different directions. At a point in our lives, when Posner and I became judges and came to use our academic insights in quite new ways, no such move was available to Patrick. Indeed, writing about his visit to America in 1968, he says – with perhaps a mite of gentle envy – about Allen Linden, whom, justly, he greatly admired, that he "was made a judge … something that can happen to Professors in America and Canada, but not in England". And so, tired of teaching and scholarship, he withdrew, and, as a result, his end-of-life writings became different in view and method and I fear overly negative and political.

It is not that there isn't something to be said for the positions he took. And had he become a judge, as Posner and I did, he might have moved in the same direction. Posner and I – as judges – both came to review and reconsider, in interesting ways, our earlier scholarly positions. But Patrick, from the sidelines as it were, wrote in some anger and so lost much of the

3 FI Michelman, "Pollution as a Tort: A Non-Accidental Perspective on Calabresi's Costs" (1971) 80 *Yale Law Journal* 647.

4 G Calabresi and AD Melamed, "Property Rules, Liability Rules, and Inalienability: One View of the Cathedral" (1972) 85 *Harvard Law Review* 1089.

5 RA Posner, "Book Review: *The Costs of Accidents* by G Calabresi" (1970) 67 *University of Chicago Law Review* 636.

wonderful nuance that make his earlier writings no less powerful, but more convincing.

All this, and much more, can be read, seen, or foreseen in Patrick's autobiography, which I believe is extraordinarily worth reading, for what it shows about a truly great scholar and human being and also for what it tells about the law and the legal academy in a fascinating time.

Guido Calabresi
July 23, 2025

Editor's Preface

A SERENDIPITOUS DISCOVERY

On 30 March 2018, Patrick Selim Atiyah, or PS Atiyah as he was known professionally, died. He was a legal scholar of the highest calibre. Writing predominantly from the mid-1950s to the late 1980s, he authored numerous works of great importance. These were concentrated in the areas of contract law and tort law. However, his interests extended far beyond these fields. He made significant contributions to understanding of the judiciary, the role of the academy, the similarities and differences between the legal cultures in Britain and the United States and the intersection between judge-made law and statutory law. His research was often enriched by insights from other disciplines, including economics, history, philosophy, politics and sociology. In 1982, Joseph Raz wrote that "Atiyah is not a philosopher using a few legal cases as illustration, nor is he a lawyer who uses the occasional philosophical argument. He is a great legal scholar who has studied the philosophical issues in detail and who speaks with equal confidence in both fields."[1] Ten years later, Tony Weir wrote that "Atiyah is unrivalled in the number, scope and quality of his contributions to English scholarship in the last 40 years".[2]

Soon after Atiyah's death, I was invited to write a memoir about him for the British Academy, of which he had been a Fellow. The invitation was very welcome. I had been a great admirer of Atiyah and looked forward to the opportunity to celebrate his accomplishments. Further, at the time I was writing a chapter concerning Atiyah's tort-related writings for a collection of essays entitled *Scholars of Tort Law*.[3] As a result, I was already immersed in Atiyah's work. After I had assembled a draft of the memoir, I was put in

1 J Raz, "Book review: Promises, Morals, and the Law by P. S. Atiyah" (1982) 95 *Harvard Law Review* 916, 917.

2 T Weir, "Book review: Essays for Patrick Atiyah" (1992) 51 *Cambridge Law Journal* 375, 376.

3 J Goudkamp, "Professor Patrick Atiyah (1931–2018)" in J Goudkamp and D Nolan (eds), *Scholars of Tort Law* (2019). For an analysis of Atiyah's contract law scholarship, see J Goudkamp, "Professor Patrick Atiyah (1931–2018)" in J Goudkamp and D Nolan (eds), *Scholars of Contract Law* (2022).

touch with Atiyah's family, who unearthed a largely unpublished autobiography that Atiyah had written in his retirement.[4] It opened up a new vista regarding him. It provided insight into his life and work that was previously unavailable. This meant that I needed to return to the drawing board as concerns the memoir. But the eventual product[5] was, I hope, far richer and nuanced in view of the autobiography. More significantly, studying the autobiography made it clear to me that it was a work of sufficient importance that it needed to be put into the public domain for the benefit of other researchers and interested readers more generally. Atiyah's personal correspondence makes it clear that he wished for it to be published, but he felt that the only autobiographies that are published are written by celebrities or full of sexual interest. His, he thought, did not qualify on either count.

ATIYAH'S EARLY LIFE

Patrick was born in England on 11 March 1931. He was the second of four children of Edward Atiyah, who was of Lebanese origins and a prolific author and political activist, and (Dorothy) Jean Levens, who was of Scottish descent. Edward and Jean met in Oxford, where Edward was reading history at Brasenose College. Jean was the sister of Robert Levens, who had long been the senior tutor at Merton College. Patrick's siblings were Michael, Selma and Joe. Both Michael and Patrick were raised in the Sudan where their father was employed as a schoolteacher and subsequently as a liaison between the Sudanese intelligentsia and the condominium administration. Patrick attended Victoria College in Egypt from age ten as a boarder on a Sudan government bursary. He did not enjoy his time at the school. He was subjected "to a fair amount of bullying" and was not "particularly successful academically, often averaging no better than halfway

4 Chapter 11 of the autobiography appears, with certain adjustments, in PS Atiyah, "An Autobiographical Fragment" in GP Wilson (ed), *Frontiers of Legal Scholarship* (1995). The autobiography is far from the only manuscript which Atiyah left unpublished. His personal papers include a large number of draft articles. These are entitled "Dorset Yacht Co Ltd v Home Office" (an article on the Court of Appeal's decision which he withdrew from the *Cambridge Law Journal* because the House of Lords delivered judgment in the proceedings before it could be published), "International Commercial Arbitration", "Liberalism and the Social Framework: The English Experience 1776–1914", "Social Change and the Law: The Last Fifty Years", "The Teaching of Tort Law", "Risk and the Law", "The Practice of Promising" and "Insurance and Accident Law in the Western World: New Trends and Prospects".

5 J Goudkamp, "Patrick Atiyah" (2020) 19 *Biographical Memoirs of Fellows of the British Academy* 149.

up the class".[6] He described "the school's religious approach [as] one of extreme tolerance, extending in practice to apathy".[7]

In 1950, Atiyah went up to Oxford. He had initially intended to read history or philosophy, politics and economics. However, shortly before he was due to take up his place he was involved in a motorcycle accident which resulted in his being convicted of a minor motoring offence. This brush with the law prompted him to switch to jurisprudence, which he read at Magdalen College. The chance collision in issue thus changed the course of his life. It is perhaps not a coincidence that the generally fortuitous nature of accidents would become a central theme in his scholarship. At Magdalen, Atiyah was taught principally by the powerhouse team of Rupert Cross (whom he admired and liked) and John Morris (whom he may have admired but did not like, and the antipathy appears to have been mutual).[8] He took his undergraduate degree with first class honours and then read for the Bachelor of Civil Law. During his studies, Atiyah married Christine Best. They had four children, Julian (1954), Andrew (1956), Simon (1961) and Jeremy (1962), who generally called Atiyah 'Pad' (in addition to 'dad').

ACADEMIC CAREER

Upon graduating from Oxford, Atiyah went on to have a glittering academic career which, in its earlier phases, was punctuated by intervals working as a government lawyer.[9] It began in 1954 at the London School of Economics where Atiyah worked as an Assistant Lecturer. His teaching responsibilities lay in the law of contract and the law of trusts. He found teaching the latter subject unrewarding, principally because the course focused on the black-letter rules divorced from their associated social context. While at the LSE, Atiyah published his first article, which concerned the tort of conversion.[10] He described the burden of that contribution as being to reject "the orthodox view"[11] that where "the defendant has not infringed the plaintiff's possession he may set up the jus tertii as a defence".[12]

6 See the autobiography, p 35.

7 ibid p 34.

8 Atiyah wrote in his autobiography p 60 that "Morris regarded me as conceited if not arrogant". It appears, however, that Atiyah and Morris may have reconciled later in their careers: see pp 112–113.

9 See the text accompanying nn 87–88.

10 PS Atiyah, "A Re-examination of the Jus Tertii in Conversion" (1955) 18 *Modern Law Review* 97.

11 ibid 97.

12 ibid 98.

In 1955, Atiyah moved (back) to the Sudan where he worked at the University of Khartoum for several years. He was appointed as a Lecturer and subsequently Senior Lecturer and headed the Commercial Law Department. One of his colleagues and neighbours was William Twining, who was a recurring figure throughout his career. Atiyah returned to Britain periodically including in 1956 in order to be called to the Bar by the Inner Temple. While in Khartoum, Atiyah wrote numerous case notes for the *Sudan Law Journal and Reports*, of which he served as the general editor in 1957.[13] These notes concerned the rights of an owner of property *vis-à-vis* its bona fide purchaser,[14] privity of contract,[15] the penalty doctrine,[16] the circumstances in which a court becomes *functus officio* and the "slip rule",[17] exemption clauses and the doctrine of frustration[18] and the distinction between a mere breach of contract and fraud.[19]

Atiyah also published in the *Sudan Law Journal and Reports* a draft Sale of Goods Bill, which he described as being "[b]roadly . . . based on the English Act, but [with] considerable alterations and emendations".[20] In addition, he wrote several substantial articles for other journals. These addressed the sale of non-existent goods,[21] the state of legal education in the Sudan,[22] hire-purchase agreements,[23] the requirement that a charity be for the benefit of the public or a section thereof[24] and equitable remedies against infants who commit fraud.[25] In his autobiography, he refers to these publications as being "the sort of fairly humdrum stuff which it is

13 See further W Twining, *Jurist in Context: A Memoir* (2019) 47–48.

14 PS Atiyah, "*Sudan Government v Bakheit Adam Mohammed* and the recovery of lost and stolen property ordinance, 1924" [1956] *Sudan Law Journal and Reports* 47.

15 PS Atiyah, "*Sid Ahmed Mohamed v Sudan Mercantile Co*" [1956] *Sudan Law Journal and Reports* 55 (note).

16 PS Atiyah, "*Roughdi Boutros v Christos Simos*" [1956] *Sudan Law Journal and Reports* 93 (note).

17 PS Atiyah, "*Hassan Khalil Suleiman v El A'Gig Ali and Christos Simos v Mohd. Ali Ahmed*" [1956] *Sudan Law Journal and Reports* 94 (note).

18 PS Atiyah, "*Abdel Gadir El Baloula v El Saggay Agricultural Scheme*" [1956] *Sudan Law Journal and Reports* 95 (note).

19 PS Atiyah, "*Sudan Government v Hirachand Jeraj Shah*" [1956] *Sudan Law Journal and Reports* 97 (note).

20 PS Atiyah, "A new Sale of Goods Bill" [1957] *Sudan Law Journal and Reports* 107.

21 PS Atiyah, "Couturier v Hastie and the Sale of Non-existent Goods" (1957) 73 *Law Quarterly Review* 340.

22 PS Atiyah, "Legal Education in the Sudan" (1957–58) 4 *Society of Public Teachers of Law* 137.

23 PS Atiyah, "Injustices and Anomalies in the Law of Hire Purchase" (1958) 5 *Business Law Review* 24.

24 PS Atiyah, "Public Benefit in Charities" (1958) 21 *Modern Law Review* 138.

25 PS Atiyah, "The Liability of Infants in Fraud and Restitution" (1959) 22 *Modern Law Review* 273.

the business of the academic to churn out".[26] Alongside these periodical writings, Atiyah published his first book, *The Sale of Goods*.[27] He would go on to produce a total of eight editions of that work, which turned out to be "the most successful and consistent seller" of the many books that he would ultimately write.[28]

After four years in Khartoum, Atiyah was "restless for change" and felt that his career was not developing as it should have.[29] He had applied unsuccessfully for positions at two Oxford colleges (one of the applications had been torpedoed by a critical reference written by John Morris) and for an Assistant Lectureship at Cambridge.[30] With the prospect of an Oxbridge post, which was then "the height of [his] ambition",[31] appearing not to be immediately on the cards, in 1959 he moved to Accra where he was employed on an eighteen-month contract by the Attorney-General's department. However, Atiyah quickly became disillusioned with both Ghana and his employment. This was at least in part due to "the general smell of corruption which hovered over government activities",[32] as well as "the increasing totalitarianism of the government".[33]

In 1961, Atiyah returned to England in order to take up employment as a legal assistant at the Board of Trade. In the same year, he published *An Introduction to the Law of Contract*,[34] which would become the classic student text on the subject in Britain and several other countries. Atiyah wrote the book, which formed part of the Clarendon Law series, at the invitation of HLA Hart acting on the suggestion of Rupert Cross. He would go on to produce a total of five editions.[35] The work was very positively received. In relation to the first edition, AG Guest wrote that the "book constitutes a most stimulating and original discussion of the basic principles of the law of

26 See the autobiography, p 74.
27 PS Atiyah, *The Sale of Goods* (1957).
28 See the autobiography, p 72.
29 ibid p 76.
30 ibid.
31 ibid.
32 ibid p 83.
33 ibid p 84.
34 PS Atiyah, *An Introduction to the Law of Contract* (1961).
35 Steve Smith was responsible for the sixth edition: SA Smith, *Atiyah's Introduction to the Law of Contract*, 6th edn (2005). It is evident from their respective prefaces that Smith and Atiyah did not see eye to eye in relation to it.

contract",[36] while JC Smith remarked that it brought a "fresh approach to old problems".[37]

In 1964, Atiyah was elected to a tutorial fellowship at New College, Oxford. He succeeded SFC Milsom, who departed in order to accept the position of Professor of Legal History at the LSE. Atiyah's law colleague at New College was the legendary Tony Honoré who had been appointed in the same year as Atiyah as a University Reader in Roman-Dutch Law. With this formidable team, New College must have had a respectable claim to being the strongest Oxbridge college in law. At the time, Atiyah's older brother, Michael, a mathematician, was a Professorial Fellow of the College (the Savilian Professor of Geometry, 1963–69). Having two Atiyahs at the same College caused no end of confusion to Oxford's mail service.[38]

Shortly before his fellowship commenced, Atiyah lost both of his parents in tragic circumstances. His mother, who suffered from severe depression, committed suicide,[39] and his father died from a heart attack while he was speaking at the Oxford Union (as Patrick and Christine were watching the debate from the public gallery).[40] These losses and their circumstances cannot but have had a profound impact upon Atiyah. It was at around this time that he discovered that he had inherited both his mother's tendency to depression as well as his father's weak heart.[41] While at New College, Atiyah wrote *Vicarious Liability in the Law of Torts*,[42] which was his first major work concerned with tort law. That monograph quickly earned positive reviews[43] and, despite its having been published in 1967, is "still the leading text on vicarious liability".[44]

36 AG Guest, "Book review: An Introduction to the Law of Contract by P. S. Atiyah" (1961) 24 *Modern Law Review* 658, 658.

37 JC Smith, "Book review: An Introduction to the Law of Contract by P. S. Atiyah" (1962) 7 *Journal of the Society of Public Teachers of Law* 42, 42.

38 M Atiyah, "Patrick Selim ATIYAH QC (Hon) FBA" *New College Record 2018* (2019) 89.

39 See the autobiography, p 107.

40 ibid.

41 ibid pp 107–108.

42 PS Atiyah, *Vicarious Liability in the Law of Torts* (1967).

43 See, e.g., JA Jolowicz, "Book review: Vicarious Liability in the Law of Torts by P. S. Atiyah" (1968) 26 *Cambridge Law Journal* 150; H Silberberg, "Book review: Vicarious Liability in the Law of Torts by P. S. Atiyah" (1969) 2 *Comparative and International Law Journal of Southern Africa* 357; PD McKenzie, "Book review: Vicarious Liability in the Law of Torts by P. S. Atiyah" (1968–70) 5 *Victoria University of Wellington Law Review* 272; cf the mixed review in H Street, "Book review: Vicarious Liability in the Law of Torts by P. S. Atiyah" (1968) 13 *Society of Public Teachers of Law* 57.

44 R Stevens, *Torts and Rights* (2007) 259.

After a few years, Atiyah found Oxford's tutorial system deadening and, when an opportunity to move to Australia arose, he took it. Thus, in 1969 he moved down under to take up a chair at the Australian National University at the relatively young age of thirty-eight. Alan (later Lord) Rodger succeeded him at New College. Atiyah initially enjoyed life and work in Australia. While at the ANU, he published what is arguably his most significant book, *Accidents, Compensation and the Law*.[45] That work, which is discussed in further detail below, offered a revolutionary perspective on tort law in that it perceived it as just one of many overlapping systems that dealt with personal injury and death resulting from accidents. Atiyah argued that chance usually determined which system (if any) applied.

In the event, Atiyah's stay in Australia was short-lived. His eldest son had become the subject of police interest or, more accurately, persecution. By 1973, the matter had become sufficiently serious that Atiyah decided that he needed to leave the country in order to protect his young family. He returned to England to work at the University of Warwick. He had been recruited by his friend Twining,[46] who had himself accepted a position there in 1972. Overall, Atiyah did not enjoy his time at Warwick, although his views may have been coloured by the fact that at around this time he became deeply depressed. He had to labour under the effects of medication that he had been prescribed in an attempt to combat the condition. In Atiyah's eyes, a redeeming feature of Warwick was, however, its library, which had integrated the law collection with materials from the other social sciences. This permitted him easily to access non-legal materials that informed his legal research. It was not a coincidence that it was at this time that Atiyah embarked on writing his *The Rise and Fall of Freedom of Contract*.[47] This work, which is a masterpiece in interdisciplinary scholarship, is addressed further below.

In 1977, Atiyah returned to Oxford to take up a chair, the Professorship of English Law, which is affiliated with St John's College. He succeeded William Wade, who had been appointed Master of Gonville and Caius College, Cambridge. Atiyah records that receiving the letter of appointment from the University Registrar "was one of the greatest moments" of his life.[48] His inaugural lecture, which was subsequently published as a short book, was entitled *From Principles to Pragmatism: Changes in the Function*

45 PS Atiyah, *Accidents, Compensation and the Law* (1970).
46 Twining (n 13) 155.
47 PS Atiyah, *The Rise and Fall of Freedom of Contract* (1979).
48 See the autobiography, p 164.

of the Judicial Process and the Law.[49] Its burden was to probe the tension between what Atiyah identified as being the two principal functions of the judicial role, namely, peacefully to resolve conflicts between disputants and to establish rules designed to encourage or discourage particular types of behaviour in the future. Atiyah's overarching thesis was that there had been a steady shift in favour of the former objective with the result that English judges were becoming increasingly focused on achieving pragmatic outcomes rather than on questions of principle.

As the holder of a statutory chair, Atiyah was not required to provide tutorials and he instead delivered a relatively small number of lectures and seminars. He found this method of instruction more enjoyable. As to his lecturing style, Atiyah was engaging and energetic and he not infrequently fulminated against judges and scholars with whose opinions he disagreed. This, coupled with frequent and pronounced gesticulations, made him a highly memorable speaker. Even when difficult to follow, he communicated his enthusiasm. Ultimately, however, he considered teaching to be something of a distraction from his research, which was his real passion.

By the 1980s, Atiyah had gained a formidable international reputation. He was regularly invited to give named lectures across the common law world. These included, most notably, the Oliver Wendell Holmes Lectures at Harvard Law School in 1981. His concern in the papers that he delivered[50] was to test against criminal law, tort law and contract law in England Holmes's theory that the primary purpose of the law is to "induce external conformity to rule" and that moral blameworthiness is not generally required for liability.[51] In 1988, Atiyah retired prematurely on account of serious health problems.[52] As well as his having been afflicted by chronic and sometimes severe depression intermittently throughout his career, he had long had trouble on account of congenital defects with his heart, having suffered from a cardiac arrest when he was around forty years old and having undergone heart bypass surgery in 1987.

Atiyah and Christine moved to Hayling Island where their son, Andrew, was living nearby. Atiyah enjoyed cooking, listening to classical music (which

49 PS Atiyah, *From Principles to Pragmatism: Changes in the Function of Judicial Process and the Law* (1978).

50 Atiyah delivered three papers. One of them was published as PS Atiyah, "The Legacy of Holmes through English Eyes" (1983) 63 *Boston University Law Review* 341.

51 OW Holmes, *The Common Law* (1963) 42.

52 Atiyah (n 38) 59.

he described as being "one of the pleasures of [his] life"),[53] tending to his garden and reading (in a range of fields but especially history and politics). Although claiming to be "bored with law" and to have given it up (at least when he wished to decline professional invitations), he published several scholarly works during his retirement the most significant of which is *The Damages Lottery*,[54] which is addressed below. Atiyah and Christine suffered tragedy when their youngest son, Jeremy, a journalist, died suddenly and unexpectedly on 12 April 2006 in Italy. Jeremy was a travel writer and at one stage wrote for *The Independent*.[55] At the funeral, Atiyah read out several letters that Jeremy had written home over the years.

ATIYAH'S SCHOLARSHIP

In this section, attention is turned to some of Atiyah's principal publications, which are taken chronologically. The selection is inevitably somewhat a matter of personal preference. The first is *Accidents, Compensation and the Law*.[56] Written for the famous *Law in Context* series at the request of Twining,[57] it presented a novel way of looking at tort law, namely, viewing it as just one of several mechanisms for delivering compensation for personal injury and death resulting from accidents. In the twenty-first century, it is easy to fail to appreciate the contemporary originality of this approach. In order properly to grasp the revolutionary methodology pioneered in the book we must put out of our minds the last fifty years of legal scholarship. When Atiyah wrote *Accidents, Compensation and the Law*, the leading work on torts in England was *Salmond on the Law of Torts*.[58] This was an important textbook that exerted a powerful influence on the courts. However, it was deeply committed to describing faithfully the law as established by the authorities.[59] By presenting tort law as merely one of many parallel

53 See the autobiography, p 50.

54 PS Atiyah, *The Damages Lottery* (1997).

55 *The Independent* published an obituary: see https://www.independent.co.uk/news/obituaries/jeremy-atiyah-6103673.html.

56 Atiyah (n 45).

57 Twining (n 13) 154. The origins of *Accidents, Compensation and the Law* and the genesis of the *Law in Context* series are explored in W Twining, "Reflections on Law in Context" in P Cane and J Stapleton (eds), *Essays for Patrick Atiyah* (1991).

58 *Salmond on the Law of Torts* was first published in 1907: J Salmond, *Law of Torts* (1907). Atiyah himself described *Salmond* as "the most influential English torts book of the twentieth century": Atiyah (n 50) 352.

59 For a searching examination, see M Lunney, "Professor Sir John Salmond (1862–1924): An Englishman Abroad" in Goudkamp and Nolan, *Scholars of Tort Law* (n 3).

compensation systems, *Accidents, Compensation and the Law* could not have contrasted more sharply with *Salmond*. Twining, who felt that as a student he had been betrayed by *Salmond* in that it presented a picture of the law of torts that was fundamentally divorced from its practical operation, puts the matter in the following understated but nevertheless revealing terms:[60]

> Atiyah's method is interesting in contrast to traditional Torts textbooks. First, his *standpoint* was of a mildly Fabian legal scholar talking *about* the Tort system in general, rather than expounding its rules in detail. Secondly, it was critical, with a clear sense of the underlying *political values and rationales*. Thirdly, it was concerned with the *actual operation* of the relevant law; fourthly, it substituted "compensation for accidents" (not a doctrinal concept) for "Torts" and "Negligence" as *the organising concept* and this provided a basis for comparing different compensation regimes and showing up the injustices, incoherence and anomalies of the situation. Fifthly, he explained the situation largely in terms of a *history* of piecemeal growth without any coherent guiding principles or ideology. Finally, the book is explicitly addressed to law students to help them to *understand* the existing system; the explicit *critique and recommendations* were largely confined to a relatively short last chapter.

The second book that deserves attention is *The Rise and Fall of Freedom of Contract*,[61] which Atiyah wrote predominantly while he was at Warwick and which he describes in his autobiography as his "*magnum opus*".[62] It explores in almost 800 pages the concept of freedom of contract in view of the environment in which, according to Atiyah, it flourished and then wilted.[63] Its overarching claims are that classical contract theory had proven to be a failure and that "far from being the typical case of obligation", contractual liability "may be a projection of liabilities based on benefit or reliance".[64] The work is a thoroughly interdisciplinary one that draws extensively on economic, historical, political and sociological literature. Indeed, to some extent, these other fields, rather than the law, were Atiyah's primary concern.

The book is divided into three temporal periods. The first is concerned with matters prior to 1770, which Atiyah regarded as the formative period for the idea of freedom of contract. During this stage, there was, Atiyah

60 Twining (n 13) 155 (emphasis in original).

61 Atiyah (n 47).

62 See the autobiography, pp 172, 178.

63 *The Rise and Fall of Freedom of Contract* was preceded by an important article published shortly before the book appeared in print: PS Atiyah, "Contracts, Promises and the Law of Obligations" (1978) 94 LQR 193.

64 Atiyah (n 47) 4.

concluded, no general theory of contractual liability and promises played a subordinate role in the creation of obligations. The second period encompassed 1770 to 1870, which Atiyah called the age of freedom of contract. It was characterised by the flourishing of general principles of contract law that were intimately linked with the development of the free market. The third stage concerned the century from 1870 to 1970. This period involved the decline and fall of freedom of contract.

A deluge of mostly favourable reviews promptly ensued. Writing in the *Yale Law Journal* Charles Gray referred to "Professor Atiyah's extraordinary mastery of literature from many fields"[65] and remarked that he had "almost singlehandedly created nineteenth-century legal history in the main stream of general history".[66] Charles Fried, while disagreeing vigorously with many of Atiyah's claims, admired "not only the compendiousness of [his] learning, but his wit and imagination as well".[67] John Baker's review was mixed. He acknowledged Atiyah's "massive work".[68] But he was somewhat critical of it as an analysis of legal history and characterised it instead as "a monument of intellectual history".[69]

In the preface to *The Rise and Fall of Freedom of Contract*, Atiyah wrote that it would be the first stage of a two-part study regarding the theory of contractual and promissory liability.[70] The second stage, he said, would "explore the interrelationship of modern contract law with the underlying theories and values of modern England".[71] Alas, the other half of the grand project was never written, although extensive notes were prepared and survive today. It is unclear why the project was abandoned. One possibility lies in the fact that Atiyah's thesis that freedom of contract had been rejected was shown by various developments in Britain and elsewhere during the 1980s to be radically mistaken.[72] It may also have been the case that Atiyah simply no longer had the energy required for another vast undertaking.[73]

65 CM Gray, "Book review: The Rise and Fall of Freedom of Contract by P. S. Atiyah" 90 *Yale Law Journal* (1980) 216, 231.

66 ibid.

67 C Fried, "Book review: The Rise and Fall of Freedom of Contract by P. S. Atiyah" (1980) 93 *Harvard Law Review* 1858, 1860.

68 JH Baker, "Book review: The Rise and Fall of Freedom of Contract by P. S. Atiyah" (1980) 43 *Modern Law Review* 467, 467.

69 ibid 469.

70 Atiyah (n 47) vii.

71 ibid.

72 Among many works concerned with the intellectual revival of freedom of contract, see FH Buckley (ed), *The Fall and Rise of Freedom of Contract* (1999).

73 See the autobiography, p 161.

In the event, Atiyah would go on to write a different book – the third in the present selection – loosely connected with contract law, namely, *Promises, Morals, and Law*.[74] This was not so much a work on contract law as a philosophical enquiry as to the nature of promises. Its thesis was that:[75]

> the mere fact of expectations and of reliance (however intentionally induced) cannot alone create the grounds upon which promises are held to be obligatory. Something else is needed before this conclusion can be reached. The extra element, it is suggested, is compliance with some socially accepted values which determine when expectations and/or reliance are sufficiently justifiable to be given some measure of protection.

The book was greeted by numerous reviews. The originality of Atiyah's enterprise was readily acknowledged but the analysis garnered few supporters.[76] Atiyah's thesis was variously described as resting "on an unpersuasive attack on prior doctrine and an unwarranted faith in the morality of social practices",[77] being "gravely weakened once [his] generalisations about the law are undermined",[78] depending on "an untenable view of promises" and "a distorted doctrine of their relation to the law".[79]

The fourth book is *The Damages Lottery*,[80] which Atiyah wrote in his retirement. Its title, an obvious allusion to Terrence Ison's *The Forensic Lottery*,[81] showed the influence of that work on Atiyah's thinking. Atiyah made two overarching claims. The first was that, subject to limited exceptions, the tort system should be dismantled. Atiyah complained that it "is as unjust and inefficient as it could be"[82] and "built on . . . rotten foundations".[83] He pointed in this regard to, in particular, the fact that it delivered compensation based on luck rather than need, that it probably had no meaningful deterrent effects and that it was delay stricken and costly to administer. In advancing this critique, Atiyah was not crossing virgin territory. Many other

74 PS Atiyah, *Promises, Morals, and Law* (1982).

75 ibid 68.

76 Hugh Collins described it as "highly innovative": H Collins, "Counsel to Philosophers" (1982) 45 *Modern Law Review* 225, 226.

77 Anonymous, "Book review: Promises, Morality and the Law by P. S. Atiyah" (1983) 31 *Michigan Law Review* 899, 903.

78 Collins (n 76) 228.

79 Raz (n 1) 938.

80 Atiyah (n 54). The book built upon PS Atiyah, "Personal Injuries in the Twenty-first Century: Thinking the Unthinkable" in P Birks (ed), *Wrongs and Remedies in the Twenty-First Century* (1996).

81 T Ison, *The Forensic Lottery: A Critique on Tort Liability as a System for Personal Injury Compensation* (1967).

82 Atiyah (n 54) 2.

83 ibid 93.

scholars, including Ison, had mounted similar attacks on the tort system, but few had done so with Atiyah's rhetorical skill. Atiyah's second claim, however, was arrestingly original. He contended that after tort law had been largely eliminated nothing needed to be put in its place. The vacuum created by the removal of the tort system would induce members of society to purchase first-party accident insurance, which he regarded as a preferable way of dealing with losses caused by accidents. It appears that Atiyah's most fundamental reason for not suggesting (as he had earlier in his career) that a social security system should fill the gap left by the retrenchment of tort law lay in the fact that welfare state ideals had fallen out of favour. In the modern age, a market solution was preferable, he argued.

Atiyah wrote *The Damages Lottery* primarily for popular consumption.[84] This is noteworthy partly because few legal scholars aim their work at the layperson, and even smaller numbers are able to do so successfully. Atiyah positioned *The Damages Lottery* in this way because he felt that reform could be achieved only if there were a sufficient shift in public attitudes concerning tort law. The public, he felt, needed to understand why the tort system had gone horribly wrong and what needed to be done in order to fix the problem. Only then could the political momentum necessary for change be achieved. Atiyah considered that the various stakeholders, including the Law Commission of England and Wales, were far too committed to the existing system to be able to effect of their own motion the type of reforms that he had in mind.[85] Atiyah's efforts, however, were unavailing, as the system continued substantially unchanged.

SELECTED THEMES

At this juncture, there are a few key themes regarding Atiyah that can usefully be identified. The first is that he had a restless disposition, which was perhaps inculcated by his having frequently travelled during his childhood.[86] This manifested itself in various ways. Atiyah switched employers reasonably regularly throughout his career. As observed above, he worked at the

84 Atiyah wrote one other book that was aimed primarily at the layperson, namely, PS Atiyah, *Law and Modern Society* (1983). He made various further attempts to bring legal issues to the public's attention. For example, he regularly wrote law-related letters to the editor of *The Times*, and participated in a television programme in which he addressed the liability of pharmaceutical companies for birth defects: see the autobiography, pp 175–176.

85 Atiyah (n 54) 173.

86 See the autobiography, p 22.

LSE, the University of Khartoum, the University of Oxford, the Australian National University, the University of Warwick and then again at Oxford and never spent more than around a decade at any one institution. Nor did he remain, during his working life, in a given country for much longer than around that amount of time either. The world was a much larger place in Atiyah's time than it is today, and his relocating to regions of the world remote from Britain (even if they were formerly part of the Empire) may have been perceived by some as somewhat unusual. One senses that Atiyah's desire for variability in his life also accounts for the fact that his research interests were unusually wide.

Another theme concerns Atiyah's interest with the practical. Although he ultimately became a career academic, he developed a significant amount of professional experience in the law. This practical work clearly left an impact on him and his scholarship. This is apparent from the fact that he dedicated chapters of his autobiography to the relevant periods of his life.[87] Furthermore, a sizeable proportion of Atiyah's work was written with an eye to the law's practical applications and effects. To a substantial extent, it was also reform orientated. Atiyah described himself as "basically an academic, with some leaning towards the world of practical law".[88]

Atiyah (like his father) was very internationally orientated, perhaps unsurprisingly given the range of countries in which he lived. He was particularly interested in the solutions to legal problems which had been arrived at in other jurisdictions, and studied the law in, in particular, the United States in detail. Unusually for a British legal scholar, both in his time and now, he wrote articles for an extensive assortment of law journals in that country.[89] His interest in the law in the United States culminated in his writing, together with Robert Summers, *Form and Substance in Anglo-American Law: A Comparative Study of Legal Reasoning, Legal Theory, and Legal Institutions*.[90]

87 ibid chs 6 and 8–9.

88 ibid p 80.

89 Illustrations include PS Atiyah, "Liability for Railway Nuisance in the English Common Law: A Historical Footnote" (1980) 23 *Journal of Law and Economics* 191; PS Atiyah, "No Fault Compensation: A Question That Will Not Go Away" (1980) 54 *Tulane Law Review* 271; PS Atiyah, "From Principles to Pragmatism: Changes in the Function of the Judicial Process and the Law" (1980) 65 *Iowa Law Review* 1249; PS Atiyah, "The Theoretical Basis of Contract Law – An English Perspective" (1981) 1 *International Review of Law and Economics* 183; PS Atiyah, "Lawyers and Rules: Some Anglo-American Comparisons" (1983) 37 *Southwestern Law Journal* 545.

90 PS Atiyah and RS Summers, *Form and Substance in Anglo-American Law: A Comparative Study of Legal Reasoning, Legal Theory, and Legal Institutions* (1987). See the autobiography, p 186.

Atiyah was a dedicated and well-organised teacher. He prepared his lectures meticulously. This is clear from those of his lecture notes that survive. To give an illustration, when he returned to Oxford in 1977, he taught part of a course in Commercial Law which was dedicated to "The Law of International Trade". His notes run to 132 pages of typed text. They read in a manner similar to a textbook. Atiyah's concern with legal education regularly manifests itself in the autobiography. He constantly compares and contrasts different methods of delivering tuition. Interestingly, however, he never considered himself to be a particularly able educator. He wrote that he "was far more interested in [his] own research", and that he was "not a particularly gifted teacher".[91]

It is obvious that Atiyah must have been ferociously hard-working, it being quite impossible for his massive volume of writings to have been yielded without relentless industry. In "manic phases", he would write around 8,000 words per day.[92] Although he would return home in time for dinner with his family, he would generally spend the evenings reading and jotting down ideas as they occurred to him. Work was a passion for him rather than a chore. At times, Atiyah was so consumed by his work that he took sedatives in the evening in order to enable his "restless mind to get some sleep".[93]

Consider, finally, Atiyah's highly distinctive writing style. It was exceptionally engaging. Joseph Raz referred to Atiyah's prose as "vigorous and lucid",[94] while AG Guest remarked that "Mr. Atiyah has a lively and interesting style which is frequently coupled with felicitous, if caustic, turns of phrase".[95] Although Atiyah was often prolix his writing was exhaustive rather than exhausting and never dreary or difficult to understand. His work was generally lightly referenced, which is consistent with his interest usually lying not in the minutiae of cases and statutes but in wider concerns although it can also be attributed, at least in part, to the fact that nearly all of Atiyah's research was done in the pre-internet age and at a time when paid research assistance was essentially non-existent. The often sparse footnoting had the advantage of preventing his readers (and perhaps Atiyah, too) from becoming bogged down in the detail.

91 See the autobiography, p 169.
92 ibid p 166.
93 ibid p 161.
94 Raz (n 1) 916.
95 Guest (n 36) 658.

INFLUENCE

It does not appear that Atiyah's thinking was shaped in any fundamental way by any one scholar. This is perhaps unsurprising given that his principal tutors when he was a student at Oxford, Rupert Cross and John Morris, were not specialists in the fields of law that became his focus.[96] Having said that, Atiyah naturally built to a degree on the work of others. Much of his research regarding accident compensation systems was influenced by writers in Canada (especially Allen Linden) and the United States (particularly Guido Calabresi, Terrence Ison[97] and Jeffrey O'Connell). Grant Gilmore's *The Death of Contract*[98] had been the catalyst for Atiyah's *The Rise and Fall of Freedom of Contract*.[99] Indeed, Atiyah was so concerned with North American scholarship that he made frequent research visits to, in particular, the United States, and spent a meaningful proportion of his career ensconced in a range of its universities. He was eager to forge personal connections with leading thinkers and to debate issues with them face to face.

In terms of influence on others, Atiyah certainly shaped scholarly debates about the law, both here and abroad. This is apparent from the fact that his research was, for example, addressed in a *Festschrift*.[100] To give another illustration, Atiyah and Summers' *Form and Substance in Anglo-American Law*[101] inspired a major international conference that was convened in 2018.[102] Conversely, Atiyah's impact on judicial decisions appears to have been rather muted overall. This is probably unsurprising given the radical nature of many of his ideas. The real significance of Atiyah's work lies, therefore, mainly in its contribution to academic dialogue in the fields in which he worked.

Extensive efforts have been made to identify doctoral students whom Atiyah supervised. Jane Stapleton, one of the great torts scholars of her generation, was among them. In 1984, she completed a doctoral thesis entitled "Compensation for Disease".[103] However, it is unclear whether Atiyah had any other research students. Given that it was much less common for

96 The main exception to this concerns Atiyah's interest in the doctrine of precedent. Here there was an overlap with Cross's research, as Cross had co-authored a book on the subject. The last edition was R Cross and JW Harris, *Precedent in English Law*, 4th edn (1991).

97 See the next accompanying n 81 above.

98 G Gilmore, *The Death of Contract* (1974).

99 See the autobiography, p 159.

100 Cane and Stapleton, *Essays for Patrick Atiyah* (n 57).

101 Atiyah and Summers (n 90).

102 The conference proceedings were published in A Robertson and J Goudkamp (eds), *Form and Substance in the Law of Obligations* (2019).

103 The thesis was later published as J Stapleton, *Disease and the Compensation Debate* (1988).

students to read for doctoral degrees in his time than it is today, it is possible that he had no other supervisees. In terms of examinees, in 1984, Atiyah assessed together with John Baker a doctoral thesis by Vernon Palmer on privity in contract.[104] Palmer would go on to have an illustrious career as a comparative lawyer. In terms of undergraduates who Atiyah taught while at New College, they included Andrew Ashworth (who would go on to hold the Vinerian chair at Oxford) as well as Gerald Barling (who would become a Judge of the High Court of England and Wales).

OVERSHADOWED BY MICHAEL ATIYAH?

It appears that Patrick felt himself as living in the shadow of his older (and clearly the senior) brother, Michael, who was one of the world's most celebrated mathematicians. As Patrick puts it in his autobiography, "whether as a result of age, ability or personality, Michael was decidedly a leader and I a follower".[105] Although Patrick had risen to the apex of the legal academy and was one of the best-known scholars in his fields in the common law world, Michael's accolades were in a different league. His many academic and state honours included being elected, at the age of thirty-three, as a Fellow of the Royal Society (1962), being awarded the Fields Medal (1966) and being made a Knight Bachelor (1983) and member of the Order of Merit (1992). In 1990, he was elected as the Master of Trinity College, Cambridge (where he had studied as a student) as well as the President of the Royal Society. Michael amassed more than thirty honorary degrees (whereas Patrick had (merely) two, from Oxford (1974) and Warwick (1989)).

Michael and Patrick argued boisterously with each other at family gatherings about all manner of subjects but especially politics, with Michael's inclinations being more to the left, and Patrick's sympathies lying to the right and increasingly so as the years rolled by. Even though they met relatively infrequently in their later lives due to their often being based in different countries, and despite there being something of a rivalry between them,[106]

104 The thesis was later published as V Palmer, *The Paths to Privity: A History of Third Party Beneficiary Contracts at English Law* (1992).

105 See the autobiography, p 18.

106 Patrick gave Michael a copy of his *Festschrift* (see n 100) and added to it the following inscription:

> "To Michael,
> from your undistinguished brother, so strangely honoured by the OUP and various authors,
> Patrick, 6 Jan 1992
> Sibling rivalry runs deep".

Patrick and Michael enjoyed a warm relationship with each other and had done so since they were young. While a student at Cambridge, Michael would ride to visit Patrick in Oxford on what he described as a "dangerous motorcycle" with James Mackay (later the Lord Chancellor) as a pillion passenger. And when Michael was appointed the Master of Trinity College in 1990, Patrick attended the ceremony and he and Michael and their brother Joe posed for photographs together.[107] Michael, who read at least some of Patrick's books,[108] died not long after Patrick, on 11 January 2019.

RIVALRY WITH GUENTER TREITEL

One of Atiyah's contemporaries at Oxford was Guenter Treitel, who was also a towering figure in the field of contract law.[109] Given that their careers and interests overlapped, they are regularly compared and contrasted with each other. Their notoriously difficult relationship is addressed in the autobiography.[110] Initially, it appears that Atiyah and Treitel got on well. Consistent with this they co-authored, early in their careers, an article about the Misrepresentation Act 1967.[111] However, things deteriorated fairly rapidly thereafter. There were several noteworthy developments in this connection.

Atiyah's inaugural lecture at the Australian National University, which he delivered in 1971, was entitled "Consideration in Contracts: A Fundamental Restatement".[112] He described it as an attempt to reinterpret the doctrine of consideration in order to take proper account of the way in which it was applied by the courts. Basic ideas usually thought to be central to the law of consideration, such as "benefit" and "detriment", were said to be neither sufficient nor necessary to amount to consideration. Treitel wrote a review of the lecture in the *Australian Law Journal*.[113] It was hard-hitting by the

107 See the autobiography, p 200.

108 Interview with Michael Atiyah (Oxford, 10 November 2018).

109 See FMB Reynolds, "Guenter Heinz Treitel 26 October 1928–14 June 2019" (2021) 19 *Biographical Memoirs of Fellows of the British Academy* 129; A Burrows, "Professor Sir Guenter Treitel (1928–2019)" in Goudkamp and Nolan, *Scholars of Contract Law* (n 3).

110 See the autobiography, pp 163, 170–172.

111 PS Atiyah and GH Treitel, "Misrepresentation Act 1967" (1967) 30 MLR 369.

112 Later published as PS Atiyah, *Consideration in Contracts: A Fundamental Restatement* (1971).

113 GH Treitel, "Consideration: A Critical Analysis of Professor Atiyah's Fundamental Restatement" (1976) 50 *Australian Law Journal* 439.

standards of the time.[114] Atiyah was said to have been guilty of a "striking omission" in failing to consider the rule that the courts do not generally have regard to the adequacy of consideration,[115] and his explanation as to why executory and bilateral agreements are enforceable was castigated as being "far from conclusive".[116]

In 1977, Atiyah was elected to the Professorship of English Law at Oxford. Treitel had also applied for the position. He was severely aggrieved that Atiyah had been appointed instead of him and considered that he had been passed over. The pill must have been particularly bitter to swallow in circumstances where Treitel was senior to Atiyah. Treitel had been a fellow of Magdalen College when Atiyah was one of its students and had seemingly taught him.[117] Further, by the time of his application, Treitel had been a fellow at Oxford for more than twenty years and, in 1974, had been promoted to the position of All Souls Reader in English Law (which apparently did not require him to be a member of All Souls). Atiyah's contributions to Oxford, by contrast, had been far more modest. He had served for a grand total of five years, as a tutorial fellow of New College, from 1964 until 1969.

Although Treitel was elected a few years later to the more prestigious Vinerian chair, this did not result in any rapprochement. On the contrary, there was further falling out over a postgraduate course entitled "Remedies in Contract and Tort" which Atiyah created upon taking up his chair at Oxford.[118] Treitel objected to its being established on, it seems, the basis that it would erode interest in a course which he was running concerned with the law of restitution. Atiyah says resigned from the Law Faculty's governing board in protest and withdrew his inaugural lecture from the *Oxford Journal of Legal Studies* of which Atiyah was the editor.[119] It appears that the two exchanged scarcely a word with each other during the remainder of their careers.

114 A kinder review was offered in JU Lewis, "Book review: Consideration in Contracts by P. S. Atiyah" (1972) 50 *Canadian Bar Review* 353.

115 Treitel (n 113) 439.

116 ibid 442.

117 See D Foxton, "Afterword" in J Goudkamp and D Nolan (eds), *Scholars of Commercial Law* (forthcoming).

118 See the autobiography, pp 170–172.

119 Treitel opted instead to publish the lecture as a pamphlet: GH Treitel, *Doctrine and Discretion in the Law of Contract: An Inaugural Lecture delivered before the University of Oxford on 7 March 1980* (1981).

THE AUTOBIOGRAPHY

It is unclear when, precisely, the autobiography was written. However, certain passages in it suggest that Atiyah wrote it in around 1989.[120] Consistent with this, the story largely peters out after this time. Whatever the position, it is apparent that Atiyah returned to the autobiography intermittently to update it. Thus, the latest date reference in the autobiography is to 2009.[121] It is evident that Atiyah wrote his autobiography with the benefit of various documents to hand. He quotes periodically from a number of sources (for example, his personal correspondence). It is not, in other words, simply a product of memory. The autobiography does not provide a specialist account of Atiyah's work. Rather, it is aimed at the general reader who is interested in the law and the state of the legal academy in the twentieth century. It is a classic illustration of Atiyah's eminently readable style. The chapters are sequenced chronologically although within certain of them Atiyah sometimes flits backwards and forwards in time.

APPROACH TO THE EDITORIAL WORK

I should say a few words about my approach to the editorial work. The autobiography had been completed to a high standard and it was clear that I was working with what was a near-final version. Atiyah had proofread it and scrawled corrections on it. As such, the work on my part in preparing the manuscript for publication has been more modest than might otherwise have been the case. To a large extent, it has been limited to correcting obvious errors, making minor adjustments to the text in places for clarity and modernising some of the language and terminology. Because there is value in presenting an authentic, unvarnished product, I have generally abstained from making substantive alterations, even where some of the views that Atiyah expressed would today be regarded as being politically incorrect. In short, Atiyah's voice has been preserved rather than replaced by my own. Footnotes offering principally citations to various sources have been added. My work has also involved selecting photographs of Atiyah for inclusion in the volume. In addition, a list of Atiyah's publications has been compiled and his family tree prepared. They form the appendices to the autobiography.

120 For example, Atiyah refers to events that took place in 1964 and indicates that he regretted waiting twenty-five years to write about them: see the autobiography, p 91.

121 ibid p 15.

CONNECTION WITH SCOTLAND

In circumstances where the autobiography is published by Edinburgh University Press, I should briefly single out some of its connections with Scotland. Atiyah was interested in the law and legal traditions in Scotland. He was often sensitive to the distinction between Scottish law and English law,[122] including in the autobiography.[123] And he had studied the works of institutional writers such as Stair and Kames.[124] The interest was reciprocated in that the Scottish courts cited (as database searches reveal) Atiyah's research not infrequently. Further, and as already mentioned, his mother was Scottish. Her family history is interestingly narrated in Chapter 1 of the autobiography. There are various other connections with Scotland of differing degrees of significance. For example, Michael Atiyah's wife, Lily, was from Edinburgh and she and Michael moved there in their old age as Lily's recompense for her having relinquished her own academic career for Michael's.

ACKNOWLEDGEMENTS

Finally, but importantly, there are numerous debts of gratitude that I have accumulated which I should acknowledge. The Atiyah family, and particularly Simon (one of Patrick's sons) and Joe (Patrick's younger brother) helpfully supplied various details and photographs. I am indebted to Guido Calabresi on account of his generously writing the foreword. Special thanks are due to Hector MacQueen who first approached me to write the memoir for the British Academy regarding Atiyah and thereafter encouraged me to propose to Edinburgh University Press, and in particular the Edinburgh Studies in Law series, that the autobiography be published. He also supported the work in numerous other ways at several junctures, not least by kindly providing comments on a full draft of the manuscript. Edinburgh University Press embraced the proposal with alacrity and I was fortunate to be able to work with Laura Quinn, Judith Mackenzie and Sam Johnson. Alexandra Braun provided careful comments on this preface and, indeed, suggestions on the project as a whole. The anonymous referees who reviewed the proposal

122 However, in *The Rise and Fall of Freedom of Contract*, Atiyah explained that it was fundamentally concerned with the position in England because he was sufficiently ignorant of Scots law that his claims should not be taken to extend to Scotland: Atiyah (n 47) viii.

123 See the autobiography at, e.g., pp 68, 136.

124 Atiyah (n 74) 13–15.

offered excellent advice which was overwhelmingly implemented. Andrew Devine was a superb copy-editor.

I also wish to acknowledge Peter Cane, Jane Stapleton and William Twining all of whom provided me with insights regarding Atiyah. Matthew Johnson was an exceptional research assistant who contributed significantly to the volume. He helped, in particular, with the preparation of Atiyah's list of publications and family tree, although his work extended well beyond these matters. Tim Wang provided excellent assistance as regards the page proofs. I am grateful to Elizabeth Wells of the Bodleian Law Library for locating numerous sources and also offering constructive guidance as concerns various research avenues. Michael Riordan, the Archivist at St John's College, Oxford, sourced the photograph of Atiyah that appears in Chapter 12. The portrait of Atiyah that appears in Chapter 14 hangs in New College, Oxford. Jacqui Julier, New College's Deans' and College Officers' Secretary, responded helpfully to queries in relation to it. Juliet Wood, who painted the portrait, kindly gave permission to use an electronic image of it. George Balkwill, the Senior Development Officer at New College, provided me with details regarding students who Atiyah taught.

James Goudkamp
Rio de Janeiro
9 April 2025

Table of Cases

Table of Legislation

Figure 1.1 Patrick Atiyah. Image reproduced with the permission of the British Academy.

1 My Family

I am the product of a mixed marriage – my father was an Arab and my mother hailed from Scotland. I came – as a doctor once told me – of poor physical stock, but good intellectual stock! My father, Edward Selim Atiyah, was a Lebanese Christian by origin who had fallen in love with all things English at a very early age, and had plotted and schemed his way to Oxford where he met my mother, and proceeded to fall in love with her too. They were married in 1926, three years after my father had left Oxford, by which time he had obtained a job in the Sudan political service, working in Khartoum. For the next seventeen years my parents' home was in Khartoum, so my elder brother Michael and I spent our early years in that remote and hot world, remote in miles from England, but even more remote in time from the twenty-first century.

My father related the story of his early life in his own autobiography, *An Arab Tells his Story*, which was published in 1946.[1] His own father, my grandfather, Selim Atiyah, was a doctor who had spent much of his working life in a British hospital in Omdurman (the twin city of Khartoum, just across the Nile) where he had gone not long after the British conquest of the Sudan at the battle of Omdurman in 1898. I never knew Dr Selim who died in 1925 just after my father left Oxford, and six years before I was born. Nearly fifty years later, on one of my occasional visits to the Sudan, I was lunching with some Sudanese friends in the old Grand Hotel, along the Nile front in Khartoum, when I happened to mention that I was the third generation of my family to have worked in the Sudan, and I asked my companions whether any of them had known Dr Selim. By way of reply one of them rolled up his shirt sleeve, and pointed to an old scar. "That was an abscess", he told me, "which was lanced by Dr Selim when I was a boy". I responded by saying that I was glad to see that my grandfather had left his mark on the Sudanese!

My father was, in many ways a very remarkable person. As he related in his own autobiography, he grew up without the modern nationalistic

1 ES Atiyah, *An Arab Tells His Story: A Study in Loyalties* (1946). Atiyah's father was the author of numerous other books, many of which Atiyah refers to below. One of the more prominent which he does not mention is ES Atiyah, *The Arabs* (1955). In addition to these works, Atiyah's father was a regular speaker on BBC radio.

appurtenances which most people acquire almost as a matter of course. He was born in Lebanon in 1903, when that was not the name of a country, but merely of a vague geographical region of the Ottoman Empire, though one with a large Christian population. His childhood was dotted with memories of rivalries, of this sect against that, this religion against that, this super-power against that. In a search for some sort of identity my father attached himself at a very early age – and long before he ever saw the country – to England, and learnt to love the English language, English history and English culture, and perhaps above all, English skills in maintaining orderly public administration throughout the Empire. As his early years were divided between the Sudan where Dr Selim worked, and Lebanon itself, where the family came from, and to which they returned at every opportunity, my father was able to contrast the orderly maintenance of public administration, law and order, and public sanitation and other such manifestations, as he saw them in the Sudan, with the general corruption, inefficiency and squalor which he saw in Lebanon itself and indeed much of the Arab world.

This early emotional attachment to England led my father to persuade his parents to send him to Victoria College, a British public school founded in Alexandria around the turn of the century, as a memorial to Queen Victoria, where he reinforced his love for English literature and culture, and made many life-long friends both among the teachers and the pupils. It was with the help of the headmaster, Mr RWG Reed, who later became almost as important an English figure in Egypt as the British Ambassador, that my father had succeeded in getting into Oxford when the time came.

His early love for the English language and literature never left him. He became in due course more at home in English than his own native Arabic, and could speak perfect English, with scarcely a hint of an accent. His written English was also graceful and elegant – his autobiography was much praised by the reviewers – and he had some minor successes as a novelist in his later years. One of his novels, *The Thin Line*,[2] a study of the mind of a person who kills, almost by accident, and of his personal relationships with his wife and friends, was particularly successful, being translated into several languages, and eventually being made into a film by the distinguished French producer, Claud Chabrol, under the title, *Juste Avant La Nuit*. This was unfortunately many years after my father's death, and he never saw the film though he had himself worked on a script for it.

2 ES Atiyah, *The Thin Line* (1951).

This film led eventually to some legal complications which, as a lawyer myself, I rather relished. What happened was that, around the time when the film was first being shown I (then living and working in Australia) received a letter from a firm of London solicitors informing me that the company which had made the film wished to buy certain residuary rights to a renewal of the copyright under American law, and offering £500 for these rights to myself and my siblings. This rather surprised me because I knew that my father had sold the film rights outright and I could not think what residuary rights we could possibly have. However, I was not a lawyer for nothing, and having a convenient law library available I burrowed away into American copyright law. I was astonished by what I discovered. It seemed that under American law, copyright lasted in the first instance for twenty-eight years but could then be renewed for a further twenty-eight years. Of course, the original author could sell the rights during his life and, if he was still alive at the end of the first twenty-eight years, his sale was binding on him and the buyer would own the renewal rights. However, if the original author died during the first twenty-eight-year period, the renewal rights passed to his wife, and after her death to his children. What was more this was still the case even if the author had sold the rights outright, and even if he had left his estate by will to any other parties. That this was the result of the American Copyright Act of 1909 was confirmed by a decision of the United States Supreme Court,[3] in which the judges had surmised that Congress had proceeded on the "author starving in a garret theory", that is, Congress had wanted to preserve to an author's wife and children the renewal rights in some work he had produced where, perchance, the work had proved much more valuable than had been expected when he first sold the rights. It was an extraordinary piece of paternalist legislation which in effect prevented an author or artist from making a totally binding sale of his own assets, and I believe it has since been repealed by Congress. But at the time my siblings and I rejoiced at being the beneficiaries of this quaint piece of legislation.

My father's other novels were less successful commercially speaking, but they all remain very readable. Two of them are set in Lebanon – *Lebanon Paradise*[4] (how ironical the title sounds today) and *Donkey from the Mountains*,[5] and one in the Sudan – *Black Vanguard*[6] – and they all contain delightful portraits in fictional guise of some of his friends and

3 *DeSylva v Ballentine* 351 US 570 (1956).
4 ES Atiyah, *Lebanon Paradise: A Novel* (1953).
5 ES Atiyah, *Donkey from the Mountains* (1961).
6 ES Atiyah, *Black Vanguard* (1952).

acquaintances, as well as providing sympathetic accounts of a long-lost social environment.

My father was fairly conservative in his literary tastes. Shakespeare was always his greatest love, and he could quote many passages of Shakespearean drama. He once embarrassed an English journalist friend who asked him if he knew the origin of the phrase *miching mallecho* because she had a vague idea that it might be Arabic; in fact, as my father delightedly pointed out, it comes from Hamlet. He introduced me to the London theatre in 1945 by taking me to one of the greatest Shakespearean productions of the century, the Old Vic performance of *Henry IV, Part I* with Laurence Olivier as Hotspur, and Ralph Richardson as Falstaff. For days afterwards we swapped delighted quotations from the play, mainly of course from the so-eminently-quotable prose of Falstaff.

As a person, my father had quite a formidable presence. Short and somewhat stout in appearance, he had an extremely loud voice, and his laughter (as well as his coughing) was explosive and rumbustious. As he was an excellent public speaker, and could moreover talk intelligently and wittily on almost any subject, he was nearly always the centre of attention at gatherings and parties. He was an affectionate father and friend, and also had something of a romantic streak in him; combined with his love of the dramatic, this no doubt explained his fondness for retelling us as children famous stories from the past – such as Darwin's discovery of the theory of evolution, and Galileo and his famous experiment at the leaning tower of Pisa (even though this later turned out to be apocryphal). During the war his Churchillian imitations were much admired, and on VE Day, a good-humoured crowd gathered round him in a London pub while he recited from memory large chunks of some of Churchill's best-known speeches.

Like many Mediterranean people he had the very un-English habit (which I have also) of gesticulating vigorously with his hands when excited, and this, combined with his powerful voice, made him a most effective public speaker. He had one of the loudest voices I have ever known. His obituary in *The Times*[7] records that "when he dined in restaurants strangers would walk across from the other side of the room to say how much they had enjoyed his conversation and ask whether they could join in". A story (almost certainly apocryphal) was told to all visitors to the government block in Khartoum where he had his office that, on a previous occasion a stranger was being shown round when my father's stentorian tones could be heard

7 *The Times* (London, 26 October 1964) 15.

bellowing from his office. "That", said the host, gesturing in the direction of my father's office, "is Mr Atiyah talking to someone in Wad Medani" – a town some 100 miles from Khartoum. "But", exclaimed the stranger, "why on earth doesn't he use the telephone?" On another occasion, when several members of the family were attending a performance of the repertory theatre at Guildford, my father began to hold forth in his usual manner during the interval, whereupon my sister Selma, with the embarrassment of a fourteen-year-old at feeling our circle to be the centre of all ears, if not eyes, tried to shush him. Raising his voice a few more decibels, my father retorted, "I have been talking like this for forty-five years and no daughter of mine is going to stop me now." Poor Selma!

He was the kind of father who enjoyed intellectual rather than sporty or athletic intercourse with his children. During the war-year summers when he was able to get away to Lebanon he would enjoy his early morning walks over the mountains from our holiday home in Aley, above Beirut, and I remember how these often served as the occasion for a lecture on Shakespeare, or English history, or even politics, with some introduction to socialist ideas which at this time he was inclined to favour after his early Conservatism. Since I was only eight when the war began, my early years were naturally dominated by this great shadow in the background, and my father was even more caught up in it, because it was a part of his job to interpret Sudanese opinion to the British officials in the Sudan. So, as I suppose must be commonplace for people of my age, war talk dominated my early years, even though I spent most of the war outside England itself. My father was a good deal more acute in his judgements on the war than many of his contemporaries. He saw it coming long before it burst; he was a great admirer of Churchill, and respected his prophecies when Churchill was still in the political wilderness in England; like Churchill, he deplored the Munich sell-out; nor did he expect, as most British officials in the Sudan did, that Russia would collapse under the first German onslaught; and he looked to America, and particularly to Roosevelt, as the ultimate saviour of Europe. One of my earliest memories is of the family in Khartoum clustering round an old wartime radio at four o'clock one morning to hear the result of the American presidential election in November 1940, when Roosevelt won his third term.

For a couple of intellectually minded boys like Michael and me, my father proved (especially as we grew older) an ideal parent. Vigorous and loud discussions and arguments became a commonplace in our family. No subject was barred, no opinion was taboo. My father was very liberal in his outlook, indeed as my mother used to say, he was fanatically broad-minded. The one thing he could not tolerate was intolerance. We did, however, learn that too many of our arguments were over matters of opinion which could be resolved by reference to the Encyclopaedia Britannica. Many times a good row was brought to an end by the cry "Ascertainable fact", whereupon one of us would turn to the Encyclopaedia, and hunt for some piece of information.

My father was not a practical man. He had been brought up in a world and a society in which domestic servants were commonplace, and he expected to leave all household arrangements to the women in the confident belief that food of the right quality would arrive at the right time, that beds would be made, laundry would somehow get done, and the house cleaned. A *bon mot* from my sister Selma once hit just the right note in describing his dependence on my mother in all domestic matters: my young brother, Joe, when a boy of five or six, inspired by Heaven knows what, once asked my father what he would do if a tiger suddenly appeared through the door. While my father hesitated for an answer, Selma said, "I know exactly what you would do. You would call, 'Jean, come and take this tiger away'"! Still, he did perforce learn a certain amount of do-it-yourself activities long before that phrase was invented. Before the war we used to spend our leaves in England, often camping, or living in rather makeshift accommodation, until my father eventually acquired a sort of summer holiday home from one of his old Oxford friends, on the terms of paying for it when he could. For some years until the war came my father used to spend his summers with a series of friends making this a more habitable place for the family.

My mother was a very different sort of person altogether. She was an intensely practical person, of enormous energy and resources when it came to dealing with family matters and domestic problems. Although her life in Khartoum was a life of leisure through the grace of domestic servants, she was never idle, but spent her time making clothes for herself and her children. During the holidays she more than made up for any leisure she enjoyed the rest of the year – and our holidays lasted for up to three months or more in the halcyon pre-war days when my father enjoyed eighty days' leave a year. On these holidays my mother had to try to provide the sort of comforts to which my father was accustomed (even at camp) as well as coping with several small children. In 1939–40 we spent the bitter English winter in our summer shack, after my father had been summoned back to Khartoum, and my mother had to cope with three small children in a house totally unequipped for winter use. We certainly had no central heating, and only one fireplace; nor was there any form of coal store, and the coal was dumped outside the back door where it froze into one large heap, and could only be prized apart with an axe or spade. The bathroom repeatedly froze, pipes burst and froze again, so that on at least one occasion we found the floor covered with a thin sheet of ice rather like a skating rink. Then the air raid warden called a day or two after the outbreak of war to tell my mother that the asbestos tiles on the roof were shining too brightly in the moonlight, and something would have to be done about them. This last problem was eventually solved by Michael and me who clambered all over the bungalow roof (which was very low-pitched) sloshing khaki distemper all over it until the air raid warden was satisfied. All this, and more, was the sort of thing my mother could cope with. She was also clever with her hands, and inventive in design. She designed a sort of two-headed doll, with one white head and one black one, with a skirt which just reversed itself over the heads, and during the war she made hundreds of these dolls which were sold for the benefit of the (Sudan) war relief fund.

But as my parents grew older there increasingly appeared a sad incompatibility between them. My mother's intense down-to-earth practicality acted as a damper on my father's romantic and dramatic temperament, and they eventually separated. When Joe went to Cambridge at the age of eighteen, my mother evidently felt that her life's work was done, and that there was nothing left for her to live for. She went to pieces rapidly after that.

Because most of my early years were spent in the Middle East, I got to know various members of my father's family rather better than my mother's. Apart from my grandmother, universally known as Mama Asma, my father's closest relative was his sister, my aunt Najla. She was eight years younger than him, and when I first became aware of her, she was married to an engaging young man called Mitri Shami. To his young nephews, his most striking feature was that he was minus his left thumb which he had shot off in a hunting accident; but later, when we got to know him better, we came to appreciate some of his other features. He had, in particular, an impish sense of humour which led him to play practical jokes on all members of the family. He specialised in April fool jokes, and went to enormous lengths to concoct ever more elaborate and convincing pranks. Once he persuaded a firm which made chocolates to stuff a box of chocolates full of salt and pepper, and wrap the whole in factory-new cellophane to ensure an appearance of authenticity. He then presented the box to the family and sat back to watch the fun. In his younger days he worked for the Palestine government as a customs official, stationed at a place called Nakkoura, on the Palestine-Lebanon border. Nakkoura was on the Mediterranean and enjoyed, of course, a glorious summer climate as well a magnificent geographical position. The beautiful sandy beaches were dotted with outcrops of rock with delightful pools in which children could play with boats, or just paddle and enjoy the deep blue water and the everlasting summer sunshine. Michael and I often stayed with Najla and Mitri for a few days on our way from school in Egypt to Lebanon where we spent our summers during most of the war years. In those days the only way to travel from Haifa, in Palestine, where the railway from Egypt came to an end, to Beirut, was by car, and a car service provided some large American limousines to enable the journey to be undertaken in some comfort. The whole of that magnificent coast-line still lives in my mind. Nakkoura is, of course, now part of Israeli territory.

Mitri was a most successful customs official who had a nose for sniffing out smugglers trying to get hashish across the border into Palestine. A special room, a sort of museum of exhibits, was kept in the customs office at Nakkoura, mostly displaying the results of Mitri's success in this battle of wits with the smugglers. False petrol tanks in cars, false back seats, a set of concrete terrazzo steps of the kind much used in the Mediterranean countries, hollowed out in the middle, and a variety of other such devices testified to the gains to be made from smuggling. Unfortunately, or perhaps fortunately in view of the subsequent Lebanese-Israeli troubles, Mitri gave up his job in about 1944 and tried his hands at a succession of business ventures, each of which proved a total disaster. He was rather like the PG Wodehouse character, Ukridge, who was able to convince others of the total plausibility of all sorts of mad ventures, even to the extent of persuading them to invest hard cash in his schemes. It began with pig farming, though his most long-lasting venture was a dream to make a fortune by exploiting (or getting someone else to exploit) a manganese mine in some remote region of Jordan. For years we heard about the manganese mine, but nothing ever came of it and Mitri spent his time in unprofitable activity, frequently trembling on the brink of destitution. Eventually my aunt Najla was forced to take a job as a teacher simply to provide a more secure source of income. They did, however, retain a small pension, paid by the British government, as a debt of honour to all ex-Palestinian civil servants, even those who, as in Mitri's case, were not themselves British subjects. (The Israeli government refused to acknowledge the claims of these former Palestine government employees.) Unfortunately this pension only covered Mitri himself and on his death nothing was left for Najla. My brother Michael then stepped in with some generosity to help her.

Najla and Mitri had a son, Michel, always known as Micho when a boy, who was three years younger than me, and just of an age to provide a constant source of irritation to older cousins. During the war years, when we spent our holidays together, we saw a good deal of them. He emigrated to Australia in 1971, when I was also living there, and almost the first news we had of him was that he had won $10,000 in the Queensland State lottery. But Michel had an unhappy life in many ways, and died young in Australia around the turn of the century. He had married and brought his wife with him to Australia, but as a couple they remained childless until rather late in life they adopted a child, who they called Michael. After both his parents had died, Michael re-established contact with other members of his family.

Najla also had two daughters, Muna and Sameera, but after 1945, when my parents moved to England, we saw little of them for many years. Muna did, however, come to England for a short holiday in 1969, when she stayed with me and my own family in Oxford, and watched the first moon-walk with us in the early hours of that famous morning. Later she suffered a numbing tragedy when her eldest son, a boy of eight, was killed by a bomb explosion in Beirut in 1983, in the aftermath of the Israeli invasion of Lebanon. We saw little of my Beirut relatives after the Lebanese civil wars began but Najla and Mitri were able to come to England for a brief holiday from the horrors of the war in around 1985 and they stayed with us and with each of my brothers for a week. Najla was in a pretty nervous shell-shocked state by this time and the peace and quiet of our Oxford garden did her a lot of good, I am glad to say. Then after the wars finally ended Christine (my wife) and I travelled to Beirut for ten days to re-establish contact with my relatives and since then we have kept in touch with Muna by visits and regular emails and even telephone calls from time to time. Najla died at the age of eighty-eight in around 2002.

Other relatives of my father who figure in my early recollections include two of his aunts and an uncle. The uncle, Samuel, who we all knew as Uncle Sam (a source of some amusement to others after America entered the war in 1941, when "Uncle Sam" came to mean something else) was living in Cairo when Michael and I went to boarding school there, and he made many of the arrangements for our travels and excursions during this time. He had two children, a girl, Leila, and a son, Fouad, who we also saw a good deal during the war years, but we did not communicate with them too easily, because they were brought up as Arabic and French speaking (as many upper-class Lebanese families were) while Michael and I resisted all efforts to teach us Arabic, and only learnt schoolboy French. Sam himself spoke

English very well, indeed too well for his own good, because his knowledge of English led him to a tragic end. He supplemented his income by doing translation work for the British Embassy in Cairo, and after the war he was persuaded to extend this work to intelligence documents, some of which were secret Egyptian government documents. Eventually he was caught, and in the anti-British turmoil at the time of the Suez Crisis, he was tried as a conspirator for his part in this intelligence work. He spent his last years in an Egyptian jail, though I believe he was given a fair trial and was not treated inhumanely even in jail.

My father's two aunts, Mary and Selma, closely resembled their sister, my grandmother Mama Asma, in appearance, but they were somewhat sweeter in temperament. Mary was unmarried and led a difficult spinster life in the kind of "genteel poverty" which afflicted people similarly situated in England in the nineteenth century, and perhaps even the early half of the last century. She had no income and no home of her own, being entirely dependent on what Sam was able to afford her, and living in a series of rather depressing pensions;[8] fortunately she died before Sam was sent to prison or she would have been quite destitute.

My father's other aunt, Selma, was a very quiet, sweet old lady, who was married to a family favourite, called Farid. He was a large, not to say, fat, man who was the only one of our relatives with whom Michael and I were able to have serious adult conversations. We talked about the war and politics, and he treated us like adults in these conversations, which made us very fond of him. We also used to play the favourite Lebanese game of backgammon with him. This was played with great gusto. The numbers were shouted out loudly when the dice were thrown (always in an old language which for years I assumed was Turkish until I was corrected recently) and the counters were banged down on the board so as to make the loudest possible noise. To my great sadness Farid died before my first return visit to Lebanon after I had grown up, so my memories of him remain those of a young boy.

Because so many of my formative years were spent out of England, I did not get to know my mother's family very well in those early years. Both her parents had, anyhow, died long before I was born. Indeed, her father, a Church of England clergyman, had died when my mother was herself only seven, leaving a widow and five children – my mother, two brothers

8 In modern parlance, the concept of "pensions" has become associated almost exclusively with regular income received by retirees. However, Atiyah used the word in a now antiquated sense to refer to guest houses.

and two sisters. For many years this grandfather was a very shadowy figure in the family's consciousness, but a large cache of letters from him to his wife, my grandmother, were discovered only a few years ago which inspired my uncle Frank to write a short memoir for the family's benefit recording what he knew of his father – my grandfather – and family. Frank's researches in fact traced the family tree back some considerable way.

My grandfather, John Thomson Levens, was born in 1862, the son of James Levens, a ship's master, himself born in 1812 or 1813. James died when JT Levens was a baby, and his mother followed, when he was only thirteen. My grandfather was then brought up by an uncle John who supervised his education. He took his Master of Arts degree with honours at St Andrews University in 1886, and later studied at the University of Jena in Germany and finally at Westminster Theological College where he took first class honours and graduated top of his class in four subjects. About a century later my brother Michael was awarded an honorary degree at St Andrews University[9] and told his hosts of his grandfather's connection with the university. They looked through their records and were able to confirm what Michael had told them. Our grandfather became a pastor in the Presbyterian Church in 1892, but transferred to the Church of England in 1899, and was from 1904 to 1914 Vicar of Alverthorpe in Wakefield.

His letters to his wife (from whom he was often separated for long periods while seeking preferment in the Church of Scotland) revealed that he was not only an exceptionally gifted man academically, but also that he was very far from being the conventional, stuffy Victorian clergyman that the family later thought. He was, apparently, reading Ibsen's plays before the turn of the century when they must have been very *avant-garde*, and found them "unpleasant but very powerful". Judging from these letters, Frank wrote in his memoir that JT Levens was

> "in fact extremely vital and energetic. He loves to get out of the city into the countryside and he cannot see a hill or a mountain without climbing to the top of it. Indeed, in the earlier years of his married life, there is quite an element of daredevilry about him. He is an avid sightseer and likes to share his impressions with his wife, hence a number of good descriptive letters during his travels."

He died shortly after the outbreak of war in 1914, leaving his wife almost penniless, with five children, of whom the youngest three were still only

9 Michael Atiyah was awarded an honorary Doctor of Science in 1981. A photograph taken at the ceremony and other details are posted on the University of St Andrews website: *https://special-collections.wp.st-andrews.ac.uk/2017/06/23/graduation-week-celebrating-honorands-medics-mathematicians-and-sportsmen/*.

thirteen, seven and five years of age. Thereafter his family survived on a very modest pension from the Church's widows and orphans fund.

My grandmother on my mother's side also died before I was born, and all I know of her and her family comes from my mother's recollections and Frank's family memoir. Frank traced this branch of the family back to his own great-grandfather, John Cochrane, who was a farmer in Scotland. One of his younger sons, Robert, my own great-grandfather, went into business in Glasgow, rose to be manager of the Guardian Assurance Company and was eventually transferred (probably in the 1880s) to London as Managing Director of that company, which today forms part of the Guardian Royal Exchange Group. Robert Cochrane left a sizeable fortune when he died in 1912, but he assumed that his married daughters were well provided for, and so left almost all the income from his estate to his widow and two unmarried daughters. Hence it was that when only two years later my grandmother lost her husband, she was left virtually destitute with her five children.

My mother's brother Robert was the member of the family that I eventually got to know best, which was in a way only fitting, because it was he was responsible for the meeting of my parents. Robert was the family genius, whose early exploits were part of family folklore. He virtually taught himself to read before going to school, and later won a series of scholarships, first to Rugby, and then as a classical scholar to Balliol College, Oxford, at a time when that was just about the highest academic success open to a British schoolboy. Indeed, Robert made so much money from a variety of scholarships that my grandmother was induced to move to Oxford while he was a student there, and he partly supported the family out of his receipts.

My father recounted in his autobiography how he came to meet Robert, and through him, my mother. My father had spoken at a debate at the Oxford Union and had been invited to meet the President at a little gathering afterwards. There he was asked to speak at a forthcoming debate on the motion that "Eastern nations should develop along Eastern and not Western lines". My father declined the invitation saying that he wanted to speak against the motion, as he was then passionately in favour of the Westernising of the Arab nations, a view he came somewhat to modify later in life. But the President of the Union told him that they were really looking for a speaker to support the motion, as they had plenty of speakers against it. Robert thereupon stepped forward and volunteered to speak for the motion. Robert – and his whole family – were somewhat *avant-garde* in those days, being rather radical in their opinions and whole outlook on life, while my father was at that time extremely conservative, a great believer in the British Empire, and all Western things. However, this did not prevent my father being much taken with Robert's family, by whom he was almost adopted in his last year at Oxford. He was particularly taken with Robert's young sister Jean who he eventually married and who became my mother.

Robert later became a classics don at Merton College, Oxford, where he spent all his working life, apart from a short spell during the war when he worked on cypher breaking in intelligence. When I got to know him he was tall, spare and rather stooping in appearance, and with many of the features often thought characteristic of the Oxford don. His absent mindedness was at times legendary. After a good family dinner, Robert would dutifully pick up a tea towel to do the drying up, spend ten or fifteen minutes drying the same plate, all the while engaged in deep conversation with those similarly engaged, and then slip the now thoroughly dried plate back into the washing-up bowl. He was one of those Oxford dons who were known as "good College men"; he seems to have written very little, though he nursed all his life the idea of doing a new edition of some classical text. In a way he was one of those clever men who were rather spoiled by Oxford – he never put his brilliant mind to proper use (except perhaps during the war) and never felt the need to do so. But he did devote much time and attention to his pupils, in the best Oxford manner, and because classics students at Oxford were traditionally thought well qualified to become permanent secretaries or ambassadors, the time came when he had ex-pupils in senior posts scattered all over the Whitehall machine, and over many of the world's capital cities as well. Robert was also an excellent literary critic, and when my father began to write novels he always submitted them to Robert for advice and usually followed it.

Robert married an attractive blonde half-Scandinavian wife called Daphne, who devoted her life to producing plays among the various Oxford drama societies. She was very successful at it too, winning many awards, and often being invited by distinguished amateur companies to produce for them Daphne lived well into her nineties and I met her again in Oxford in 2009 when her younger daughter Karin was celebrating her seventy-fifth birthday. Robert and Daphne had three children. In addition to Karin, they had, a son and another daughter, but tragedy hit them. The boy, Andrew, was killed in a road accident while visiting Russia, at the age of about twenty-one, and Karin's first husband was killed in an air disaster.

My mother's other brother, Frank, was two years younger than she was. He did not have Robert's early genius, and lacking financial support, missed out on university education, but he did have a gift for languages, and picked up half a dozen or more which came in handy when he got a job with a firm of publisher's representatives, whose business involved placing advertisements in newspapers all over the world. Eventually he came to be managing director of this firm, the only member of the family of his generation who ever seems to have had any success in business life. Frank was always a warm family man, who liked to keep in touch with us, and was also very interested in the family's ancestry. He once travelled to Scotland hoping to find the original home of the Levens family, and did, I believe, find a village somewhere with several Levenses in the churchyard. When Robert died Frank inherited from him a trunkful of letters written by his father, my grandfather, and it was with the aid of these that he wrote the short memoir to which I have previously referred. Frank married an Austrian woman who knew even more languages than he did, but she died childless at a comparatively young age, and then Frank married again and had a daughter, Ann, who was more or less a contemporary of my second son, Andrew.

I saw very little of my mother's two sisters, Janet and Betty. They were both a lot older than my mother, and Janet became almost a complete invalid not long after we returned to England after the war. I do, however, remember paying her a visit in her house in Rushden in Northamptonshire in around Christmas 1945 when I was amazed to discover that she still had gas lighting in her house. Her only son, my cousin Phil, (though an American citizen thanks to his father) was a bomber pilot with the RAF and lost his life in a raid over Germany around 1944. My aunt seems to have been completely unhinged by this, and convinced herself, as well, it seems, as some Air Ministry officials that he had not really been killed but had "disappeared" because he was engaged in some secret intelligence work. However, she was eventually visited after the war by another member of the bomber crew who had succeeded in baling out of the doomed plane; his story left no doubt of my cousin's fate.

My immediate family circle, in which I grew up and spent my first years, consisted of my parents, my brother Michael, and myself, and a little later my sister, Selma, and later still, my brother Joe, so-named, (it is now a trifle embarrassing to remember) because he was born in 1943 at a time when my father had some admiration for the Russian dictator Stalin. The daily companion of my early years was, of course, my older brother Michael, now Sir Michael, OM, former Master of Trinity College, Cambridge, President of the Royal Society, and one of the world's leading mathematicians. His bent for mathematics appeared at a very early age. A family story that my parents used to relate had Michael at about the age of four or five listening to my mother go through the household accounts with the cook in Khartoum, adding up the figures in his head as they went along. But though Michael was clearly precocious in mathematics he was not (perhaps through lack of opportunity and early advanced education) a child prodigy like Ruth Lawrence, who took first class honours in mathematics at Oxford at the age of fourteen, and who Michael later supervised for her DPhil, which she got at the age of eighteen. Nor do I think he was one of those early mathematical geniuses like GH Hardy who (according to CP Snow) ask questions about large or infinite numbers before they are three. All the same, when we went to Victoria College in 1941 Michael quickly displayed unusual powers as a mathematician, and when we moved to England at the end of the war, it was evident that he had rare talent which needed developing. Michael was sent to Manchester Grammar School, then the leading school for mathematics in England. From there he won the top scholarship to Trinity College, Cambridge, and his career never looked back from then on. Within a few years he was a Fellow of Trinity College, he won the Smith's Prize (which was typed for him by Christine) and became a Fellow of the Royal Society at thirty-three, the youngest fellow for many years. This was a source of great pride to my father who kept on his mantelpiece a framed cutting from *The Times* announcing the election. In the end Michael had, so far as I could judge, clearly surpassed these child prodigies as a mathematician.

Michael and I got on well together as boys, and indeed we have continued to get on well as adults, although our relationship has occasionally become strained by the odd argument and disagreement, mostly on matters of politics and economics and such like. For the first ten years of my life we were daily companions, and for the following three or four years when we were at Victoria College, we were still largely thrown on each other's company during the long summer vacations, and also at Christmas time when we travelled back to Khartoum together. As boys we did many of the things that boys no doubt usually do together, but also some that were perhaps less usual. We played chess together a great deal until we both became quite proficient at it. (I myself became school chess captain when I was seventeen, and later played occasionally for the Oxford second team, whose standard was, however, considerably below that of the first.) Sometimes, as when travelling, we even tried playing chess without a board, trying to emulate the great masters who played a game blindfold, but differing from their procedures in that we had no board at all, and nobody to keep a record of the moves. These games were pretty difficult and I am not sure that we ever got beyond six or seven moves each. We also played a lot of bridge, which was rather more difficult as there were only two of us. We were occasionally allowed to join my father and his friends in a round of proper adult bridge, and we would always snap up a willing visitor for a three-handed game. Failing that, we were quite willing to spend hours playing two-handed bridge, in which each of us bid and played two hands. Monopoly was another favourite which absorbed many hours, but we found the ordinary version rather tame. One summer Michael made up his own, larger and more elaborate version of the game, in which instead of buying and selling streets in London, the players bought and sold the major cities of the world. As the board was a good deal bigger, there were more properties to be disposed of, and prices were all set somewhat higher. The first attempt at this game led to a severe liquidity shortage as we had failed to match the more expensive and numerous properties with an adequate money supply, but we soon remedied that, adding £1,000 and £5,000 notes to the usual monopoly money. It was my first lesson in public finance.

Neither Michael nor I was particularly athletic or good at physical sports (though he was much better than I was, and did once win a cup for the under sixteen hurdles at Victoria College), but we spent a great deal of time in these early Khartoum years swimming. My father had installed a small swimming pool in the garden when we were very young. It was a crude affair without a filtration plant and had to be emptied and refilled once a week. Not surprisingly, we spent a great deal of time in it. For many months of the year the average maximum temperature in Khartoum exceeds 100 degrees Fahrenheit so it is hardly surprising that we should have learnt to swim very young (my mother claimed I swam at three). We raced, we dived, we swam under water, we tried to keep afloat in large round rather flat washing bowls (known as "tishts"), we jumped out and ran round the garden, and then dived back into the pool. My earliest recollections of Khartoum all centre round the pool.

Michael was nearly two years older than I was, and was definitely marked out for great things even then. By contrast I showed little special ability, and my mother related that my father had rather unkindly put me down as a moron at the age of three. At any rate, whether as a result of age, ability or personality, Michael was decidedly a leader and I a follower. Among other things this meant that Michael always won at games. I accepted that Michael as the older brother would naturally swim and run faster than I could, and I also found it quite natural that he should invariably beat me at chess. I was, however, more frustrated at the fact that he always seemed to win games in which chance played a greater role, like bridge and monopoly. Once in a while I would persuade him to play even simpler games like ludo or snakes and ladders – games which Michael rather despised – in the hope that where no skill at all was involved, the law of averages would give me an occasional victory. But it never seemed to work. It seemed a law of our relationship that Michael would always come first and I second. Generally I think I took this well enough, though there were the occasional tears and sulks. Michael (though he would probably dispute this) got to take his position as number one rather for granted and was not a good loser. Luckily for him, he has, throughout his life, rarely been in the position of a loser. I, on the other hand, learnt from an early age what it was like to be a loser. This made my rare successes all the sweeter.

I had one glorious moment of triumph. We both went to the same school in Khartoum, the Clergy House School, mostly for the children of British officials. This school was run as a simple primary school for children of all ages, so it was impractical to divide them into classes, and each age group did work appropriate to their age, while all were taken together for other subjects, and when it came to examinations, all the children were ranked even though not all had done the same questions. Throughout my years at the Clergy House, Michael was always top in the annual examination – except once. On this one occasion I was placed first and Michael second. When school finished, we both grabbed our bikes and raced home, I to announce my triumph, and Michael to give vent to his disappointment and rage at the unfairness of the teacher. I remember in particular Michael's characteristic indignation that the teacher (no doubt making some allowance for the age difference) had given him a lower mark than me for the geography test – which for both us had been to draw a map of Britain from memory. Mine, though not too accurate (Michael indignantly pointed out that I had left out Wales) was drawn in the approved fashion with wiggly lines. Michael had drawn his with very straight coast lines, and argued that wiggly lines drawn from memory could not possibly represent the real coast line, so it was more honest and rational to draw straight ones. This extreme rationalism was rather characteristic of Michael, and I have always assumed it was tied in with his mathematical mind. Unfortunately it also led (and still leads occasionally) to a somewhat infuriating dogmatism; and an absolute conviction in the correctness of his own views. I remember also another occasion when I felt that Michael begrudged me a modest degree of success which did not even challenge his superiority. When I was about thirteen and Michael about fifteen we were invited one Sunday to visit an old friend of our father's who lived in Alexandria and who treated us sumptuously to a magnificent meal cooked by his wife. This friend, named Meg, was an excellent chess player and we had both played against him from time to time on previous visits. On this occasion Meg complimented me on my improvement as a chess player since we last played which had in fact been evident from the game we had played. Although this was not in any way a comparative judgement on our relative skills, Michael seemed put out that he also had not been complimented by Meg and insisted that he had also improved.

Of course Michael was not the only one of us with strong and perhaps dogmatic views. As I am also a person of strong views, and rather positive opinions, who likes to lay down the law within my home, my own children grew up to regard me as a somewhat domineering parent who usually knew (or thought he knew) the answers to all their questions. So they were somewhat astonished one day at some family gathering to hear Michael overbear me with an emphatic, and loud, "No Patrick, you're WRONG". Indeed, they roll around with laughter at the mere recollection of this incident, though I am not sure whether it was the sight of my discomfiture or Michael's cocksureness which tickled them more.

This dogmatism of Michael's could sometimes leave quite an unpleasant taste as happened once when we were holidaying in Italy together with various members of his family in 2005. A question was raised about the temperature of the pool in our rented villa and Michael having told me it was something like twenty-seven degrees Celsius, I noticed on checking the thermometer a little later that it was well below this, and mildly suggested that he may have misread it. This resulted in an astonishing outburst from Michael who insisted loudly and aggressively that he had NOT misread it. We had the impression that Michael was simply unused to being contradicted even on trifles, and did not like the experience at all. I would not like to leave the impression that Michael was frequently aggressive or unpleasant to me or my family. In fact he was very generous in many ways, especially financially, so for instance on this holiday in Italy we were his guests in the luxurious villa which he had rented.

But Michael was certainly a very competitive person from his earliest days. I remember one incident in particular from our schooldays which illustrates this very well. We were in Beirut at the time, in charge of one of our relatives who dumped us at the sports day of the American University although we had no great interest in this event. After a while Michael thought we could enliven the proceedings so far as we were concerned by backing rival teams. He chose to back the dayboys and I was left with the boarders. It soon appeared that Michael had chosen the wrong side and he began to fret and fidget and show increasing irritation as the boarders won event after event. Seeing this I, who could not care less who won, offered to exchange sides with Michael, but this was evidently not the right thing to do at all. Michael dismissed my offer with contempt, and had to continue watching "his" team suffer increasing defeats, which I noticed with increasing anxiety myself as his mood deteriorated.

My younger siblings, Selma and Joe were not childhood companions in the way Michael and I were. Selma was six years younger than I was, so she was still quite a tot when I left for Victoria College at ten. Joe was another six years behind Selma, so I have quite vivid memories of his birth and babyhood. He was born in Lebanon in the summer of 1943 during our annual holiday in Aley. My father was not yet on leave and my mother with characteristic, if not foolhardy, courage had arranged to have her baby in a nursing home about two miles from our house, even though, were the birth to come at night, transport might well be non-existent. In the event, when the time came – inevitably in the middle of the night – she *walked* to the nursing home, accompanied by the gardener who carried her case. None the worse for the effort, she gave birth to Joe a few hours later. I calculated a few days later that my father had completed his fortieth year the same day that Joe completed his fortieth day.

2 Childhood

I am not one of those prodigies with memories of babyhood. Not until I was about eight or nine – coinciding roughly with the outbreak of war – do my memories begin to form a continuous series of events. Until then I have a number of isolated random recollections of a misty kind. Most of them are, not surprisingly, associated with travel which played a major role in my early life. Before the war, expatriate Sudan government officials were allowed annual leave of eighty days, with assisted passages for themselves and their families to cover the cost of travel to and from England. Rather to his surprise, my father discovered that he was eligible for this assistance even though he was not then a British citizen. At first he had moral scruples about accepting the benefit of these leave regulations, thinking that it was through some accidental loophole that he was entitled. But he consulted some senior colleague who told him not to be a damned fool, a piece of advice for which my father was eternally grateful, so the annual leave journey to England became a regular event. Indeed, my parents took advantage of it to ensure that Michael, I and Selma were all born in England, which then automatically conferred British citizenship on us, and so spared us a possible source of trouble in later years.

The houses in Khartoum were at least equipped with electricity, and most now had electric refrigerators and ceiling fans which made life possible in temperatures which regularly exceeded 100 degrees Fahrenheit for many months of the year. But air conditioning was quite unknown, and it was the climate which dominated the pattern of life.

To accommodate oneself to living in such extreme heat, the secret was to make as much use of the outdoors during the hours of darkness as possible. For many months of the year, people would, once the sun had gone down, sit out on their lawns or terraces, eat out, and even sleep out. Since it only rained for about two months of the year (mid-July to mid-September) for the rest of the hot weather season it was quite safe to sleep out of doors, and many houses were equipped with flat roof terraces for this purpose. Only those who have experienced it can know the delicious feeling of sleeping out in the (relatively!) cool night air after a day of searing heat. As the temperature climbed rapidly after daybreak, people rose early, with the sun, about 6 am, took a leisurely cup of tea, and often started work at 7 am, doing perhaps a two-hour stretch before breakfasting at 9 am. Work would be resumed at 10 am, and continued until 1.30 or 2 pm, though during the war years my father often did not get home until 2.30 or 3 pm. A good lunch was followed by a siesta under a ceiling fan, which enabled one to stay up late to enjoy the cool of the evenings. Hard-pressed officials in the war might also work another couple of hours in the evening. In our case, the routine might differ somewhat because of our swimming pool, so that my father often took a quick dip when he got home, before lunching, or perhaps had a more leisurely swim after the siesta at 4 or 5 pm.

All this meant that gardens were as important as houses, and many of the gardens of the British officials were beautifully tended and colourful creations. Large lawns, magnificent flowering shrubs, and massive shade-providing trees went together with roses and sun-loving flowers like zinnias and carnations. Given the absence of rain for almost ten months of the year it may be wondered how it was possible to keep such gardens going, but the Khartoum water supply was quite abundant in those days, and much could be done with hoses. In addition, the first three or four streets running parallel to the river were watered from the Nile by an elaborate network of pumps, small canals and ditches which enabled the lawns and flower beds to be flooded once a week by the government gardeners who were responsible for their maintenance. In our own case, the weekly emptying of the swimming pool ensured an adequate supply of water to all parts of the garden by means of strategically placed pipes.

The pattern of life also required, of course, an abundant supply of domestic servants, and there was certainly no shortage of these in Khartoum. During the period of which I am writing we always had at least two, and often three servants. There was the cook, an old family retainer who had been trained in Lebanese-style cookery, and who remained with us for nearly twenty years. His first name was “Allagabu” which means “God brought him”. Then there was a series of house-boys, a term never used in Khartoum, however, where they were always known as “suffragis” – literally waiters, but in fact their duties extended also to cleaning and perhaps doing the household washing. We also often employed a gardener, though perhaps not full-time. When there were small children on the scene a nanny was also a common addition to the household. In the larger and better off households of the British officials there were often two or three more servants per household than this. The salary of a servant at this time would have been about two or three Sudanese pounds per month (though many lived in and had their food provided) at a time when my father was earning about 800 or 900 Sudanese pounds per annum. This will no doubt seem like outrageous exploitation to some people, but at that time everyone accepted it as perfectly natural, just as the Victorians did in England a hundred years ago. It was, in any event, a free economy, in which servants' wages had to be competitive with what could be earned elsewhere.

The war must have caused shortages in the shops, but I do not remember the pattern of life being seriously disrupted by shortages. Petrol was not, I think, rationed, nor were foodstuffs. I believe whisky, an almost staple drink among the British officials (and many others) was scarce – a bottle a month was the unofficial household ration. There were one or two tiresome shortages – ink, for instance, was almost unobtainable for some years, and this was a real nuisance before the ballpoint pen was ever invented. Imported clothes were certainly difficult to find, but local tailors had plenty of materials and could run up most items without difficulty – though I remember that shirt buttons were almost unobtainable for some time, and locally made substitutes of appallingly bad quality had to be used.

Entertainments were somewhat limited which no doubt partly explains why so much social activity went on. But there were one or two cinemas – open-air cinemas, of course – and Michael and I were particularly fortunate in having the free run of the "Coliseum", only about five minutes' walk from our house. One of my father's duties during the war was to act as a film censor (to ensure that local morale was not too depressed by the war news, rather than to protect the community's sexual morals), and this naturally brought him into regular contact with the cinema owners. The Coliseum was owned by a Greek named Mr Likos who must, I suppose, have instructed his cinema attendants that we were to be allowed in without charge. At any rate we certainly came and went entirely unchallenged, and as the programme was usually changed three times weekly, we spent many evenings there. The film diet was a mixture of British and American films, and it was here that we got our ration of Errol Flynn swashbuckling as Robin Hood (which was actually shown for a whole week, so we saw it three times), of American Westerns, and of British war films, such as "The First of the Few", the story of the Spitfire.

There was also boating on the Nile during the season, that is, when the river was not in high flood. Many people owned small sailing boats which were moored by a derelict old barge at the side of the river, reputed probably apocryphally, to have been part of Kitchener's fleet in 1898; but sailing was too strenuous for my father, and he acquired a half-share in a rather battered old motorboat christened appropriately "May Day", though it was a long time before I appreciated the joke. We would go out, usually taking a picnic tea in the afternoon, putter along to Tuti Island (which lay between Khartoum and Omdurman when the river was low, but which almost disappeared altogether when the river was in flood), or perhaps more adventurously further upstream along the Blue Nile to a spot where swimming was possible. Although crocodiles were occasionally sighted, they were not really native to this northern part of the Sudan, and we were never troubled by them. A friend once told us that he had spotted a crocodile from his house in Khartoum North, went to get his gun to take a shot at it, and when he returned saw my mother swimming at the very spot, but that was about as close a call as we ever had. On one occasion a tremendous storm blew up while we were at Tuti Island (fortunately not then a complete island) and we had to abandon the boat, and make good way across the island to Omdurman where we obtained help and transport, but most of our outings were sedate enough affairs.

There was also the Khartoum zoo, situated by the river, almost at the junction of the Blue and White Niles, which provided pleasant entertainment for children, though the lions often seemed as overcome by the heat as everyone else. (In the night, their roars could often be heard halfway across the town, and sitting in one's garden one could easily imagine them to be just around the corner.)

For children, the rainy season itself provided entertainment of its own. For a little over two months of the year Khartoum would by smitten by tremendous thunderstorms, perhaps eight or ten times all told. The storms usually came in the evening or at night, after a slow build-up of many hours of intense windless and humid heat. When the storm finally burst, the streets would become awash, the rain would be lashed onto the verandas by high winds, the temperature would drop by ten or twenty degrees in a few minutes, and mattresses and bedding would hastily be brought in from the outside beds and deposited on the verandas (it was still far too hot indoors), where children could play and tumble amongst them.

There was, of course, no air travel from Khartoum before the war, and the normal route was by train to Port Sudan, and then by ship. But for us there were many variations: sometimes we travelled overland to Alexandria, and caught a ship there, sometimes we took the ship only to Marseille, and travelled across France by land. Sometimes we went or came back via Lebanon so that we could spend part of my father's leave with his relatives in his own country. My mother generally went somewhat earlier than my father, and often returned later, so that our "leave" period in those pre-war days might run to four or five months. I have a number of vague memories of these pre-war journeys. I remember on board a ship my mother once giving me a severe telling off for being "abominably rude", and spending the rest of the afternoon wandering round the ship, rolling round my tongue this new and lovely word, "abominably". On another journey I remember the ship's loudspeakers telling us of Hutton's record score of 364 against the Australians in the Oval test match, though I had some vague notion that a "test match" was some kind of a trial or experimental game rather than a real match. That must have been in 1938, and in fact the journey back to Khartoum that year provides a number of other memories. That summer my father had bought a new car in England, a Ford V-8 (it cost just £240, and was rather a large, bulbous shape by today's standards) and planned to take it back to Khartoum. We shipped the car across the channel – no drive-on ferries, of course and I remember seeing it slung overhead by crane – and spent a few weeks driving through Europe to Trieste, where we took ship for Beirut, taking the car with us on the ship. I remember only a few high-spots of our European tour. A dreary first night in a dreary Brussels hotel, with those dreary white counterpanes then found all over Europe; our first glimpse of the famous *autobahns* of Germany, the earliest motorways in Europe designed to take Hitler's armoured divisions – on which my father proceeded to reach eighty-three mph, urged on by his eager sons; feeling car-sick driving through the Black forest, and moaning repetitively, as children will, "Daddy, I'm going to be sick", to which my father replied with a brisk "Nonsense", and drove on, with predictable consequences, and all over the nice new car, too; seeing the two enormous wine vats in the *schloss* at Heidelberg, a memory so vivid that when I revisited Germany for the first time in 1976 with Christine, we paused en route through Heidelberg so that I could see them again, to find, inevitably that they were not so large as I had remembered them; glimpses of the Swiss alps; a hot day in Venice where we took a swim at the lido; and then Trieste where, by pre-arrangement, we met Gucki.

Gucki was a member of a Jewish family of whom we came to see a good deal, and I am glad to be able to record here the way in which my father helped this family. They were three sisters, Austrians, Marion, Lisel and Gucki. Marion was married to an Englishman who worked in the Sudan government, which was how my father came to hear of them. After Hitler took over Austria and the persecution of the Jews there had begun in earnest, my father used his good offices with the Sudan government to help the other two sisters to escape from Austria. Gucki was the youngest, and unmarried, and my parents agreed to engage her as a governess for a year so as to help her to obtain an exit permit. This sounds much grander than it really was, or was intended to be. My parents were never well enough off to be able to afford a real governess in the English style; but Gucki was young and impoverished, and desperately anxious to get out of Austria where (as later became obvious enough) her life would have been in danger. My parents offered her board and lodging, and a little pocket money in return for help with the children, what today would be called more of an au pair arrangement.

We had arranged to meet Gucki in Trieste, where she joined the ship that took us to Beirut, and so on to Khartoum. In fact Gucki was not an easy person, being rather prickly and inclined to be bossy. She quarrelled with the servants, and did not get on too well with us, her charges, either. I can remember being greatly shocked when she persuaded me to take a quinine tablet – there being a malaria epidemic – by sticking it into a teaspoonful of jam and, in response to my suspicious questions, swearing that there was no tablet. It was my earliest experience of a deliberate cold-blooded adult lie, and I never forgot it. Gucki eventually left us to go and live with her other sister, Lisel Weiss. Lisel was married and had a son a little older than me called Herbert. With sympathy from the Sudan government, and some assistance from the Jewish authorities in Khartoum, she and her family came to Khartoum in 1939, arriving virtually penniless in the ferocious summer heat, and knowing almost no English. They were allowed to live in a single room in the grounds of the local synagogue, and were provided by a few sympathisers, including my parents, with some of the bare necessities of life, but not much else. Lisel's husband, Richard, luckily had some entrepreneurial skills, and they soon began to make a living. He began by making, bagging and selling potato crisps at the local cinema; then he started a scrap iron business. One thing led to another, and within a year or two they had rented a house, bought a car, and had joined the very international circle of friends round whom my parents had made their social life.

A year or so after they had arrived in Khartoum, Herbert joined us at our boarding school in Egypt (Victoria College), again with assistance from my father. In characteristic fashion my father had asked his old friend Mr Reed, who was still headmaster at Victoria College, to transfer to Herbert the exhibition (or bursary) which I held, so as to help the Weisses with the financial burden of boarding school fees. My father could not really afford this sacrifice, and was later embarrassingly reduced to writing to Mr Reed to ask whether it would be possible to restore my bursary without depriving

Herbert of his. Fortunately Mr Reed was sympathetic, and everything was sorted out.

I am sorry to say that Michael and I were not as sympathetic or considerate to Herbert as we might have been or (I hope) as we would have been if we had had adult understanding of what he had been through in Austria. Indeed, on one occasion we teased the poor boy to tears by accusing him monstrously of being a "little Hitler". His father later gave us a severe lecture for this, which we well deserved, and my parents made us apologise for our behaviour, but it was difficult for children to grasp the relationship between the world events that we were vaguely aware of, and the personal human tragedies that grew out of them.

My first series of connected memories dates from the beginning of the war. The family was spending the summer of 1939 in England, as customary, when my father received a telegram summoning him back to Khartoum. A ship had been chartered for Sudan government officials, on which there was no room for families, so for the time being we remained behind. Indeed, we wintered in our holiday home – with our prescribed air-raid shelter dug in the garden – and waited for the opportunity to return to Khartoum. This came just in time, shortly before the end of the "phony war", early in 1940. About March or April we travelled across France by train, took ship from Marseille and paused in Beirut to see my father's relatives. Indeed, we spent some months there – I do not know why – living in dreary pensions, and Michael and I actually attended a local school for a short time. Of the school I have no real memory, though I do recollect discussing in the playground the rival merits of France as a land power and England as a naval power. This was a French (and Arabic) speaking school, and most of the children thought France the strongest land power in Europe. A few weeks later the battle of France was over, and Hitler was master of Western Europe.

In June we moved up to our house in Aley, in the mountains above Beirut. My father had, by a stroke of good luck and foresight, built this house in 1935 or 1936 mostly (as was usual with his adventures) with borrowed money. The land itself – some two or three acres – was owned by my grandmother, having been acquired many years earlier by my grandfather, the doctor, and had been left unused and unbuilt on ever since. But it was a magnificent site, on a sloping hillside overlooking the Mediterranean, and my parents had themselves designed the little villa to obtain the maximum benefit from the position. There was a large terrace, naturally facing the sea view; the usual large lounge off which most of the other rooms led, and enough bedroom space for the whole family, including my grandmother and Najla and Mitri.

The garden was terraced in the customary Mediterranean manner, and a number of excellent fruit trees and vines were planted, so that by the time the war came, and we were no longer able to travel to England on leave, this house provided a delightful holiday home for the family through a series of long Mediterranean summers. It was not equipped with any form of heating, however, and as these mountain villages could be pretty cold in winter, was not regarded as habitable except from about May to October. If Michael and I were staying in Beirut at the time of the move to Aley, the day of the move itself was a time of great excitement. A very early start, a lorry if possible for baggage and some furnishings and equipment, taxis, luggage, passengers, a time of great confusion and excitement, the drive up the mountainous roads (no fear in childhood of the rash driving which could make the hairpin bends something of a trial for adults), the first glimpse of the little white villa with its green shutters, its disappearance again as the car rounded the next bend, the final straight over the bumpy unmacadamised length of a mile or two, and then we were there. Again, great excitement, unpacking, rushing round the house and garden, re-exploring loved and remembered spots, trees and views.

On this occasion, however, the excitement was short-lived. Only a day or two after we had arrived, a family confabulation among the adults after we children were in bed, led to a decision to return to Beirut again the following day. Once again, world events impinged on our lives. With the fall of France, the entry of Italy into the war looked imminent; and no one then knew what that would mean. The immediate fear was that Italy might bomb some of the obvious lines of communication in Lebanon, and the mountain road to Aley was also the main road from Beirut to Damascus. If my father had been there perhaps we would not have had such groundless fears; but the family was troubled, so back to Beirut we went, much to my disgust. Pension life in dirty, smelly Beirut was dreary indeed compared with our mountain home. But we did not stay long. Shortly after on return to Beirut we were on our way back to Khartoum to rejoin my father.

The reunited family now had to face another problem which the war had created for us. Khartoum offered no satisfactory secondary school facilities for English-speaking children. All the British officials in the pre-war days had sent their children to boarding school in England at the age of eight or nine. The Clergy House school could cope with children up to about nine, or even, at a pinch, ten, but not later. Michael was ten in 1939, and the intention had been that he should go to Victoria College in Alexandria in the autumn of that year. Indeed, we had even bought his school outfit during that summer of 1939. But with the outbreak of war, Alexandria seemed a much more threatened place than Khartoum. In those early days of the war nobody was sure what bombing would mean, nor for that matter, was it at all clear which cities could expect to be in serious danger from bombing. It was generally assumed that Italy would join Germany and try to make war in the eastern Mediterranean, and Alexandria, as one of the major naval bases of the British fleet, seemed a pretty obvious target. So when the war came the family took it for granted that Michael would not go to Victoria College, and indeed for the whole of 1939–40 our schooling was pretty disrupted. When we finally got back to Khartoum it was anyhow mid-summer, and schools were shut for the year, so nothing could be done immediately. But my mother tried to repair the damage of the past year, and for a few months we had regular morning lessons with her, and once or twice a week we took French lessons from the wife of one of my father's colleagues, a Lebanese lady who was herself French-educated and spoke French fluently. When the autumn came the Clergy House school agreed to extend their age limit to help families like ours, and so we returned there for another eighteen months or so. It was during this period that I got to know Khartoum rather better, with the aid of a newly acquired bicycle, and my earliest memories of the town are mostly of this year.

Despite the grim war news Khartoum remained then a very solid part of the old British Empire, which in those remote regions, seemed an impregnable and eternal institution. Khartoum's very physical appearance was a constant reminder of what the Empire involved. There was, for example, the magnificent riverside avenue, which ran the whole length of Khartoum from the bridge over the Blue Nile to Khartoum North at one end, to the bridge over the White Nile to Omdurman, at the other end. Many elegant houses and gardens abutted this avenue, occupied almost exclusively by senior British officials. In those parts of the Empire one measured one's status as an official not (as is sometimes said of the modern civil servant) by the thickness of the carpet pile in one's office but by the position and size of one's house and garden. Those nearest the river were the largest and grandest, and were reserved for the most senior officials. The grandest of all, of course, was the palace itself, built more or less at the centre of the site of the original palace where Gordon had been killed in 1885, and now occupied by the Governor-General. As one moved to the roads away from the river, one still found reminders of the Empire. In the second road from the river was situated the buildings of the Gordon College (later transmuted into the University of Khartoum), the Anglican cathedral (where also the Clergy

House school was situated), and the statue of Gordon, seated on a camel, which was taken down after the Sudan became independent and returned to the British government – who handed it over to the Gordon Boys' school in Surrey. The story was told to every visitor of the British official who took his small son to see and pay homage to Gordon every day, until the boy was due to be dispatched to school in England. When his father asked him if there was anything he wanted to know before he left, the boy summoned up his courage to ask who was the man sitting on Gordon's back!

As one moved further away from the river, the houses and gardens became progressively smaller, as befitted their occupants, the less senior officials. We ourselves lived in fact some considerable distance from the river, partly no doubt because of my father's lack of seniority, but also because he had spotted and applied for a house with a large piece of adjoining waste land which, he had correctly anticipated, could by persuasion of the right officials, be annexed to the house itself to provide a much larger garden than could normally be expected at that distance from the river. Later, as Khartoum burgeoned and diplomats arrived from around the world to set up embassies and offices, many modern houses and beautiful new gardens sprang up a long way from the river, and indeed far into the desert, but when I was a boy the town of Khartoum hardly extended south of the railway line.

3 Schooldays and Holidays

Early in 1941 the family came to a momentous decision. The war had settled to a steady pattern, Egypt did not for the present look like a war zone, and above all, Victoria College had moved its boarding section to Cairo from Alexandria. With Michael nearly twelve, and myself ten, the Clergy House school could no longer afford us an adequate education, and after a disastrous one-day experiment at the local Coptic secondary school which Michael and I absolutely refused to attend for a second day, it was finally decided that there was no good reason why we should not both be despatched to Victoria College. Indeed, as the Clergy House school refused to take Michael after he was twelve in April 1941, we began our boarding school life during the summer term of that year. We remained there until the end of the war, though during the last year the school moved back to its principal premises in Alexandria. For these next four and a half years our lives followed a fairly set pattern. School during the academic year (a somewhat short year by English standards), the Christmas holidays back in Khartoum, the summer holidays in Aley. The Easter vacation we remained at school as my parents could not afford the fares for the extra journey back to Khartoum, and though the school did try to lay on a few entertainments for the handful of boys who stayed on, like us, it was rather a dreary time.

Victoria College had changed a good deal since my father's time. The Cairo premises, in the suburb of Shubra, consisted of an Italian day school, requisitioned by the Egyptian government after Italy's entry into the war, leased to Victoria College, and hastily converted to meet the needs of boarders so (to quote from my first letter home) "The dormitories are classrooms with black-boards in them". The demand for places at the school proved so great that during our second year there (1941–42) the school rented a house (known as the "villa") a mile or two away, which acted as an overflow for boarders. This was not a convenient arrangement for anybody, least of all the boarders, as it meant that we had no access to our dormitories from the time we set out about 8 am, until we returned for bed about 9 pm. Michael and I were accommodated in the villa for a year or more. The "villa party" was in the charge of an ex-British army sergeant called Sergeant Mulloy who would shepherd us to and from the villa each day, and keep order while we were there. There were also a number of Italian air raids during that first year – though I am not sure that any bombs were actually dropped on Cairo – and from time to time we were dragged sleepily out of our beds to troop into some sort of makeshift air raid shelter. Here the sergeant tried to keep everyone awake and cheerful by playing a game called "Buzz" which consisted of everyone in turn saying a number, in sequence from one onwards, but in which the number seven (or multiples of seven) had to be replaced by the word "buzz". If you did not get it right you were out.

It was not only the buildings that had changed at Victoria College. The whole character of the school had changed. In my father's day the school was designed as a British public school, offering British education and culture to people who, in principle, wanted to acquire it. In our time many of the teachers were not themselves British – it was understandably very difficult to recruit British teachers in Egypt during the war – and the great majority of the boys were now Egyptians. Although most of them presumably were sent there by parents who still had some admiration for British education, or anyhow thought it the key to success in the world they knew, the world itself had changed since the First World War when my father had first gone to the school. No longer was it universally assumed that everyone in the "inferior nations" should study English language, history and literature because these were somehow more important than their own language, history and literature. Many of the Egyptians boys were strongly nationalist in their feelings, and no longer particularly friendly towards Britain. Many of them, indeed, were fairly indifferent as to the outcome of the war, regarding it as a quarrel between foreign powers in which they were not directly concerned. Many of them were outraged when British tanks ringed King Farouk's palace in 1942 and he was compelled to appoint a pro-British Prime Minister. What was more, although the school remained an English-speaking school and all lessons (except for foreign languages) were given in English, most of the boys were not native English speakers. Amongst themselves they often spoke Arabic or (in many cases) French.

It remained the aim of the school to live up to is motto, *E pluribus unum*, and to some extent it succeeded in doing so. Indeed, looking back on it today after sixty years of rivalries, wars and conflicts, it is remarkable how little was the sense of political or religious hostility among the boys. For the boys were indeed a remarkable hotchpotch. Although more than half were probably Egyptians, there were also large numbers of other Arab boys, Sudanese, Lebanese, Palestinians (King Hussein of Jordan went there, though after

I had left); there were the boys of the very cosmopolitan trading classes that lived in Egypt in those days, Greeks, Armenians and Jews; there was a small handful of English boys, and a scattering from other places and backgrounds throughout the Mediterranean and North Africa, from Malta, to Turkey and south to Ethiopia. I remember little sense of hostility between the Arab and the Jewish boys – indeed none of a political nature. Nor was there any religious fanaticism at all. Perhaps the religious tolerance practised by the British in the Empire was still influential in encouraging the people in countries like Egypt to practise religious tolerance too. Certainly the school's religious approach was one of extreme tolerance, extending in practice to apathy. There was no chapel, no compulsory services of any kind, virtually no religious instruction indeed. The school did not even make the gesture (as the Sudan government did) of replacing the Western weekend with holidays on Friday (the Muslim holy day) and Sunday. At Victoria College all boys had classes on Fridays, and though some of them no doubt said their Muslim prayers, and the Jewish boys may have attended synagogues, I have no recollection of this being at all obvious.

Some of the traditions of the English public school continued to be maintained more or less successfully even in these unpromising surroundings and times. English games were, of course, compulsory – football in winter and cricket in summer. The school teams played weekly matches mostly with teams from British army regiments, and some of our best players were Arabs and Jews. At cricket our fastest bowler was an ebony-black Sudanese who subsequently became a high government official in Khartoum.

One day in our first summer at school we were in for a particularly exciting cricketing event. Bill Bowes, the English fast bowler had (so it was rumoured) been recently released as a prisoner of war, and was presently stationed in Cairo. He agreed to come to the school and give a demonstration of fast bowling. A large crowd gathered round the nets to watch the demonstration. The school cricket captain, an Egyptian boy who was actually a very capable cricketer, and who later joined the school as a teacher, was at first put into bat against Bowes, but after he was narrowly missed by a rising ball, the master in charge decided not to risk him again, and Bowes bowled at the vacant crease. He told us that he would knock each stump out in a particular order, and proceeded to do so in three balls, which for someone recently released from a prisoner-of-war camp, and presumably short of cricket practice, seemed a pretty impressive performance to us.

I myself was not very happy at Victoria College, particularly during my first two or three years. I was perhaps a little emotionally tender, and I was small, even for my age; my position was made worse because most of the boys at the school, coming from non-English speaking backgrounds, were less advanced academically by English standards, so both Michael and I were placed in classes with boys whose average age was almost two years above our own. To arrive at boarding school at the age of ten, and be thrown into the company and dormitory of boys of twelve, was quite a shock to me. I was subjected to a fair amount of bullying, but perhaps to more teasing and riling, and I did not take it very well. Michael seemed much happier, perhaps partly at least because, as he was soon established at the top of his class academically, he won the respect of the other boys in a way I did not myself. I was not particularly successful academically, often averaging no better than halfway up the class, though I did rather better in English and could occasionally come second or third in class, but hardly ever first. Michael was also much better at sports than I was, and played from time to time in house football and cricket teams; I was utterly useless at all sports except swimming.

Although I was often unhappy at school, there were friendships and pleasures and amusing incidents. Not long after we arrived at the school Michael and I (filled by my father with the story of Galileo and the experiment he conducted from the leaning tower of Pisa) were shocked to discover that the other boys had not merely never heard of this famous story, but flatly refused to believe that two objects of the same shape and different weights would fall at the same speed. There was clearly only one thing to be done: Galileo's experiment had to be repeated. Unfortunately we had no leaning tower, nor did we happen to possess two balls of copper and lead, so we had to make do with the materials available. The tower could, we thought, simply be replaced by dropping our objects from the dormitory windows into the playground below. The balls were more troublesome, and the only objects we could lay our hands on were somewhat unsuitable, but we did eventually hit on a couple of those flat metal cigarette tins in which fifty cigarettes used to be packed, one of which contained dominoes, and the other a collection of stamps. Indubitably one was heavier than the other, so with these unpromising articles we proceeded upstairs while our sceptical schoolmates gathered down below. The two tins were held aloft and dropped at the same moment, but alas, we had not allowed for the protruding ledge at the base of the upper story, and both tins hit this ledge and flew open. Dominoes and stamps were scattered everywhere. But still, it was conceded that the two tins had hit the ledge simultaneously, and the sceptics were silenced. Galileo was vindicated!

My mother preserved some of my early letters, but they reveal little signs of epistolary skill on my part. I quote a few extracts, with spelling and grammar unchanged.

> *May 8th (1941)*: Thanks for congratulating me on spelling Mediterranean but I asked Michael how to spell it.
>
> *May 15th (1941)*: The war does not seem to be getting on to well for the British. I wonder if the Germans will take Tobruk. And this business about Hess is rather funny. But it is good news (if it is true) that the British shot down 120 aereoplanes in the first nine days of May.[1]
>
> *May 23 (1941)*: There is only one thing I don't like about your letters is that nearly half the letters are correcting my mistakes.

Although we often went out on Sundays to spend the day with relatives and friends of my parents, the school year seemed a long time to me, given that we did not return home in the Easter vacations. But Christmas was a wonderfully exciting time. Not only did we get home, but we also had the four-day journey each way, itself a marvellous experience, especially at that time of year when even the Sudan's fierce climate relented somewhat. Because of the length of the journey, and the fact that the Cairo-Khartoum service only ran twice-weekly, the headmaster allowed us to leave a day or two before the end of term, and return a day or two late. Every year a "Sudanese delegation" as Michael once put it, would call on the headmaster to negotiate the number of extra days we would be permitted. We usually managed two or two and a half weeks in Khartoum plus the journeys, so the headmaster was fairly lenient with us.

I used to love these journeys which were undertaken in great luxury, the trains and steamers being of course largely designed for British officials in those halcyon days of the Empire. The journey began with the train from Cairo which left at 8 pm. We always had a double sleeping compartment on this train and the sleeping car was of French design. A tiny washroom was situated between each pair of compartments, with doors to both compartments, and an ingenious lock which locked both doors with one movement of the bolt. The train arrived at Shellal, near Aswan (present-day site of the high dam constructed by Nasser) around noon the following day, after a pretty fast journey through Upper Egypt. The railway line kept close to the river, and it was common to see from the windows the peasant farmers

1 Atiyah observed that the parenthetical text in this letter "owed something to the skepticism of my schoolmates who told me that British claims of victories were just so much propaganda".

operating a sort of hand-pump called an Archimedes screw because (or so it was said) it was based on a design of Archimedes. It consisted of a pipe or tube of about ten or twelve inches in diameter with a twisted, spiral-like wall running down its interior length. If the lower end of the pipe was inserted in water, and the spiral then turned round and round (a handle was conveniently provided) water was pumped up and poured out of the upper end. This may sound primitive but it was the height of modernity compared with some of the extraordinary gadgets which we used to see operating on the riverside in Khartoum, where a large horizontal wheel was driven round and round by an ox, and this in turn drove a second wheel set vertically into the river. This second wheel had a series of pots lashed to it, so that as each dipped into the water it filled and as the wheel turned round the pots came up and discharged their water into a gulley or trench.

Upper Egypt, especially in the winter, looked green and lush by the river where the railway ran, and in the early mornings one could sometimes see a morning mist over the fields. This part of the journey could be comparatively cool in December and January when we travelled it, but we were heading south to hotter, harsher terrain. In one of my letters home, after returning to school in January, I wrote that it had been so hot on the first night of the journey from Khartoum that we had the fan on, but that early the following morning it had felt "absolutely freezing". Going south, we left the Egyptian train at Shellal and boarded the Nile steamer which carried us for about thirty-six hours to Wadi Halfa just inside the borders of the Sudan. This was a relatively short distance compared with the two railway segments of the journey and I do not know why the railways lines were never joined up (though I believe they may have had different gauges) so that the total journey time could have been virtually halved. But so far as I was concerned, the steamer section of the journey was an idyll. The steamers were very flat-bottomed boats, with huge paddles at the rear; they must have been (I imagine) a little like the famous Mississippi paddle steamers of the last century. On board every comfort was to be found. The cabins, especially the deluxe top-deck cabins which we nearly always had, were a delight. They were equipped with washbasins and bunk beds (Michael and I regularly fought over whose turn it was to have the upper bunk). The floors were covered with a fleck carpet whose pattern lives vividly in my memory. The cabins were also supplied with electric fans, wardrobes and other little furnishings. There were actual bathrooms at the rear of the boats and of course flushing toilets. The decks were spacious and well provided with comfortable chairs and tables where one could just sit and watch the view, or read, or play bridge. Servants glided about, ready at one's call to produce tea, or cold drinks for which one just signed a chit, to settle at the end of the journey. At mealtimes a servants would parade the decks, banging a little hand-gong. The dining room also seemed luxury to me (I had rarely eaten a meal in a restaurant at this time) with beautiful clean table linen, and heavy silver cutlery stamped with "SR" for Sudan Railways, and the meals themselves, as I remember them, consisted of three or four courses each.

The view from the steamer was not generally very exciting, as we were now approaching the desert regions, but if there was time the steamer would stop for an hour or two at the famous temple of Abu Simbel. This ancient Egyptian temple was bodily removed when the high dam was built at Aswan, in a gigantic UNESCO-sponsored exercise which cost many millions of pounds. It consisted of four immense seated statues of ancient Egyptian figures, carved into the rock face, the head of one of which had long since broken off and crashed to the ground, shifted, presumably, by an earthquake.

We spent two nights on the steamer, and on the morning after the second night we woke to find the steamer tied up at Wadi Halfa. This whole town has now been submerged by the waters of the high dam, and its populace moved, but in those days it was the connecting point for train and steamer on the Sudan Railways service. Later, for a few years, it also became an important staging point as an airport. Again, there was the excitement of getting off the boat – we never had to worry about carrying luggage, of course, porters were plentiful – and walking down the long white train looking for our sleeping car. There were no platforms, just sand, the endless sand of the Sudan. The trains were very long, the coaches very white with small windows and (at least for the more privileged passengers like ourselves) tinted glass and shutters. (These trains were actually made in the Sudan at large railway workshops in Atbara, a very successful Sudanese industry.) I loved them. Like the steamers, though of course, less spacious, they offered every comfort, even (what the sleepers on the Egyptian trains did not) individual washbasins in each compartment. We also felt more at home with the Sudanese of the Sudan Railways, and the service seemed pleasanter and more like what we were accustomed to in Khartoum.

The trains were very slow, and the journey from Wadi Halfa to Khartoum took about twenty-eight hours. The line ran southwards across one of the most scorching and barren deserts in the world. Not far south of Halfa, the line left the relative comfort and security of the riverside, and ran across the great bend of the Nile, a distance of several hundred miles of pure waterless desert, and merciless heat. A few railway halts had been constructed alongside the line – not stations in the ordinary sense – where a handful of railway workers lived, and where the train would pause for a few moments, puffing exhaustedly, before resuming its southward journey. It was a one-track line, and the train had therefore to pull in occasionally at a halt or station to allow the northern-bound train to pass. Apart from these rare events, the journey across the great bend offered little to look at except the desert itself. But the desert could sometimes be quite spectacular, especially in colour. It was not just a flat sandy desert, but had hills and rocks, sometimes of striking and strong colours, brown and purple and orange. At sunset the range of colours would be extended by the dying glow of the sun's rays until the train melted into the surrounding countryside in the blessed relief of the dark night. The railway staff would then open the carriage doors, and squat on their haunches by the doorways to get what comfort they could from the breeze created by the train's gentle movement.

Eventually, at Abu Hamed, the railway line rejoined the river, and from here until it reached Khartoum, the line ran continuously down the east bank of the Nile, the very line, in fact, which Kitchener's army had constructed on their way to Omdurman in 1898. Finally, around lunchtime the following day, the first outposts of the capital would be seen, the train would cross the bridge from Khartoum North over the Blue Nile, circle the city, whistling continuously, and draw up triumphantly at Khartoum central station.

These four-day journeys were, apart from the summer holidays, almost the high-spot of my year while I was at Victoria College. On the way home for the Christmas holidays, one had the anticipation of home, family and Christmas, to look forward to and savour for four days while luxuriating in the comfort of the journey itself. And on the way back to school, they did at least provide a buffer between leaving home, during which one could gradually accustom oneself to the grimmer days (as I thought them) that lay ahead. Frequently we made the journey in company with other friends at Victoria College who also lived in Khartoum, and so we had companionship as well as comfort. We would talk, play bridge, or chess, read, and relax at meals. Freed from the tensions and stresses of boarding school life we would often have quite serious arguments about the war, politics and other issues. I remember once Michael arguing vigorously (I am not sure how seriously) that it was stupid to take prisoners of war who had to be fed, and guarded, and might live to fight again. They ought just to be shot. But most of us tempered our rationalism with rather more humanity, and could not stomach this logic.

Occasionally, we would strike up an acquaintance with some British officers of whom there were always a good many travelling this route during the war years. Once a group of officers disembarrassed themselves of some acquisitions in the form of a number of parakeets and a souvenir consisting of an Italian naval cutlass, and we arrived in Khartoum, to be greeted by our rather bemused parents, carrying these mementoes. On another occasion Michael and I persuaded an officer to join us in a three-handed game of bridge, and we sat playing happily for some hours on the floor of our cabin on the Nile steamer. It did not occur to us to find it odd that a British army officer would enjoy whiling away a few hours in our company playing bridge; but by a strange chance my father later encountered this officer, who turned out to have been a headmaster in private life, so perhaps he had found our company enjoyable in a semi-professional sort of way.

One day, in 1942, a few days before the Easter vacation was due to start, our school life was interrupted by near tragedy. The previous morning Michael had been taken ill, and had to be helped to walk from the Villa to the "Sick Flat" in the main buildings. I had seen him looking extremely pale, but it is not the way of children to worry about such things, and at first I had no reason to connect Michael's illness with the strange things that were now happening. For what we now saw was that the buses carrying the day-boys to school were being turned away as they arrived, and presently rumours began to spread that the school was closing for the holidays a few days early. I was summoned by the headmaster's wife, Mrs Reed, a very kindly lady who ran the Sick Flat. She explained to me what was going on, although at first I did not take it all in, and it was only later that I heard the full story. Michael, it seemed, had been stricken with an attack of meningitis, and was in fact found unconscious in his bed by Mrs Reed the previous evening. The school doctor, hastily summoned, accurately diagnosed the disease and was able to get some M & B tablets[2] down Michael's throat despite his unconscious state. In those pre-penicillin days M & B was by far the most effective drug in combatting this dread disease and the doctor had warned the headmaster of the imperative necessity of obtaining further supplies without delay. This was no easy matter in wartime Cairo, especially late at night, but the good Mr Reed set off for a tour of Cairo's chemists at midnight, and finally located a supply. Later, Michael was taken to a British hospital in Cairo, telegrams of warning were despatched to my parents, and it was decided to close the school early for fear of the possible spread of infection.

2 These were an antibacterial medication.

When Mrs Reed spoke to me the next morning Michael was still desperately ill in hospital though she naturally did not stress this fact to me. All that I gathered was that my mother was due to arrive in Cairo that day by seaplane from Khartoum, and my father in fact arrived a day or two later having secured a lift with an Air Force Blenheim conveniently on its way from Khartoum to Cairo. My father had telegraphed one of his Lebanese friends, George Toutounji who met him on arrival, and pressed into his hands a cheque for £200, saying, "Edward, you are bound to have expenses, just take this and repay me when you can". Somehow, my father had a capacity for making friends like that.

Within a few days Michael was out of immediate danger, though he remained for a few weeks very ill indeed. My mother was put up at the school – now empty of boarders – and my father stayed in Cairo with friends. So I had a strange life that Easter vacation. I took some of my meals with Mr and Mrs Reed when they were entertaining my mother; on other occasions we went to visit friends and relatives in Cairo; part of the time I just remained the schoolboy boarding at the school during the vacation. Michael spent his thirteenth birthday in hospital and I spent a few piastres of my pocket money buying him a book – a Baroness Orczy adventure story. I was not allowed to see Michael myself, as it was judged best not to take any risks with such a deadly disease even though the risk of contagion is extremely small; but of course my parents visited him daily and brought me news of him. His first question, on regaining consciousness was to ask if the Japanese invasion of Australia – then daily expected – had yet begun. My father, who had some ability as a poet, was moved by this association of Michael's illness and the war to write a dramatic poem depicting the struggle, of which I only remember the first verse:

Michael you have been a battlefield,
Like Libya or the Russian front,
Where mighty armies clashed and reeled,
But your defenders bore the brunt.

As Michael's recovery was well under way he seemed to suffer from a slight relapse which worried the doctors and my parents for a day or two before it was discovered that he was now ill with a mild attack of measles. This prompted my father to add a postscript to his poem of which I only remember the final two lines:

Like Mussolini, after Hitler, making war,
Like measles after meningitis.

When it became clear that Michael was going to make a complete recovery, but would need a period of convalescence, my parents decided that my mother would, instead of returning to Khartoum with my father, proceed immediately to Beirut as soon as Michael was fit enough to travel with her. They would remain for fussiness over such matters, and I was after all a well-seasoned traveller, although in the past always in the company of parents or at least of Michael. This time I had to travel alone. My father's Uncle Sam collected me from school, put me on the train, and handed me my passport, a bunch of tickets and a little money. The journey was complicated by the fact that there was then no bridge over the Suez Canal, although one was later built by the British forces. But at this time the train stopped at Suez, it was necessary to get off, catch the ferry over the canal, and then re-embark in another train on the other side. It was only there that the sleeping cars were available. Crossing the canal also meant moving from Egypt to Palestine, and there was therefore a passport control office at the entry point to the ferry. The train from Cairo arrived at the canal late at night, and I can remember sitting sleepily on a pile of luggage out in the open air, adjoining the passport officer's window. From time to time he would bark out a name as he went through the pile of passports in front of him, the passengers presented themselves for inspection, received their passports back, and proceeded to the ferry. Who looked after the luggage, and ensured that it got from the one train to the ferry and then the other train, I now have no idea, but somehow it must have worked out. I got to the other side and found myself sharing a two-berth sleeper with a British army officer who must have been a bit surprised at his companion. At Haifa, the next day, I was met by my uncle Mitri, and despatched to Beirut by car. I then had the task of getting myself from Beirut to Aley though I have absolutely no recollection of this part of the journey. I do not know if my mother was at all perturbed at the thought of an eleven-year-old boy making this journey on his own, but I suppose people were inured to difficulties of this sort during the war. In 1944 I had to make the journey alone again because that year Michael had to stay on after the end of term as he was doing the then School Certificate examinations. But by then I was an even more well-seasoned traveller and I had no difficulty coping even though my train was delayed by many hours, so I had to spend a night in Haifa with nobody to meet me or look after me. Fortunately I had encountered a family on the train who knew my grandmother, and they took pity on me, and put me up for the night in Haifa, which was their home.

Back in Aley, life was very pleasant indeed. Perhaps this was when I acquired my taste for the Mediterranean climate, a taste which I have never lost. The school holidays were almost, if not fully, three months long. From early July to the end of September, throughout the years 1942–45 we stayed in my father's house in Aley, except that in 1945 our stay was cut a little short by our return to England. My father himself would join us when he could. For the first year or two his leaves were very short, but as the war went on he was able to take longer leaves and in 1942 he was with us for a month or more. He greatly enjoyed the clean mountain air, the wonderful Mediterranean views, the smell of pines on the hillsides, the beautiful clear springs which gushed forth clean, cold and quite drinkable water. Sometimes we would gather wild herbs, growing profusely – oregano and thyme, I think – and take these home where they would be crushed into a powder in a pestle and mortar, and used freely on various local foods. We would often take early-morning walks and picnics over the mountains from our home. There was in particular a footpath which ran from Aley across the mountains to the small village of Suk-el-Gharb, my father's birth-place, where his uncle Farid, and Aunt Selma invariably summered. Sometimes we would rise early and walk to Suk-el-Gharb to take breakfast with Farid and Selma. On other occasions we would take sausages and eggs and cook our own breakfast at the mountain top, using the ever-present stones and rocks and sticks to construct makeshift camp-stoves. Later in the summer, Michael and I would sometimes get up very early, climb the large old fig tree in the garden and pick a basket of lovely purple-coloured figs, still moist with a hint of Mediterranean dew, and carry them with us to offer to Farid and Selma.

It was during these long summer holidays that Michael and I were particularly thrown on each other's company – there were few other boys around of our own age for us to play with – and it was at this time that we played many games of chess, endless rounds of two-handed bridge, and a variety of other games, often home-made. There was Michael's version of the monopoly game, and I also remember another elaborate board game, made by Michael, and based on some contemporary war game, in which the players represented either the Allies or the Axis, and moved military counters around a map of Europe. Again, as with the monopoly, Michael's version was much more elaborate than the rather tame manufactured one which had given him the idea.

I often think that in some ways life in Lebanon in those years must have resembled life in England in earlier centuries. There were, for instance, the coffee houses, perhaps resembling London's coffee houses in Dr Johnson's day. Here the men (rarely the women) would sit for hours, reading newspapers, drinking coffee, smoking a hubble-bubble (called there, a "nurgeely") and usually playing backgammon. Much vigorous banging of counters and throwing of dice always accompanied this game. From time to time a bootblack-boy would appear, offering to clean one's shoes. These boys carried a sort of long wooden box, with a leather strap, slung over their backs, and a small rush stool in their hands. The box would be unslung and placed on the ground, and the boy would seat himself on his stool. And to call them "boxes" fails to convey the elaborate gadgets which were attached to them, or contained in them. Neat little flaps opened to reveal shoe polishes and tins and brushes of every kind. Decorations and ornaments were also attached to the boxes revealing some pathetic attempt at artistic expression with what was very likely the owner's sole possession. The shoe cleaning itself was also an elaborate ritual, no casual polishing. First each shoe was washed with a piece of sponge, and then carefully dried. Then the polish was applied and brushed. Then a final coating of wax was applied and all finished off with a duster so that the shoe glittered like a mirror.

Again, there was "visiting", much as described in Jane Austen's novels. As the women of the household were mostly free from household chores, they would frequently set off on a morning of visits to their cousins or friends. Children would also be dragged along to be admired and petted. How I hated those "visiting days"! Forced to submit to the humiliations of being washed and dressed up in smart clothes, then being required to parade before the hostess, and perhaps even to submit to kisses, and ultimately being compelled to sit still while the adults nattered on for hours, with perhaps a cake or a sweet the only relief from the tedium. Naturally the conversation centred round family gossip – who was getting married who was having a baby (this not too loud with children present) – and so on. Oh, the insufferable boredom of it!

Other social institutions of the time may have had their English counterpart in earlier days, though I have not myself read accounts of them. There was, for example, washing day. Once a week a washerwoman would come in to do the family washing, an immense pile of laundry would be collected – there were often ten or eleven in the household – and she would set to, with a bar of old-fashioned kitchen soap, to wash her way through this load. Of course, being in the Mediterranean summer, all this took place out of doors. The washerwoman would sit herself comfortably on a small rush stool, adjusting her seating with as much care as a concert pianist, and proceed to scrub away at the laundry in a large flat round washing bowl. At her side would be placed a primus stove on top of which a can of water would be heating – the can was always one of those ubiquitous four-gallon kerosene or petrol cans used by the army during the war which became a familiar sight to all in war spheres. As fast as she used up one can of hot water, it would be replaced by another. At lunchtime she would pause for refreshments – she expected to be provided with lunch, of which, judging by her size she needed a goodly amount – then returned to her task. We had of course an inadequate washing line for this enormous quantity of laundry, so it was spread around on any available railings, chairs or even trees and shrubs. There was never any trouble getting it dry.

Another great event was baking day. It was customary for people to make their own bread – round flat loaves of the type recently popularised in England under the name of "pitta bread". Carefully stored in a large bowl, wrapped in moist cloth, these loaves could be kept for some weeks, so it was possible to bake a family supply for several weeks at a time. But we had no oven in the kitchen – few people in Lebanon at this time had modern cookers, most cooking being done on primus stoves – so the bread had to be sent down to the village bakery. The proceedings began rather like the weekly washing. A woman would call, and be presented with a huge sack of flour; she would sit down on a rush stool and proceed to mix and knead this in a large bowl, and roll it into the necessary round shapes. They would then be piled, one on top of another, perhaps as many as a hundred such loaves, wrapped in a suitable cloth, and replaced in the bowl. This would then be carried down to the village bakery a mile or two away, often followed by Michael and me, come to observe the fun, and if possible to snatch a hot loaf straight from the oven and eat it at its most delicious.

The bakery itself was of a very old-fashioned kind, not nowadays seen at all in the Western world, though it's like may have been common enough at one time in England, for all I know. The oven was built into the wall of the bakery, with openings underneath for the fire, and openings above (without doors) for the bread. The baker would take eight or ten loaves and, working with incredible speed, would deposit them in a row, as though laying a handful of cards down on a long plank-like implement, narrowed at one end to afford a handle. He would then slide the plank into the oven, turn all the loaves off onto the tiled oven floor with a flick of his wrist, and proceed to the next plank. Meanwhile, one could see through the oven openings the loaves rapidly swelling like balloons, as this kind of bread does, being hollow in the middle. A few moments later came the most difficult trick of the baker's art. He would slide the plank underneath the whole row of part-baked loaves

Figure 3.1 Victoria College, Alexandria, Egypt. Patrick is first from the left in the second row. His brother, Michael, is second from the left in the first row. Credit: Atiyah family.

and flick them over to do the other side. A few more minutes and the plank would again be slid under the loaves and they would be withdrawn from the oven, steaming hot and absolutely delicious. An hour or so, and the family's bread supply for several weeks would be baked.

4 Post-War England

As the war drew to its end my father began to talk more and more of retiring from the Sudan and going to live permanently in England. He had always had this idea at the back of his mind, and in 1944 an opportunity seemed to open up before him. About that time the Arab countries joined in a rare act of political agreement to establish the Arab League, and a Palestinian Arab called Musa Alami conceived the idea of setting up an Arab publicity bureau in London, under the auspices of the new League, to ensure that after the war was over the Arab case on a variety of issues was presented to the British public.

Many intelligent Arabs felt that after the First World War their voice had not been adequately heard in the West, which had proceeded to carve up the former territories of the Ottoman Empire without regard to Arab wishes. They wanted to be sure that this did not happen again, and that the Arab countries of the Middle East emerged from the war with their independence recognised by the West.

Above all there was the problem of Palestine, and the urgent need to see that the West did not simply assuage its guilt for the wrongs done to the Jews by the Germans by perpetrating further wrongs on the Arabs themselves. It was by this time clear that when the war was over, the Arab-Jewish conflict over Palestine would be renewed, and thoughtful Palestinians like Alami were concerned that the Arab case should be adequately presented to British public opinion. The Jewish case never lacked spokesmen in Britain; there were, after all, Jews in Parliament, in business, in the professions and in all walks of life. The Jewish Agency in London was an effective propaganda office, lobbying governments and bombarding the public. And above all, the Nazi persecution of the Jews, and the horrifying stories and pictures coming out of Belsen and Dachau and the other terrible concentration camps as the Allied armies poured across Germany, had roused the conscience of the world, and greatly increased sympathy for the Jews. It was evident that one very practical form which this sympathy was going to take was going to be a demand for increased emigration of Jews into Palestine, where the Arabs were now in danger of becoming a minority in their own land.

Musa Alami and other Palestinian Arabs wanted the British government and the British people to realise that the Jewish problem could not and ought not to be solved at the expense of the entire Palestinian Arab nation. They were looking for a spokesman who could establish an Arab office in London, and could speak to the British people as effectively as the Jewish Agency. Alami first approached a major in the British army, Albert Hourani, who was himself of Lebanese origin, and who had met my father during the war. Hourani directed Alami to my father. Endless discussions took place between them, and my father agreed to take on the post; he persuaded the Sudan Government to allow him premature retirement on a small pension, and flew to England early in 1945. There he established the Arab Office, under the auspices, and with the financial support, of the Arab League. For some years my father ran this Office and did excellent work, publishing pamphlets and information bulletins, writing letters to *The Times* (my father claimed to have written the longest letter he had ever seen in *The Times*, extending over more than one full column), meeting and briefing British MPs and generally acting as a very successful publicist for Arab interests. He was also in great demand as a public speaker, presenting the Arab case before the British public in many different places and centres. Twice he was invited to speak at the Cambridge Union, and one of the people he influenced there was Dennis Walters who subsequently became a Conservative MP and a strong supporter of Arab interests. In his autobiography, *Not Always with the Pack*, published in 1989,[1] Sir Dennis paid tribute to my father's influence on him some twenty-five years earlier.

After my father's departure for England in early 1945, my mother took my younger sister and brother to Lebanon for a few months, and Michael and I completed the year at Victoria College, before we too proceeded to Lebanon for the summer. It had been an exciting last term, with the surrender of Germany and the end of the European war. The prospect of going to live in England was also one which we welcomed, though we had little idea of what life in post-war England was going to be like. At any rate we had one final glorious Mediterranean summer in our mountain home in Aley, before telegrams arrived, instructing us to proceed to Egypt where we were to pick up a boat sailing to England. After a frustrating few weeks' delay in Cairo, when nobody could tell us when and if we would be able to sail, such was the chaos of these immediate post-war months, we finally found ourselves on board the *Winchester Castle*. It was, as Michael said, good to feel solid deck

1 D Constable, *Not Always with the Pack* (1989).

underfoot once again. The *Winchester Castle* was an old P&O liner which had been converted into a troopship during the war, and it was crammed with passengers who had been unable to get back to England during the war years. My mother and the younger children had to share a cabin with five or six other passengers, while Michael and I were accommodated in a large saloon converted into a kind of dormitory with tiers of bunks. Conditions on board were crowded, but after boarding school, it was luxury to us. We did not even know what port we were sailing to when the ship left, but a day or two out from Port Said, the captain announced that we were making for Southampton which suited us admirably, as it was the nearest major port to our Surrey home. We arrived on 23 September 1945.

My father met us at Southampton, and for a while we conducted a very loud Atiyah-style conversation between him on the quayside, and ourselves on board, much to the amusement of the onlookers. Eventually, we disembarked, and crowded ourselves and an immense quantity of luggage into my father's Morris 18 and set off for Surrey. Our home was not in a very comfortable, or even habitable condition. It had never been more than a summer holiday house, and five years of neglect during the war had hardly improved it. It contained only one fireplace and two bedrooms, though there was an annexe with another two bedrooms and a sort of habitable garden room which was comfortable enough in the summer, though scarcely usable in winter. My father was not used to dealing with efficient and incorruptible bureaucracies administering a mass of regulations, and he had made no attempt to secure the necessary licences and permits to enable him to improve the house or refurnish it. He had even been reduced to buying sheets on the black market. But at least it was just about habitable, and later my father was able to have the house extended and finished to provide the space needed to accommodate a family with four children. We settled down to a new life.

The first things to be organised were schools for Michael and myself. After Michael's performances in the School and Higher Certificate at Victoria College, there could be no doubt that he was marked out for higher things in mathematics. However, my father was still partly under the influence of his socialist, almost communist ideals, and he had vaguely thought of sending Michael to work in a factory for a year or two after leaving school before proceeding with higher education. But when he had suggested this to the senior Mathematics master at Victoria College, the response had been distinctly frosty. Characteristically, my father then went to the other extreme, and made inquiries about the best school in the country for mathematics.

The answer, and it was the right answer, had been Manchester Grammar School, but as this was not a boarding school, my father had had to arrange digs for Michael in Manchester, and he was now despatched there for the next eighteen months. As my father had been at Oxford, it was at first assumed that Michael would follow him there, but at that time Trinity College, Cambridge had the reputation of being the best place for mathematical studies, and it was for Trinity that Michael therefore aimed when he took the scholarship examination just before Christmas, 1947. In the event he obtained the top scholarship, receiving the rare distinction of a commendatory letter in which his work in Geometry was described as "outstanding"; the second and third Trinity scholarships were also obtained by his colleagues from Manchester Grammar School, which therefore made a clean sweep of the top awards that year.

As for me, I was sent to the Woking County Grammar School, which was of course a day school, and I greatly welcomed the change from boarding school life. I participated in a number of school activities, particularly the Debating Society, which I enjoyed very much (winning in my last year the pompously entitled Declamation Trophy for public speaking), and the Chess Club. I even managed a few minor successes of a sporting nature, in the annual swimming contests, though I was quite useless at all other physical games, and compulsory physical education was a weekly torture to me.

For the next few years my life was relatively uneventful. It was largely dominated by school, though in retrospect, I remember more of the outdoor activities of the two glorious summers of 1947 and 1949. During those wonderful summers, we swam a lot at the Woking swimming pool, we took cycling holidays, we followed the cricket, and generally did what growing teenagers always do.

Among other things, I began to cultivate a taste for classical music. Although I am myself almost tone deaf, cannot sing a note, and can scarcely identify which sounds emerge from which instruments, classical music has long been one of the pleasures of my life. The foundations for a lifelong attachment to the great classical composers were laid during these years, mostly through records, but occasionally with visits to the Proms. In those days it cost only two shillings to get into the Albert Hall for a feast of music during the Promenade Concerts, although the cost for us living in Surrey was inevitably inflated by the journey. I remember once Michael and I went to hear the Beethoven Sixth and Seventh Symphonies on the same night. At that time I was not very well acquainted with the Seventh and I expressed the view that the Sixth was the greater work. Michael disagreed.

In the event, I found myself overwhelmed by the mighty crescendos of the Seventh, as I stood there in the crowd of music-lovers at the Albert Hall, and when Michael asked me afterwards if I did not now agree that the Seventh was the greater symphony I could only gulp my agreement.

I shared my growing interest in classical music (and in particular a taste for Beethoven) with a number of schoolmates, though they, like myself, were unable to play any instruments or even to sing. As a group we puzzled, indeed, rather incensed our music master at school who was programmed to give the sixth formers one lesson a week of musical appreciation. He was the traditional musical Welshman who had probably learned to sing at Chapel, and he would fulminate against our worship of Beethoven. "Beethoven could not write music for the human voice", he would pronounce in his sing-song Welsh accent. He dismissed us with withering scorn as a group of "gramophone virtuosos".

Academically I began to find myself more successful than I had ever been at Victoria College, and in the summer of 1946 I took the School Certificate with some success: I obtained four "Very Goods" and four "Credits." One of the credits, to my utter astonishment, was in Art, at which I had not the slightest talent, and which I had vainly sought permission to drop. Although some of my best results were in mathematics and science subjects, and the science teachers tried to persuade me to go onto the Science Sixth form, I never had any doubt that I wanted to pursue Arts subjects, and especially history.

My parents' standards for judging academic success were set by Michael, who had obtained eight Very Goods in the School Certificate – though, as I was fond of pointing out, he had also failed in one subject (Arabic). They did not seem to see my results as particularly distinguished, and my father continued for some years to think of me as an unacademic and unintellectual sort of boy. He occasionally tried to persuade me that I did not have to think of going to a university, as there was nothing to be despised in less intellectual careers. These were, I think, partly the relic of his socialist and idealist years, but partly they were also due to a massive misjudgement of my temperament – which had some influence on me, because I also tended to think of myself as unintellectual in those days.

However, I never had any doubt that I was going to try for a place at Oxford, though I was not confident of success. In those days the Oxford scholarship examinations were held in Oxford, and candidates had to spend a few days there, lodging in the colleges. When I asked my father for a few pounds as I was about to go to Oxford for the examination in December 1948, he handed them to me saying that he felt like a punter laying money on a long shot. I think I was almost as surprised as he was when the long shot came off and I was awarded an Entrance Exhibition funded by the Ministry of Education in Modern History at Magdalen College.

I had intended at first to "read" either History or PPE (Politics, Philosophy and Economics) at Oxford, but while I was waiting to go up to Oxford there occurred one of those chance events which was to change the whole course of my life. One day, returning from the Oval where I had driven by motor-bike to see Surrey play, I ran into an unfortunate pedestrian who was crossing the road in front of me without looking where he was going. Somewhat surprisingly, perhaps, I was more hurt than he was, as I gashed my leg which bled profusely, while he escaped with nothing more than a shaking. In due course I was summonsed before a London magistrate for driving without "due care and attention". I was, in fact, only a learner driver at the time, and I dare say the accident was partly my fault, though I certainly thought the fault was not all mine. Anyhow, when I appeared before the magistrate I decided to defend myself, and I cross-examined the witnesses vigorously, if inexpertly. The magistrate still convicted me, but fined me a nominal £1, and then he asked me whether I was a law student, saying that he thought I might have been from the way I had conducted my defence. As I left the courtroom I pondered these words, on the way home in the train I turned over in my mind the idea of becoming a barrister, and by the time I had got home I had pretty well made up my mind to read law when I got to Oxford. I have never regretted that decision.[2]

I was lucky in my change of subject. At that time Magdalen College had one of the strongest tutorial teams for law in Oxford. My first tutor was Rupert Cross who was a very remarkable man. Rupert (as he was universally known in Oxford) was blind, and had been blind since he was a year old when he had an operation for cancer on his eyes. He had qualified and practised as a solicitor for some years, until (as he put it) he decided that he

2 Atiyah was due to start at Magdalen in October 1949. In the event, his arrival was delayed. The reason for the delay is unclear. Correspondence held in Magdalen College's archives reveals only that the delay was arranged to "allow time for [Atiyah] to get over the whole disturbance of the affair and for any mentions of it in the press to be forgotten": letter from the President of Magdalen College to Edward Atiyah dated 7 October 1949. It is possible that the affair was the motorcycle accident, but the position is ultimately unclear. Other correspondence, including a letter from John Morris to the President dated 13 December 1949, indicates that Atiyah started his studies in Trinity Term 1950 (i.e. the final term of the 1949–1950 academic year). He was prescribed some reading to do at home in the interim. I gratefully acknowledge Frank Rose for alerting me to these items of correspondence and for providing me with copies of them.

had divorced too many couples and sought an academic job. He blossomed in his new career, proving exceptionally successful and popular as a tutor, while at the same time finding the time to write very extensively, mostly on criminal law and the law of evidence. Later in life he also sat on a number of law reform committees for which he eventually received a knighthood, to the great pleasure of his old students. In 1964 he was appointed to the Vinerian Professorship of English Law, and gave up his tutorial fellowship at Magdalen for a professorial fellowship at All Souls. By 1979 three of Oxford's six law professors were old pupils of his.

I got on very well with Rupert, and I think he enjoyed having me as a student. Certainly, my tutorials often seemed to stretch well beyond the statutory tutorial hour, and when my essay was still unfinished after one-hour-and-forty-five minutes, and the next student was knocking at the door, Rupert would insist on my coming back to finish the essay later in the week. He was the kind of person who always got the best out of his students, because nobody ever wanted to let him down. He was also an astonishingly knowledgeable lawyer, despite his inability to pick up learning through browsing – which has always seemed to me one of the most important ways of learning, especially for an academic. You could rarely catch him out. Many a time, when asked some apparently arcane question, Rupert would say: "Ah, yes, there's something about that in Bloggs on Rape" (or whatever) and he would grope his way to his bookshelf, feel along the volumes, pick out the book, hand it to you, and add, "Somewhere around page 250 you'll find a discussion of that point".

During my second year Rupert had the misfortune to be involved in a motor accident as a result of which he had to remain on his back in bed for some weeks, and he was accommodated in the Nuffield Sanatorium on the Banbury Road. He did not, however, allow this little incident to get in the way of his teaching, and tutorials were still conducted in his room at the Nuffield. If one had a tutorial at 6 pm. Rupert would surreptitiously suggest, in a conspiratorial sort of way, that if one looked in such and such a cupboard one might just possibly find a bottle of sherry, and one was invited to partake of it on condition of keeping Rupert's own glass steadily replenished. This was all very well but it meant that if the tutorial hour ran much past 7 pm. one was in great danger of missing dinner in college which was, of course, invariably at 7.15 pm.

My first term's tutorials – on the criminal law – enabled me to stretch my mind in new and fascinating ways to which I responded readily. I read voraciously, and took great pains with my essays. At the end of the term Rupert told me that I ought to be thinking in terms of getting a "first" in my degree, "unless", he added in his inimitable manner, "you take to drink and fall by the wayside in the meantime". That was the first time I had ever thought of myself as having a "first class mind" (especially by Oxford definitions) and the thought perhaps went to my head a little. I became a little brash and perhaps even arrogant. This was another of those chances which had an impact on my life later on, largely through the reactions of my other tutor, John Morris.

Dr Morris was already something of an Oxford law character when I first arrived at Oxford. He appeared to cultivate two distinct roles: with his students he adopted a quiet, somewhat menacing and frightening severity of manner. With his colleagues he adopted the role of a "cantankerous old cuss" increasingly as the years went on. When I first went to Magdalen, Morris had a higher academic reputation than Rupert Cross, having obtained the DCL degree[3] a year or two earlier at a fairly young age, as these things went at the time. He had also just spent a year as a visiting professor at the Harvard Law School, which was a rare distinction for an Oxford fellow. I found Morris a strange man. He had a formidable physical presence – tall of stature and massive in girth, he must have been all of fifteen or sixteen stone. He could be pompous, severe, and cantankerous, and many of his students found him quite terrifying – including (by his own admission) one of my contemporaries, Nicolas Browne-Wilkinson, later a Law Lord. But I often found that Morris's severity and cantankerousness was a deliberately cultivated exterior, and that if one stood up to him, and punctured the pomposity, he could quite easily respond with a sort of grunting laugh. He was not unfriendly to me, and certainly was complimentary on my work; but I learnt afterwards that he had resented the fact that I always seemed to have an answer to everything, and had put me down as brash and bumptious, which may well have been unhappily true, anyhow for a time. I also learnt that Morris was nothing like as popular a character in the Magdalen Senior Common Room as Rupert who was loved by one and all.

Another tutor who took me for a couple of subjects was Charles Monteith, a Magdalen graduate who had been elected a Fellow of All Souls, and was doing weekend teaching while he tried to establish himself at the Bar. (He eventually gave up the Bar, and went into publishing, where his greatest

3 The "DCL", or Doctor of Civil Law, was one of the higher doctoral degrees then awarded by Oxford. It was conferred on the basis of a scholar's publications. Atiyah himself would receive it: see p xxv.

coup was to select William Golding's *Lord of the Flies* for publication, a book for which Golding ultimately won the Nobel Prize for literature.) Monteith had rooms in the High Street, almost opposite the University Church, and I happened to be having a tutorial there in February 1952, just after the death of the King, when the Accession Proclamation was solemnly read out by the Mayor of Oxford in front of a crowd of assembled dignitaries. I suggested to Monteith that we should abandon the tutorial and watch the ceremonies, and so we did, having one of the best views in Oxford. It seemed a better lesson in Constitutional Law than reading out my essay.

I enjoyed my time in Oxford very much, though looking back I probably spent too much time on academic pursuits, and too little on other things. I did join the Labour Club, being an ardent and idealist socialist in those days, and was even elected a member of the committee for a term or two. Two of my friends at the time were Bill Rodgers, also at Magdalen, who later became a Labour MP and eventually one of the leaders of the SDP; and Gerald Kaufman who became a crony of Harold Wilson's and a Minister in Wilson's last government. But I found the Labour Club rather a puerile institution. What I particularly disliked about it was the kind of knee-jerk reaction politics which operates rather like a game: mention a certain word, or phrase or idea among the cognoscenti, and a predictable response is triggered off – derisory laughter, or an alternative word or phrase, or perhaps name. For a long time I thought that Gerald Kaufman – judging by what I read of him in the press – hadn't changed much in these respects. Perhaps it was the influence of the Harold Wilson years. But later he seemed to me to shed some of these puerilities, and became a more mature politician.

One illustration of the puerility of the Labour Club stands out in my recollection. We invited Sir Waldron Smithers as a guest speaker one night. I don't suppose many people today even remember Sir Waldron, but he was a sort of right-wing Dennis Skinner. He was a Conservative MP on the far-right of the party – not the sort of far-right which gets close to fascism, but an old-fashioned, courtly, far-right. He was, in short, an old-fashioned sort of Victorian gentleman and we in the Labour Club thought he was a bit of a buffoon who would have the audience all rolling about in laughter at his absurd Toryism. In fact he wasn't a buffoon at all, and the whole evening back-fired on us. He was a charming old man, full of old-world courtesy. At a preliminary tea-time committee meeting at which he had been invited to attend, we had all been seated round a table when our lady secretary had to leave the meeting early. While we, her male colleagues, sat around slouching in our usual scruffy undergraduate way, Sir Waldron leapt to his feet, dashed to the door and held it open for our secretary as she went out. I rather think we felt more shamed than amused by this behaviour, and much the same was true at his speech during the evening meeting. It would be agreeable to say that this encounter began my personal slide from socialism to conservatism, but in fact my move to the right was a long slow process which only began after I left Oxford.

I enjoyed the debates at the Oxford Union in my first few terms and would have liked to try my hand as a speaker, but the chance never came. The President of the Union in my second term was Jeremy Thorpe, and in those days would-be new speakers had to put their names down in advance and meet the President. I waited for a debate on the Law on which I particularly wanted to speak, had my interview with Jeremy Thorpe, but then discovered that few new speakers had a chance to take the floor on the first occasion that they put their name down. No later debate attracted my interest that term, and after that it seemed too late. The style of speaking was extremely artificial, of course, and rather arch. One had to know how to tell good jokes, or have some other facility like mimicry in which Jeremy Thorpe excelled. Some of the speakers could be exceedingly funny, but the endless political debates were rather repetitive, and there was an unpleasant type of audience reaction by way of ironic laughter which (it may not be overdramatic to say) played a part in causing my father's death in 1964.

There were a number of other activities I took part in – college swimming competitions (when I learnt how utterly exhausting was water polo!), chess (I played for the university second team occasionally), and even bridge, when I formed a scratch pair with a friend and went in for the university bridge contest, to come seventh out of eight teams. And of course there was the theatre and the cinema and other entertainments. But most undergraduates had a much less interesting and varied life in those days than they seem to now. We ate out very little, for instance; accommodation was either in college or in digs – there was no "house sharing" as today, with all the freedom that entails. We didn't – or at least I and my closest friends didn't – frequent the pubs which nowadays seem crammed with undergraduates. But mostly, my time was spent on reading in my subject – Law, Law and more Law.

To most people that probably sounds very dull, but I did not find it dull; and I very much regret that law is in England regarded as an arcane subject, a husk of technicalities of no real interest or concern to the public. Law is the cement of society; it is law which enables people to live in their teeming millions, pursuing each their own purposes within a relatively peaceful framework which protects all. The reconciliation of the needs of stability and predictability with the desire for individualised justice, which is at the heart of all law, is a matter of the utmost concern to societies and individuals and it is here that lawyers have an experience and expertise which goes far beyond the role of the technical craftsman. These are matters which ultimately became the central concerns of my professional life and work, and as an undergraduate at Oxford I laid the foundations for a future academic career, rather unintentionally because it was originally the thought of becoming a barrister that had attracted me to the subject. I read far more widely than I was required to, and I read critically. Revelling in my newfound powers (or recognition of my powers) I was often scornful of the reasoning of lawyers and judges, and felt that things could be improved.

One of my most exciting occasions was a moot held in Magdalen before Lord Denning. A moot as conducted in Oxford (or elsewhere) is a sort of mock appeal in which legal arguments are presented before a judge, on the basis of a statement of assumed facts. It is not a mock trial, as the public might think of that, because there are no witnesses, and the "facts" of the case are given, as so much data. There are always two counsel on each side, and a well-set moot is designed to raise at least two distinct points of law which can be argued by each pair of counsel. The mooters are expected to present their arguments as though they were in one of the higher appeal courts in England, addressing the judge (or judges) in barrister-like fashion as "My Lord" and saying at frequent intervals, "I submit" and so on. The fatal error is ever to say, "I think" because (in the standard joke) barristers never think – they submit.

The annual dinner moot at Magdalen was at that time (and I hope they maintain the tradition)[4] quite an exciting affair. We usually had a distinguished judge to preside, the occasion was (in the usual Oxford tradition) a black tie one, and we had a good dinner before adjourning to the Magdalen Law Library where we held our moot, sipping our port in most un-barrister-like fashion! Although most moots are quite serious affairs, at the Magdalen dinner moot there was usually a certain element of humour permitted, either because the subject matter of the moot was whimsical, or because the arguments of the mooters were sometimes tongue in cheek. On this occasion the guest judge was Lord Denning, who was an old member and an honorary fellow of the college. He was already (this was 1952) very well known among the legal profession as an innovative judge (indeed, in those

4 The moot continues to this day. In 2007, I participated in it before Sir John Mummery, and in 2008 before Lord Neuberger.

days, he was thought "unsound" and John Morris once predicted gravely, but absurdly, that he would eventually be removed from office) but he was not at that time known to the wider public. I was given a particularly difficult task – namely, trying to persuade Lord Denning that he should not follow one of his own earlier decisions. Although I did not succeed, I did extract from him an admission that some of his earlier obiter dicta were perhaps in need of modification, which, in the circumstances, was, I felt, no mean achievement. Fifty years later I gave the opening address at a conference at the University of Buckingham to celebrate Lord Denning's hundredth birthday.[5]

While I was doing Law at Oxford my brother Michael was doing mathematics at Trinity College, Cambridge. During my first year, and his second, we exchanged visits. I joined a Labour Club group on a coach visit to Cambridge where we had lunch and were addressed by one of the rising young men of the Labour Party, Anthony Crosland, who later became an MP and a senior minister in the Wilson and Callaghan governments, before dying tragically shortly after being appointed Foreign Secretary. Michael returned the visit on his motorcycle, bringing with him a pillion passenger named James Mackay. Mackay was a Scot who was also doing mathematics at Cambridge, but intended to change to law after getting his first degree and to practise in Scotland. He became a good friend of Michael's and in fact acted as best man at Michael's wedding which took place in Edinburgh in 1955 (Michael's wife being a Scot who came from Edinburgh). Mackay became a very distinguished Scots advocate, was appointed Lord Advocate and later served a spell as a Lord of Appeal before being appointed Lord Chancellor in 1987. In that capacity he made me an honorary QC in 1989. When he reminded me of his visit to Magdalen in 1952 I could not help having irreverent visions of him as an Iolanthe-like Lord Chancellor riding pillion on a motorcycle with his wig flapping and his gown billowing!

Life at Oxford then had, and I expect still has, certain privileges. One of them was the chance to meet the eminent who came from time to time to speak at university clubs, and who would usually take drinks, or dine with members of the club's committee. As a member of the Labour Club committee I was fortunate enough to meet Mr Attlee shortly after his government had been defeated at the election of 1951. I cannot say that I remember much of this meeting, though I do recall one anecdote which seemed rather

5 PS Atiyah, "Lord Denning's Contribution to Contract Law" (1999) 14 *Denning Law Journal* 1. See also PS Atiyah, "Contract and Tort" in JL Jowell and JPWB McAuslan (eds), *Lord Denning: the Judge and the Law* (1984).

characteristic of Mr Attlee. He told us that since he had lost office he had taken to travelling by underground in London. On one occasion a fellow passenger stared at him for some minutes and then leant over to say: "Do you know, you look extraordinarily like Mr Attlee." To which Mr Attlee had responded: "So people tell me."

There were also eminent men in embryo at Magdalen itself. Indeed, while I was an undergraduate, we nurtured a future Prime Minister of Australia, Malcolm Fraser whom I never knew; and a future Prime Minister of Canada, John Turner, who was like me, doing law, so I did know him, though not closely. Some twenty years later, when I was teaching at the Australian National University in Canberra, Turner visited Australia in his capacity as a minister of the Canadian government (not then Prime Minister, an office he only held for a very short time), and was invited to the Law School. I said, as one does on these occasion, "I don't suppose you remember me", when Turner interrupted with a glassy politician's smile, "Of course I remember you", but I was quite sure he did not, and I did not want to embarrass him by putting his memory to the test, so I hastily reminded him of Magdalen.

During my third year at Magdalen I acted as research assistant to a visiting professor from Harvard, W Barton Leach, who had been collaborating on a book with John Morris on that most recondite of legal subjects, *The Rule Against Perpetuities*.[6] Leach must be the only lawyer in history to have written an article on that subject which was hilariously funny. It abounded in mysterious characters such as "fertile octogenarians" and "precocious toddlers" who were presumed by the law to be capable of procreating at the ages of eighty and five respectively![7] My duties for Leach were simply to go and look things up in the library for him from time to time, but he was a most entertaining man to work for, and quite unlike Oxford professors. He made a speciality of noting famous examples of legal blunders, which he would use as entertainment for his students, and also as a stern warning against carelessness in the practice of law. While I was acting as his research assistant he discovered that the lawyer who had prepared Sir Walter Raleigh's settlements in the seventeenth century had made just such a catastrophic blunder, and I was required to dig out the complete story for him. It seemed that a whole and vital sentence had been left out of a crucial document whereby

6 JHC Morris and WB Leach, *The Rule Against Perpetuities* (1956).

7 WB Leach, "Perpetuities: New Hampshire Defertilizes the Octogenarians" (1963) 77 *Harvard Law Review* 279.

Raleigh had intended to settle his lands on his heirs, only retaining for himself a life interest. When he was executed for treason the result was that all his lands were forfeited to the Crown, whereas if the settlement had been properly drafted the lands would have passed to his heirs. Leach rubbed his hands with delight at this story. It was just the kind of thing he enjoyed.

He invited me to dinner one night, and rather surprised me by his drinking habits. In my youthful innocence I had assumed that the Oxford tradition – sherry before dinner, claret with dinner, and port afterwards – was universally observed. Leach put me right on this: he drank Scotch before dinner, Scotch with dinner, and Scotch after dinner. When I presented Leach with my bill at the end of the term he decided it was far too modest, and doubled the amount I asked for. He also aroused my interest in Harvard, and I began to think of it, as I have continued to do, as perhaps the greatest law school in the world. I tried to arrange a visit there several times while Leach was alive, but by the time the opportunity finally came, he was dead. I was sorry to have missed him in his own environment.

I was one of those rare students who quite enjoyed examinations, and I was blessed with a good examination memory, and a lucky examination technique. So I enjoyed a fair measure of academic success. I obtained a Distinction in "Law Mods",[8] and was awarded in my second year the University Winter Williams Law Scholarship. In my third year I shared the Gibbs Law Scholarship with Ian Brownlie (who would later become the distinguished Chichele Professor of International Law at Oxford) and Magdalen promoted me to an honorary Demyship (the Magdalen term for a scholarship).[9] I felt very confident before taking my final examinations, "Schools" as it is known at Oxford, and indeed, after the final weeks of hard revision, I took three days off altogether before the examination started. At the annual "Schools" dinner, after the examination was over, at which all the Magdalen candidates and their tutors were dined at college expense, John Morris took it into his head to go round the table asking all the candidates what class of degree they hoped to get. He began with me, which caused me some embarrassment because I knew that Morris regarded me as conceited if not arrogant. But I took the bull by the horns and replied that if Morris wanted a completely truthful answer, then of course I must say that

8 "Law Mods" is short for Law Moderations. These are examinations that first-year students sit at Oxford at the end of their second term.

9 Historically, demies were paid half the salary of a fellow (hence the name of the scholarship, which is derived from *demi-socii*) and had certain entitlements within the College.

I hoped for a first, but if he merely wanted me to be modest, then I would say (untruthfully) that I hoped for a second.

I duly got my "first" and was later told that mine was the best first of the year.[10] Michael had obtained the best first in maths at Cambridge the previous year so the family had some justifiable cause for pride in our achievements. I returned to Magdalen to do the postgraduate Oxford law degree, known as the BCL.[11] During that fourth year I began to think more seriously about my future career. Although I still hankered after a career at the Bar, with its apparent glamour and excitement, I was now married, and my wife was expecting our first son, and I did not see how I was going to support a wife and child while I waited for clients at the Bar. Scholarships at the bar in those days did not provide nearly enough to live on, and legal aid had not yet begun to provide a ready income to young and impecunious barristers. Unless one had some independent source of income, it seemed an impossible profession.

Despite my double first at Oxford (I obtained a first in the BCL to add to my first in Schools) financial prospects did not appear good in any direction. It did not occur to me that my qualifications were somewhat out of the ordinary, and that I might therefore pitch my sights somewhat high. Today, anyone with a double first from Oxford could be expected to get a warm welcome from a dozen firms of London solicitors who would probably compete vigorously for his custom; and he might even be welcomed into Chambers in London with substantial scholarships from the Inns of Court; but in 1954 competition (and success) were dirty words in England. I was in any event beginning to be attracted to the idea of an academic career, which my university successes appeared to place within my grasp, so I decided against entering either branch of the practising profession and I began to apply for jobs in the university world. I soon struck lucky and was offered an Assistant Lectureship in Law at the London School of Economics (which had a strong law department at that time), which was universally known as "the LSE". I was employed at the princely salary of £500 a year – shortly to be increased to £600 through the generosity of RA Butler, then Chancellor of the Exchequer. (I believe the lift-man at the LSE earned more than I did.)

10 Atiyah completed his undergraduate degree in 1953.
11 The "BCL" is an abbreviation for Bachelor of Civil Law.

5 Back to Khartoum

I began my academic life in October 1954, teaching at the London School of Economics. In those days Assistant Lecturers were not expected to give lectures, but were employed solely as tutors. My job required me to take about eight tutorials a week, each consisting of about fifteen students. I was asked to take five tutorials in the law of trusts and three in the law of contract. Although I quite enjoyed some aspects of tutorial teaching, there were other aspects which I did not like. In particular I did not like the repetition involved when I had to take five tutorials a week in the same subject, going over the same problems, and the same questions. Nor was I particularly interested in the law of trusts, an area of the law which is in many ways exceedingly technical, and lacking the excitement of a social dimension which I have always found the most interesting aspect of law. As a newcomer to the department, I had, of course, to teach the subjects which I was asked to teach, which usually meant those found too dull by everybody else. I was much more interested in the law of contract, which has indeed remained one of my main academic interests throughout my career.

There were also other features of teaching at the LSE which I did not much enjoy. The LSE was a large building in the middle of London (alas for the Oxford quads and gardens!), which meant that one lived a commuting life, one did not meet students out of class, and academic staff seemed to take virtually no part in extra-curricular activities. All this was very different from Oxford, and I missed the intimate atmosphere of college life. During my year at the LSE Christine and I lived with her parents near Woking in Surrey, and our eldest son was born in December 1954. I had to commute by train, and as I had evening classes twice a week, I was late home on those two evenings; indeed once a week I did not get home until 10.30 pm. I seemed to have many of the disadvantages of working in London with few of the advantages. I found it hard to settle to any interesting academic research, and spent a large part of the year preparing for the Bar examinations which everyone advised me to take, even though I now had no intention of practising. I also began to have great difficulty in seeing how Christine and I were ever to afford to have our own house on a salary of £600 a year.

Early in 1955 my father happened to be on a visit to Khartoum where he met the then Principal of the University College, Mr Lewis Wilcher, an Australian who later became Warden of Queen Elizabeth House in Oxford. Wilcher told my father how the University College was having great difficulty in recruiting teachers in the Law Faculty, and had been completely unable to fill its Chair of Law for some years. When my father mentioned my academic record to him, Wilcher responded by saying that I was the sort of person they were looking for, and though I could hardly expect a Chair at the age of twenty-four, if I went there as a Lecturer I could expect rapid promotion. My father communicated this news to me, and I decided to pursue the opportunities which it held out. I was offered and accepted an appointment as a Lecturer, on the understanding that, if my work justified it, I could expect promotion to a Chair within four years or so.

So it was back to Khartoum after an absence of ten years. How far away it all seems now! In 1955 Khartoum was still governed by Britain, though it was proceeding sedately towards a planned independence. The expatriate civil servants had traditionally had the great privilege of annual leave, with fares paid for themselves and their families, and this privilege extended to the university staff who were still, in those days, regarded as quasi-civil servants. Expatriates were also provided with government housing, at low rents, and the style of life remained very much as I had remembered it during the war. Servants' wages had increased a good deal in real terms, however, and most households were now somewhat more modest than they had been; but everybody still expected to employ a cook and a houseboy, and in fact when our second son was born we acquired a nanny as well.

The academic year at Khartoum ran from the beginning of July until March (thus avoiding the hottest months of the year which were April to June, when the expatriate staff all went on leave) so I flew out to Khartoum early in July 1955 and Christine followed me a few weeks later with Julian, then a baby of eight months. The flight in those days was by Viking, and it took two days, in five separate hops, with an overnight stop in Malta. I had gone on ahead in order to acquire some of the household necessities to equip the house with which we were provided – a house, it turned out, which had at one time been tenanted by some very good friends of my parents. It was, like all Khartoum government houses, very primitive in many ways. There were no flush loos (the town still lacked a sewage system) and the old buckets were still in use. Bathrooms lacked a hot water supply which only mattered for two or three months, because the rest of the year one just took cold showers. With a maximum temperature which rarely fell below eighty or ninety degrees Fahrenheit, and was often well over 100 for about six months of the year, and with water pipes not far below the surface of the soil, even cold water was far too hot to drink until refrigerated, and quite warm enough to shower in – except for those two or three months, when we were reduced to various makeshift expedients.

Like most government houses ours made up for a lack of internal refinements with verandas, a terrace and a pleasant garden. For a large part of the year we slept out of doors and, as the sun went down, chairs, tables and lights were carried out onto the terrace and we sat there during the late afternoon and evening.

We found much to enjoy in Khartoum. We had our own house, we had scraped together (and borrowed) sufficient money to furnish it and equip it reasonably well, we had bought a very cheap and battered old Morris, and we were able to live reasonably comfortably. Servants, of course, continued to make life more comfortable for the expatriate, and in our case we had actually obtained the services of the same cook who had worked for my father for many years. He had been trained to cook Lebanese food of which I have always been extremely fond, though he could also cope with traditional English fare such as the usual turkey at Christmas. In Khartoum, however, turkeys were bought alive and were slaughtered and prepared by the cook. On one occasion I well remember how Christine and I, sitting on the terrace, noticed our cook frantically pedalling down the adjoining lane on his bicycle. When I asked him later where he had been going in such a hurry he explained that the turkey, tethered loosely to a tree in the garden, had escaped and fluttered off into a nearby tree, so he had had to set off in hot pursuit of our Christmas dinner.

Social life also continued in very enjoyable ways. Outdoor dinner parties, given in gardens and terraces were the chief source of entertainment in a town which lacked many others. So a continuous round of parties helped to keep one's mind off the discomforts of the climate, and very enjoyable they were too. What was more – and very much to our liking – was the fact that there was almost a complete absence of any racial unpleasantness in Khartoum, so that social life was for those who wanted a really mixed life. Parties often included Sudanese and British as well as representatives of other nationalities. The university, indeed, had begun recruiting academic staff from many different countries, and we soon made friends from many parts of the world.

At this time the relations between leading Sudanese and the British were extremely good. As it became clear that Britain was going to leave the Sudan without having to be pushed out by riots, demonstrations and the usual paraphernalia of independence movements, British and Sudanese mixed on very good terms. The Sudanese knew that they were going to need the services of many expatriates for some years to come, particularly as university teachers, but also in many government and technical positions, and many expatriates were only too willing to stay on even though they knew that the top positions would shortly be assumed by Sudanese.

Because of my personal background, and my father's long years in the Sudan, we ourselves had a particular advantage in this respect. We already knew many Sudanese in prominent positions in the country. One of whom we were particularly fond was Sayed Mohammed el Khalifa Sharrif, who was married to a daughter of the Mahdi, the leader of the revolt against which Gordon had lost his life in 1885. Her brother, a posthumous son of the Mahdi, was Sayed Abdel Rahman el Mahdi (universally known as SAR), the leader of the Umma religious sect, and a powerful political and spiritual figure in the Sudan. He had co-operated with the British in various ways, as a result of which he had become in British eyes the uncrowned King of the Sudan and (more prosaically) was made a KBE.

Sayed Mohammed, as we always called him, had known my father very well, and he welcomed me to the Sudan as the third generation of my family to work there. He became a particular friend, and not long after we arrived a line of three large American cars appeared at our house. The first two contained splendid gifts – a silver tea service, and a living room carpet, and the third car contained Sayed Mohammed himself. When I asked him why he wanted three cars, he replied that one was for himself, one for his wife, and one (in broken English) was "Isbare"! He was immensely rich, having made a fortune from cotton plantations, and often travelled to England where he frequented Sotheby's and Harrods. He had bought an extremely valuable dinner service which had once belonged to some ancestral aristocratic family in England, and used to take great pleasure in using the service for everyday meals. He had also bought a massive chandelier which hung in his drawing room, and which had allegedly belonged to the Duke of Wellington. It was probably a valuable antique, but Sayed Mohammed may well have reduced, rather than increased its value, by having the gilt paint on it restored by local craftsmen.

Sayed Mohammed liked to entertain visitors at breakfast, which in his house was a splendid meal, along positively Edwardian lines (though with modern additions). Grapefruit, cornflakes with real cream, eggs, fish, and English-style toast and marmalade were all provided. After eating pretty well himself, our host would take a couple of anti-acid pills explaining that his digestion was not what it had been!

Sayed Mohammed had a son, Ishaac, who we also knew well, as he had been at Victoria College at the same time as Michael and me, though he was several years older than both of us. Ishaac had been sent to Oxford to complete his Western-style education, but while there he had been married, by proxy, without his knowledge or consent, to a cousin, a daughter, in fact, of SAR. Ishaac had been thunderstruck by this marriage though his father, the good Sayed Mohammed, in his simplicity and steeped in the customs of his country, had no idea of the terrible thing he had done to his son. Shortly before we went back to Khartoum in 1955 my father had published a novel (called *Black Vanguard*),[1] which was largely based on this extraordinary story. Although Ishaac eventually accepted the marriage, and lived with his wife (who we met, and indeed stayed with at their farm in Kosti in 1956) the story had no happy ending. She was herself a victim of the schizophrenia which led to a Sudanese woman being educated in the Western style, and then expected to behave like a traditional Sudanese wife. She eventually became insane.

Ishaac himself was an extraordinary man. He had become very interested in Western philosophy during his time at Oxford, and had also dabbled with painting. My father had once persuaded him to paint a mural in our house in Surrey, and Ishaac had spent many hours daubing a panel on the dining room wall. On one occasion we noticed the smell of burning from the room and discovered Ishaac's smock smouldering from contact with an electric wall heater, while he painted away all unconcerned. Ishaac had, in what capacity I do not know, been present at a meeting a year or two earlier between SAR and Churchill, who was still Prime Minister at the time. SAR spoke no English and his interpreter had been Ibrahim Ahmed, a distinguished Sudanese in his own right, who was in fact Chairman of the University of Khartoum Governors when I was first appointed. But Ishaac told me, with some indignation, that Ibrahim Ahmed had been guilty of suppressing an important statement by SAR in his interview with Churchill. When Churchill had asked SAR whether the Sudanese leaders had considered the possibility of remaining within the Commonwealth after independence, SAR had replied in Arabic that they had not considered the point expressly, but that if they had done so, the answer would certainly have been "No". According to Ishaac (who of course was fluent in English as well as Arabic),

1 See p 5.

Ibrahim Ahmed had only translated the first part of this reply. Which perhaps goes to show the importance of interpreters at international meetings!

In the university itself we also made many Sudanese friends. One of our closest friends was Saad ed Din Fawzi who was appointed Professor of Economics the year after I joined the Law Faculty. Although young for such an appointment, he was a very gifted man, who had taken three degrees in British universities, and was well qualified for the post. He was married to a Dutch wife, Ellie, and we became very good friends. The four of us would often go together into the souk to buy some brown beans ("Ful medames") and felafel (called "Ta'miya" in the Sudan), and make ourselves a simple dinner of local foods. Tragically, Saad ed Din was struck by cancer while in England in 1958, and though operated on in London that year, he had a recurrence the following year from which he died at the age of thirty-six. It seemed a cruel fate, not only for his wife and children, but also for his country which desperately lacked such able and qualified men.

Another good friend was in the Registrar's department in the University, Mohammed Omar Beshir, known to everyone as MOB. He was a delightful person, with an impish sense of humour, and we maintained contact with him for more than twenty years after leaving Khartoum. But by the 1980s, as the Sudan lurched from disaster to disaster, he became more and more demoralised and dispirited. It was desperately sad to see people like him, educated and trained by the West to learn and approve Western styles of democracy, freedom and scholarship, while retaining their sense of national identity, superseded by nationalistic and religious-minded leaders of greatly inferior abilities, who gradually tore their country apart.

It is today unfashionable to proclaim the virtues of old Western imperialism, and many young people appear to have grown up since the virtual end of the Empire who have been educated to believe that the imperial system was simply a cover for ruthless exploitation by the imperial powers. Not long ago, while on an academic visit to a Scandinavian university, I was asked about my years in Khartoum, and tried to explain something of the achievements of British rule. But my explanations obviously ran counter to everything that the students had learned and one young woman student, probably born after my years in Khartoum, insisted that "Of course, the whole basis of the Empire was exploitation". Those of us who actually knew these places during the imperial era find it impossible to accept this version of history. Whenever I read accounts of what is happening in Lebanon or in the Sudan, I find it hard to avoid comparing the condition of these countries as I knew them in the 1940s and 1950s and their condition today. That of

Lebanon is well known to the world; but that of the Sudan sounds scarcely better. Riven today by civil war, and economic disasters, the Sudan appears on the verge of economic collapse. By 1989, accounts were appearing in *The Times* of conditions in Khartoum depicting a town (of a million or more people) on the verge of total collapse. Electricity supplies are failing daily; the telephones rarely work; petrol is scarce and often unobtainable, and even water supplies are inadequate. The tide of refugees from the civil war camping in the desert on the edge of the town threatens to overwhelm not only the UN refugee workers, but the whole of Khartoum – and this is the capital city of this vast country. By 1991, warnings of mass starvation were becoming commonplace. It is painful to think of these things, and I return to my memories of happier days.

Life in Khartoum for me was not, of course, simply a social round. I had my work in the University College, or (as it became the following year) the independent University of Khartoum. It was, even in the 1950s, rather odd that English-qualified lawyers should find themselves recruited to teach law in the Sudan. But the English judges and lawyers who had come in to help administer this country after the battle of Omdurman in 1898 had, quite naturally, resorted to their own legal system, which was the only one they knew, as the basis for the Sudan's laws. As in India and other parts of Africa, British (or more strictly English) law was never applied to matters of personal and family status. These remained subject to customary law, which in the most developed part of the country (the whole of Northern Sudan, including Khartoum) was Islamic law, or the Sharia. A system of Sharia courts was therefore allowed to continue, side by side with the civil courts, which administered what was basically English common law. For reasons of practical necessity, however, the English criminal law and criminal procedure law (which in England itself was a rather messy mixture of statute law and case law) was superseded by codes based on the Indian codes. These were the Codes originally drafted by Lord Macaulay, which were themselves based on principles of English law cast into more modern and accessible form.

By the time I went out to teach in the University of Khartoum there were quite large numbers of Sudanese lawyers who had been trained in English law, either by studying for the Bar Exams in England, or by passing some courses previously developed in the predecessor of the University of Khartoum (the old Gordon College – at which my father had taught briefly in the 1920s). Many of them had sat as magistrates, and a few had been promoted to the High Court Bench. The Chief Justice was himself a Sudanese. And so it seemed perfectly natural, and indeed, inevitable that we should train lawyers in the English common law at the University of Khartoum. By the mid-1950s the university was turning out about twenty-five or thirty law graduates a year.

There were, however, great problems in the background arising from the use of English law, which subsequently developed into one of the most serious political problems which the Sudan had to face. The English common law has flourished well, not only in England itself, but also throughout the Commonwealth and the United States; but it does not flourish easily in countries where English is not a universal language. Now the people of the Northern Sudan, the Muslim Arab population which dominated the country, were not English-speakers. Moreover, unlike the situation which prevailed in India and some other African and Asian countries, English did not even serve as a universal secondary national language for the Sudan. It was unnecessary for this purpose because Arabic was the universal language of the Northern Sudanese. For these people to learn to train as lawyers, therefore, it was necessary for them to master a second language sufficiently for them to read technical legal materials – cases and legislation and so on. Although some of the older generation of Sudanese (such as our friends Ishaac, Saad ed Din and MOB, and nearly all who held positions of power and responsibility at the time of independence) spoke and read English fluently, most of our students had much more difficulty with the language. This was an inevitable result of the gradual spread of education and training among the Sudanese so that (for example) the language of instruction in the secondary schools which had at one time been English, simply because most of the teachers were English, had by this time become Arabic, as Sudanese school teachers replaced British teachers. So by the 1950s a crisis was impending, from the simple fact that all the existing Sudanese lawyers had been trained in English law and the English language. The continuation of this system was plainly a matter of great difficulty.

But the language difficulty was only part of the story. There were two other complications. The first was that with the growth of nationalist and above all Islamic fervour, there were increasing demands that the English-based civil law system should be replaced wholly by Sharia, or Islamic, law. This was, however, bitterly opposed by the Southern Sudanese who, unlike the Northerners were not Arabs, nor generally Muslims either. The Southerners were Africans, of completely different racial origins from the Arab Northerners. Additionally, education in the South had largely been Christian missionary education. So most of the Southerners (at least the ones who had emerged from tribal simplicity) were Christians, they spoke little or no Arabic, and they certainly had no desire to be governed by Islamic law.

But it was not only the Southerners who objected to the idea of Islamic law replacing the whole of English law. Business people and entrepreneurs of every kind, many of them from the cosmopolitan commercial classes who always seemed to spring up in these countries – Greeks, Syrians, Armenians and so on – preferred the safe certainty of a commercial legal system, based on Western private enterprise traditions to the (to them) unknown and unsophisticated Islamic tradition. Certainly there were features of the Islamic tradition (such as its complete prohibition of lending at interest) which appeared to make it unsuitable as the basis of the commercial law of a modern state. I remember discussing this problem with one of my Sudanese colleagues on the Faculty of Law at the University of Khartoum, Hassan el Turabi, who was for a long time the leader of the Muslim Brothers, a fundamentalist Islamic political group. Turabi assured me that even an Islamic legal system could operate without open recognition of the need for interest to be paid on loans. Remarkably enough, he cited to me the typical English hire-purchase contract as a device which enabled commercial operations to be conducted without open payment of interest. I found it strange that Turabi thought that a technical legal device of this kind could satisfy Allah as easily as it had satisfied English judges, but his attitude was probably not very different from that of the Christian mediaevalist lawyers who had argued over the lawfulness of usury with as much subtlety 500 years before. After we had left the Sudan, Turabi became more active in politics, and was later destined to spend alternate periods as a government minister (Presidential adviser at one time, when the legal system was totally Islamicised) and in jail. It all depended on whether the extreme political group which he headed was being courted or opposed by the more dominant political parties and leaders.

The third complication was that the University of Khartoum had so far preserved a virtual monopoly on legal education in the common law system for the Sudanese (other than the sons of the very rich who could travel to England). But many Sudanese were now being educated in Egyptian University Colleges (branches of the University of Cairo) where they were learning Egyptian law. Modern Egyptian law was no more Islamic-based than Sudanese law, because the Egyptians had adopted a version of the French Codes, but at least the materials were available in Arabic, and there were by this time commentaries and textbooks in Arabic for Egyptian lawyers. These graduates of Cairo University were not allowed to practise law in the Sudan; but there were increasing political pressures for them to be admitted to the legal profession, even though many of them knew little English and no English law.

So it was probably inevitable that the existence of an English-based legal system was bound to develop into a major political problem; and indeed it did, though after I had left the University of Khartoum. In the successions of coups and counter coups which began in 1958, the legal system became a political pawn, if not plaything. Under the regime of General Nimeiry, when Turabi's Muslim Brothers were in favour, a Presidential decree simply swept aside the whole of the English-based legal system and replaced it with Islamic law. Thus overnight, virtually every trained judge and lawyer in the country was expected to learn and operate a completely new legal system. I have no idea how they coped, though I suspect that there was a combination of chaos and a flat refusal to operate the new system. Some years later Nimeiry needed to recruit a new Attorney-General and he summoned a young Sudanese called Zaki Mustafa. Zaki had been one of my best pupils at the University of Khartoum, and he had been sent to England to do a postgraduate degree at the LSE after completing his first degree. When he returned to Khartoum he had taught at the university and eventually become Dean of the Faculty of Law in the late 1960s. (In that capacity he had invited me to spend a term as visiting professor in 1968, during the summer vacation when I held a teaching post at Oxford.) When Nimeiry pressed him to become Attorney-General, Zaki insisted that the English common law first be reinstated as the basis of the Sudanese legal system. Nimeiry complied, and so everything went into reverse gear again.

But Nimeiry had insisted that if the common law was to be reinstated, some attempt must be made to codify it, because a legal system which required the use of thousands of volumes of English reported cases was simply unsuited to the country's needs. Zaki promised to make the attempt, and he got in touch with me again when I was teaching at the University of Warwick in 1974. He invited me to visit Khartoum and draft some new codes for the Sudanese legal system. I flew out to Khartoum for a brief visit and got some briefing for the codes that were needed. It was heartwarming for me to see that some of the fundamental principles of the English common law appeared to be flourishing again in the Sudan. I was told, for instance, that when Nimeiry had in 1971 nationalised the Western banks operating in the Sudan, Zaki had insisted that an independent tribunal be established to which the banks could appeal in the event of disagreement over the value of their assets and the amount of compensation to be paid.

But alas, the difficulties must have been too great. Although I did a little work on the projected codes, Zaki shortly afterwards quit the government, tempted by the opportunities of private practice and business. My connection with the project came to an end, and I never visited the Sudan again. In 1983 Turabi was appointed Presidential adviser by Nimeiry, and Islamic law was once again reintroduced into the Sudan and there were some much publicised and ghastly accounts in the world's press of the introduction of amputation as a penalty for theft. (By 1985 Turabi was again out of favour with Nimeiry and he went back to jail, though Islamic law remained the basis of the legal system. After Nimeiry was overthrown Turabi was once again released, but the last news I heard of him was that the new regime, even more fundamentalist than he was, had re-imprisoned him because they did not regard him as extreme enough.)

All this, however lay in the future while I was teaching at the University of Khartoum, and at that time my own private research work had very little to do with the peculiar legal problems of the Sudan. Most of the time I simply read and wrote on English law. In my first year I wrote a short students' book on *The Sale of Goods*[2] which was, of course, on *the law* of sale of goods and not a thriller as my uncle Frank said it could have been, judging solely from its title. I had been struck, while still a student at Oxford, by the fact that there seemed no adequate book on the subject, which is of course one of very great practical importance, since the contract of sale of goods is about the most important kind of contract there is. I determined, therefore, to try to fill the gap, and set to with sufficient energy to complete a draft of the book during my first year as a teacher. To finish the book I needed to read a few cases which were not available in our library in Khartoum, so I applied for home leave which was not usually granted to lecturers at the end of their first year. Leave was granted, the book was duly finished and duly published at the price of twenty-five shillings in 1957. It was well received by the critics, being surprisingly widely noticed for such a slim volume by a hitherto unknown and junior lecturer. In later years it has been repeatedly re-written, to keep the material up to date, and the eighth edition was published in 1990.[3] It has been the most successful and consistent seller of all my books, and (though nobody could live on the royalties of an academic writer) it has provided me with a very agreeable subsidiary source of income for many years.

2 PS Atiyah, *The Sale of Goods* (1957).
3 PS Atiyah, *The Sale of Goods*, 8th edn (1990).

Although I thus got to England to finish my book, I was only offered half the cost of my return fare, so we had to travel on the cheap. However, this suited us, because it gave me an opportunity to visit Beirut and introduce my wife to the family there. We flew to England but returned overland, by train to Rome, where we spent a few days, and thereafter to Naples where we took ship to Beirut. After a month's holiday in Beirut we boarded the same ship, bound this time for Alexandria, whence we were to take the train for Cairo, and there pick up the four-day twice-weekly Cairo to Khartoum service on which we had sleepers booked. Unfortunately things began to go horribly wrong when I realised that I had not allowed sufficient time to get to Cairo from Alexandria. The boat had been due to dock at about 2 pm, and as the Khartoum train did not leave Cairo until 8 pm. I had assumed there would be ample time to get from Alexandria to Cairo (only a couple of hours by fast train). All our plans had been made on the assumption that we would simply whisk through Cairo to catch the Khartoum train, and I shuddered to think what would happen if we missed it – I had very little money on me, for one thing, and had no idea whether we could rebook our sleepers on the next train, for another. In fact the boat was very late docking, and by the time we had cleared immigration and customs it was nearly 5 pm. We grabbed a taxi, and asked the driver whether he could get us to Cairo by 8 pm. He assured us that he could, so I offered him £5 (which seemed a lot then) if, but only if, we caught our train. He accepted this deal, and we set off.

It was a hot mid-summer day, and the desert road from Alexandria to Cairo was fairly good; but even so I watched the milestones closely and realised after a while that we would not make it at that speed. I passed this on to the driver, who responded by increasing his speed, though at great risk of over-heating his engine – it boiled over alarmingly when he stopped to refuel and to top up his water supply. For two unnerving hours I measured our speed by checking the milestones against my watch, thinking that it would be absolutely touch and go whether we would make it. Then, just as I was about to give up all hope, the driver suggested that we should aim for Mina, a suburb of Cairo, which was actually on our way to Cairo, but on the way out for trains going South. By doing this, we could gain an extra half an hour, and he assured me that the train would stop there. He was right, and we made it with about ten minutes to spare. I have never been more relieved to catch a train.

So in July 1956 we were back once again in Khartoum, and our life continued on a fairly even keel for another three years. Our second son, Andrew, was born at our house during this second year (with the help of an Egyptian midwife) and shortly after that we acquired a nanny. Life continued comfortable and pleasant, and we were a good deal better off in our second year, thanks to some generous salary increases. Towards the end of that year the Suez crisis threatened for a time to blow the Middle East apart, but our own position never became worrying or even unpleasant. Although there were Sudanese demonstrations and protests against the British action in Suez, and angry public anti-British gestures, personal relations between us and our Sudanese friends were never in the least threatened. Indeed, we (in common with almost the whole expatriate community) were so horrified at the British government's behaviour that we were entirely in sympathy with the Sudanese reactions. I myself joined my friend Saad ed Din in drafting a letter to *The Times* protesting that the British action was "politically, morally, and militarily wrong" in the hope that we could persuade many of our colleagues to sign it. But as so often happens on these occasions, by the time the letter had been redrafted half a dozen times the crisis was over, and it never got sent.

In 1958 there occurred the first Sudanese coup. My first news of it came from my friend Saad ed Din who telephoned early one morning to warn me. At that time Christine was working as a senior hostess with Sudan Airways and she was at the airport when Saad ed Din phoned. So I rang to warn her, and suggest that she should come home for the rest of the day. She told me that she had wondered what the soldiers and machine guns at the airport were all about, which made me more insistent that she come home. In fact there was no trouble, the coup on that occasion being bloodless. Alas, there was plenty of violence to come later, after we had left the Sudan.

Throughout these next few years, my own private research continued in a quiet, academic sort of way. I wrote a couple of articles and notes[4] – the sort of fairly humdrum stuff which it is the business of the academic to churn out. Then in my fourth year I received a letter from Professor Hart, the distinguished Professor of Jurisprudence at Oxford, inviting me to write a new book on the law of contract, which was to be one of a series of introductory legal books (the Clarendon Law Series) to be edited by him, and published by the Oxford University Press. I owed the invitation to my old Oxford tutor, Rupert Cross, to whom I had once confided my ambition to write a book on the law of contract. Cross was a close friend and colleague of Hart's, and

4 These included PS Atiyah, "Injustices and anomalies in the Law of Hire Purchase" (1958) 5 *Business Law Review* 24; PS Atiyah, "Public Benefit in Charities" (1958) 21 MLR 138; PS Atiyah, "The Liability of Infants in Fraud and Restitution" (1959) 22 MLR 273.

had recommended me to him for the contract book. This was, of course, a distinct feather in my cap, and I accepted the invitation with alacrity. I wrote the book in a little over a year, went over it carefully with Hart when I came home on leave in 1959, and it was eventually published in 1961.[5] Although it never sold in the same numbers as the book on sale (there were a lot more books on the law of contract) it was all the same fairly successful; and has also run through several new editions. The fourth was published in 1989.[6] This book was to prove the beginning of a lifelong connection with the Oxford University Press.

5 PS Atiyah, *An Introduction to the Law of Contract* (1961).

6 PS Atiyah, *An Introduction to the Law of Contract*, 4th edn (1989). Atiyah would go on to write a fifth edition: PS Atiyah, *An Introduction to the Law of Contract*, 4th edn (1995). Steve Smith was responsible for the sixth edition: SA Smith, *Atiyah's Introduction to the Law of Contract*, 6th edn (2005).

6 Interlude in Ghana

After four years in Khartoum I began to be restless for change. Although we had enjoyed our time there, I did not think my career was progressing as I felt it should. Despite my academic successes there seemed no prospect that the University of Khartoum would promote me to a Chair at the age of twenty-eight – Lewis Wilcher had by this time left the university, and his successors appeared to take more conventional views about the age at which a person could expect to become a professor. I had applied without success for fellowships at two Oxford colleges during my Khartoum years, as well as for an Assistant Lectureship at Cambridge. I learnt later that I had come within a whisker of being elected at one Oxford college,[1] but my prospects had ultimately been blasted by a letter from John Morris who had told the fellows that I was bumptious and arrogant. At any rate it seemed that I had little immediate prospect of an Oxford fellowship which was then the height of my ambition. So when a new opportunity appeared to open before me while we were on leave in 1959 I seized it with both hands.

At this time Ghana was apparently one of the most exciting states in Africa. One of the first of the African states to obtain complete independence from Britain, it was then very prosperous thanks to the high world prices for its chief crop, cocoa. The rest of the world watched Ghana with interest and some admiration as its leader, Kwame Nkrumah, made speeches around the world about the need for recognition of the "African personality" and for some tangible steps towards inter-African unity or at least co-operation. Of course Ghana, like all newly independent African states, was short of well-qualified public officials, and Nkrumah had recruited to his personal staff, and later to the office of Attorney-General, a former English Labour MP called Geoffrey Bing. Bing was a very political animal whose sympathies were with the left of the English Labour Party, as it was then constituted, and he also shared Nkrumah's grandiose visions for the development of the former British African colonies. Although nominally Attorney-General, he

1 It is unclear to which colleges Atiyah applied. However, likely candidates include Christ Church (which appointed Murray McLagan) and Queen's (which appointed John Kaye). Candidates for these posts included David Bentley, Michael Furmston, Leonard (later Lord) Hoffmann and Francis Reynolds.

was really more in the nature of a personal political adviser to Nkrumah, and his job was largely to keep Nkrumah informed as to how Western governments would be likely to react to the ideas and proposals streaming out of Ghana at the time. At the same time, Bing did appear to be genuinely attempting to help Nkrumah to modernise the Ghana legal system, to revise and update its laws, and for this purpose, he was building up a strong legal department under himself, as Attorney-General.

As in most of the Colonies, but unlike the position in Whitehall, the government departments did not have their own legal advisers; so the Attorney-General's department was in effect the legal adviser to all the government departments. Furthermore, it was also responsible for all criminal prosecutions in serious cases, which were conducted before senior judges, and tried, not by juries as in England, but with assessors, whose views were merely advisory and could be rejected by the trial judge. In addition, the department seemed sometimes virtually to take over the implementation of policy once some major step had been decided upon, such as the decision to boycott South Africa and embargo all South African goods and personnel. With Bing also having direct lines of communication to Nkrumah, the Attorney-General's department was thus something of a powerhouse at the centre of the government machine, and from time to time found itself undertaking special responsibilities, such as conducting an investigation into Ghana Airways, whose management left something to be desired.

Bing had recently pulled off something of a coup by persuading Professor LCB (always known as "Jim") Gower, of the London School of Economics, to draft a modernised Companies Act for Ghana. Gower shared Bing's general left-wing sympathies, and was (as were indeed many at the time) sympathetic to African nationalist aspirations. He was also England's leading academic expert on company law, and much later, in the 1980s he was called on to advise the British government on the new self-regulation structure of city financial institutions. At this time I knew Gower slightly myself – he was a good friend of Rupert Cross, and it was he who had recommended my book, *The Sale of Goods*, to Pitmans for publication a couple of years earlier. When Bing asked him about likely young prospects for recruitment to his department, Gower had mentioned my name to him, and it was in this way that I first came into contact with Bing in the summer of 1959. He offered to arrange payment of my fare to Ghana en route for Khartoum at the end of my leave, so that I could discuss the possibility of joining his department, and I was favourably impressed by what I saw in Ghana. I was offered very good terms and so agreed to transfer to Ghana in the autumn, at the end of the first term at Khartoum. I flew to Accra direct from Khartoum in September 1959, and a week later Christine and the children joined me.

One of the things that had impressed me about Ghana was that it simply offered a more comfortable lifestyle for an expatriate with a growing family. Life in Khartoum was still in some ways very primitive in 1959, and things had been getting worse rather than better. As the Sudanese foreign trade had deteriorated, and the number of expatriates had dwindled, many consumer goods had simply disappeared from the shops. Even the shops which had formerly catered for the expatriate community began to close or halve the size of their stores. Ghana, on the other hand, was thriving in 1959. Accra had three large Western-style department stores, stacked with consumer goods at very moderate prices. Cars, so heavily taxed in Khartoum as to be prohibitively expensive, were cheap in Ghana (and we were able to buy a brand new Ford Consul with a government loan, repayable from my salary). Roads were very good, and opportunities for outings far greater. Khartoum was simply an oasis in a desert, and it was impossible to go anywhere by road outside the urban area itself. But in Ghana one could drive on decent roads to Takoradi, 150 miles along the coast, or inland to the Ashanti area of tropical forest. Then there was the sea. Accra itself had a modest beach, where Christine and the boys swam almost every afternoon for many months. But thirty or forty miles out of Accra, on good roads, there were glorious tropical beaches, skirted by beautiful palms which swayed gracefully in the sea breezes. And the climate also appeared, at any rate, at first encounter, to be much milder than that of Khartoum. Temperatures rarely exceeded eighty-five degrees Fahrenheit in Accra, and sea breezes were pleasant, while Khartoum heat was well-nigh intolerable for many months of the year. There also appeared to be better schools available, and with our eldest son, Julian, now nearly five, this was beginning to be important. So Ghana appeared to offer the prospect of a more comfortable life in many ways.

I was also thirsting after some more practical legal work, and had looked forward to handling real legal problems. The Attorney-General's department had certainly appeared to offer me a chance to practise my legal skills in an exciting environment, and I had looked forward to this. At first things went quite well. Once again, we found ready-made friends. I was expected under my contract to do some part-time teaching at the University of Ghana, and the Dean of the Law School at this time was John Lang, whose wife Jean was a good friend of a friend, and who we got to know very well. John Lang had been recruited by Bing, in characteristic style after Lang had, in a much-publicised move, been sacked as ICI's[2] chief legal adviser, on the insistence of the British government who claimed he was a security risk, and could not be trusted to handle secret government–ICI contracts. The basis of the allegation was that his wife, Jean, had been a communist in her youth, which was true, but then so had many other left-wing sympathisers, including indeed, many members of Attlee's Cabinet in the post-war Labour government. We did not discuss these matters which were plainly sore wounds with the Langs, and Jean herself evidently felt very bitter that her own activities had blasted her husband's career; but I must say I never saw or heard anything to suggest that she still retained communist sympathies, let alone that she was still an active member of the Communist Party. They had no children of their own, and Jean became very fond of Christine and our own children. After our return to England we visited them in their charming Surrey home. Jean died rather tragically some years later, when, after a tiff with John, she took an overdose of sleeping tablets, walked out into the woods and lay down to a sleep from which she did not awake.

Another good friend we made was a Ghanaian, Austin Amissah, who had been educated in England, at school and at Oxford. He spoke English and altogether sounded exactly like an Englishman, but he was another of our African friends who later suffered from great difficulties because of his ambivalent position vis-à-vis his own country, although in his case the difficulties were not matters of personality. Although he himself was a full-blooded Ghanaian, he had married a very attractive Finnish wife, called Stella, and they had several children. When we went to Ghana in 1959 Austin appeared to have excellent prospects before him, and in fact he later served a spell as Attorney-General and eventually as a judge of the Court of Appeal in Ghana. But as coup succeeded coup, and those who worked for these temporary governments came to be regarded as enemies by their successors, Austin and his wife began to feel distinctly ill at ease in his own country. After one coup he was arrested and for a few hours did not know whether his next destination would be the firing squad or the Attorney-General's seat. After this he decided that enough was enough, and he left Ghana to live a difficult life, trying to earn a living as a wandering, virtually stateless, legal and business consultant. He was several times pressed to return to his country to take up high legal office, but never felt that it was safe enough to do so.

There was also working in the Attorney-General's department in 1959 an Englishman, on secondment from the Parliamentary Counsel's Office

2 This is a reference to Imperial Chemical Industries, which was a British chemical company.

in London, called Francis Bennion. Bennion was head of the drafting section of the Attorney-General's Office and did all the most important Bills. He also drafted the new Constitution under which Nkrumah became President although that Constitution only lasted a few years, until, along with Nkrumah himself and his statue, it was swept away by the first military coup of post-independence Ghana.

Bennion and I became great friends, and we remained friends, give or take a few knocks, for many years. He had two little girls, and we had two boys of similar ages. His third daughter and our third son were both born in Ghana within a few weeks of each other. So we had much in common as families, but our main ties were intellectual ones. He was a government lawyer, with an academic turn of mind, and I was basically an academic, with some leaning towards the world of practical law, so we got on very well. He had one of the sharpest minds I ever knew, and we greatly enjoyed just talking over legal problems at the highest intellectual levels. I had recently written an academic article, which had been already accepted for publication by an English legal periodical, and I showed it to Bennion. He expressed interest and some agreement, but also criticised parts of the article; so I invited him to join with me in rewriting it, and we spent many hours doing so. It was eventually published as a joint article.[3] Francis Bennion was not, in all respects, an easy man to get on with. He did not suffer fools at all gladly; indeed, he was sharp and impatient with them. And even when dealing with those who he did not think of as fools, he could be extremely impatient with arguments he disagreed with. Working with him required constant forbearance and tact.

It was Bennion who introduced me to the work of the Parliamentary Counsel's Office in England. Indeed, I had never heard of this Office before I met him, an ignorance I suspect I shared with many English lawyers,

3 PS Atiyah and FAR Bennion, "Mistake in the Construction of Contracts" (1961) 24 MLR 421. This was one of only a handful of occasions on which Atiyah collaborated with another scholar. Atiyah wrote only two other co-authored pieces, namely, PS Atiyah and G Treitel, "Misrepresentation Act 1967" (1967) 30 MLR 369 and PS Atiyah and RS Summers, *Form and Substance in Anglo-American Law: A Comparative Study of Legal Reasoning, Legal Theory, and Legal Institutions* (1987). It is unsurprising that Atiyah co-authored just three works. His style did not lend itself to collaborative work. His ideas were often sufficiently atypical that many other researchers would have found it difficult to subscribe to them, and one suspects that given the speed with which Atiyah wrote, he would have been frustrated by the slower rate of work that collaborative research inevitably involves. It is ironic that Atiyah teamed up, in particular, with Treitel given that Treitel's style could not have been more different from Atiyah's. Whereas Treitel tended to focus intensely on microscopic features of the case law and was a far more orthodox scholar than Atiyah, Atiyah's interests lay primarily in grand, sweeping ideas.

because the Office kept a very low public profile. Although I was still not sure that drafting legislation was itself the most interesting type of legal work, I learned enough about the Office to make me feel that the work there was a real intellectual challenge. I gathered that the Office was very hard to get into and that the entry standards were extremely high, but when I began to express some interest in the possibility of joining it, Bennion volunteered to write to his chief, Sir Noel Hutton. It seemed, however, that there were no vacancies there then, so nothing came of these moves at the time.

Francis Bennion later became a rather celebrated, or even notorious public figure. He left the Parliamentary Counsel's Office and in the 1970s he set himself up as a one-man defender of the Rule of Law, which he thought was being violated by Peter Hain and his associates who threatened to disrupt the South African cricket tour to England by means which Bennion thought to be plainly illegal. Bennion was no lover of the South African government, as I well knew. He and I had cheered together when we were in Ghana, and it was announced that South Africa was being forced out of the Commonwealth. But Bennion was a great lover of free political institutions, and could not be diverted from his insistence that violence was not the way to prevent the South African cricket tour. It was a matter for Parliament to legislate upon – he publicly offered to draft a Bill for Hain which would have made the tour illegal, suggesting that Hain should achieve his ends by peaceful, parliamentary means. But Hain scorned these tactics, and Bennion launched a private prosecution against him, after failing to persuade the police and other authorities to do so. It was a courageous act, but one fraught with risks. If the prosecution had completely failed Bennion could have been saddled with costs of £50,000 or more; in the event Hain was convicted on one charge only, and Bennion's costs were ordered to be paid out of public funds – a clear indication that the judge thought the prosecution was justified in the public interest. But Bennion paid another price, in a different form, for all this public and obsessional activity. His marriage broke under the strain, and he even became totally estranged from his three daughters. This was an aspect of his character Christine and I could never understand, because to us, family relationships with our children were more important than any public events could ever be.

My own work at the Attorney-General's Office in Ghana began in quite an interesting way. I found myself doing a lot of commercial work, drafting contracts and advising government departments. I also undertook some legislative drafting in which I may have been bolder than my skills justified. I drafted a new Criminal Code which drastically simplified and slimmed down the number of crimes in the old cumbersome Code. I also drafted a Sale of Goods Act for Ghana, which modernised the old English Act on which the law had hitherto been based, and drew on my own knowledge of the subject for this purpose.[4] In addition I tried my hand – just for interest's sake – at a few criminal prosecutions. My most interesting case concerned a local government official who over a period of years had embezzled large sums of money from the funds of his council. He had consistently fooled the auditors, who had always warned him when they were coming, by creating fictitious balances which purported to have just been paid into the council's bank account (when the auditors checked the council's ledgers and petty cash) or to have been just drawn out of the bank and put into the petty cash (when the auditors checked the bank balance). This may have looked plausible in the early days when the sums involved were only a few pounds, but how the auditors could have accepted the idea that there was over £14,000 in the petty cash I never understood! His last desperate throw was to forge two paying-in slips, which had originally been for a few pounds each, to make it seem that over £7,000 had been paid into the bank with each slip. But the forgeries were clumsy, and the game was up at last. The case was quite difficult because an enormous amount of work was necessary to track the movements of the fictitious balances, back and forward over five or six years, as well as of some real money which had been obtained from the bank on forged cheques. It was also quite difficult to explain all this with sufficient clarity to the judge and the assessors, but I must have managed it reasonably well because I earned the congratulations of an English police superintendent, on loan from the fraud squad of Scotland Yard. The accused was sent to jail for several years.

After the case was over I wrote to the government department responsible to point out that the council's bank had paid out large sums of money on forged cheques, and these sums might be recoverable from the bank. The department authorised me to pursue the bank, and I did so. Although advised by competent English solicitors they agreed to pay up the whole amount without a fight, and without full investigation of the circumstances. This rather surprised me because although I had no doubt the bank was prima facie liable, I had been troubled by a legal complication which they might have raised by way of defence. The point was that although the bank had undoubtedly paid out on the forged cheques, much of the money thus

4 It is likely that this was based on a draft Sale of Goods Act that Atiyah had prepared for the Sudan a few years previously: see p xii.

paid out did (if only temporarily) find its way into the council's coffers as a means of hiding the deficiency in its funds. If the full facts had been investigated by the solicitors they might have afforded at least a partial defence to the bank, but I did not feel it was my duty to point out these difficulties to the bank, and the local council, as well as the responsible Ministry, duly thanked me for recovering their lost moneys.

After a time I began to be very troubled by some aspects of my work. One problem was the general smell of corruption which hovered over government activities. The contracts which we were constantly drawing up for the government – usually with foreign concerns who were being invited to invest in Ghana – were often no sooner signed than we were getting instructions to cancel them. Of course cancelling valid contracts meant that the government had to pay compensation, and huge sums of public money were being thrown away because of this. But in addition, I began to have great suspicions about the way some of these contracts had been agreed in the first place. I was morally certain that substantial bribes were being paid to Ministers by foreign businessmen as the price of getting contracts with the Ghana government; and naturally enough, it was the size of the bribes which tended to determine which foreign concerns got the contracts.

The signs of financial waste were all around us in the Attorney-General's Department. Apart from the possibility of actual bribery and corruption (which of course was never proved) I was involved for some months in the liquidation of a public body called the Ghana Timber Marketing Corporation. This body had been set up with public funds to organise the orderly marketing of timber for export, which was quite a sizeable trade at that time. Within eighteen months the entire capital of this body – some half a million pounds, I think – had disappeared into the pockets of the adventurers who controlled it. When we came on the scene to wind it up, there were no assets, the officers had all disappeared, and the offices were closed. We tried to prosecute one of the leading members of the corporation but it was impossible to prove the charges and he was acquitted.

Then there was Ghana Airways which (as I have said) was the subject of a special investigation by the Attorney-General's Department. The development of this airline was one of the things that had first impressed me when I went to Ghana. They were flying large modern aircraft between London and Accra, and had also inaugurated a Pan African service which flew to Beirut all the way from Ghana. What I had not at first appreciated was that much of this was a sheer waste of money. The traffic simply did not warrant the Beirut service, but it was part of Nkrumah's grand vision of a Pan African airline service, though the only part which ever materialised, I think. It was, in other words a prestige service, introduced for political reasons. But prestige was carried to ridiculous lengths. The Accra–London service was in fact largely controlled by BOAC (the predecessor of British Airways) which leased the aircraft to Ghana Airways and painted the appropriate colours and name on the fuselage. But the responsible Ghanaian Minister was highly indignant when he flew on the service and was fed off BOAC plates. He insisted that Ghana Airways must have its own plates. It was in vain pointed out to him that the cost of this would be enormous because an adequate supply of plates would have to be maintained wherever the aircraft stopped to take on catering supplies. Once again, political reasons dictated the result.

Another aspect of my work which began to worry me was the increasing totalitarianism of the government. One day a Ghanaian breezed into my office who I did not know. "We have decided to take over the *Ashanti Pioneer*" he told me (this was the opposition newspaper), "You must draft the necessary Bill". I paused for a moment, and then asked who "We" was. He told me his name which I recognised as that of a Cabinet Minister, and added that he had just come from a cabinet meeting, at which this policy had been decided. I refrained from pointing out that the Attorney-General's department did not generally get its instructions to draft Bills in this way, but I could not avoid asking a few basic questions. I pointed out that there were many different ways of "taking over" a newspaper (the government could compulsorily buy up the shares in the company, or seize its assets, or take legal powers to control its contents, etc). What exactly did the government want to do? The Minister could not answer my questions, and he accused me of being obstructive, saying as he left that he would speak to the Attorney-General about it. I never heard anything more about it personally, but sure enough the *Ashanti Pioneer* was soon closed down.

As time went on, other aspects of life in Ghana also began to pall on us. The climate, which had seemed so much milder than that of Khartoum at first impression, proved to have a kick in its tail. The problem in Ghana was not the temperatures but the humidity which remained at 85 or 90 per cent, day and night, all the year round. After some months, both Christine and I found these levels of humidity extremely tiring, and we often went to bed, exhausted at 9 pm. And although Ghana was no longer quite the "White man's grave" it had been in the nineteenth century, it was still hard to escape the occasional attacks of malaria. Despite religiously taking our anti-malarial tablets, Christine and Julian and I all went down with it, and it knocked a lot out of us.

We also found the Ghanaians in the mass a less likeable people than the Sudanese. Although we had some good friends among the Ghanaians, there were some aspects of Ghanaian behaviour which we found very unpleasant – in particular the eternal demand for tips (known as "dash"). Once on the road to Kumasi in the North, our car skidded off the road into a ditch; fortunately nobody was hurt, and the car itself undamaged, but I could not drive it out of the ditch without some assistance. However, there were people around and we sought their help. They came eagerly enough, but they would not lift a finger before we had agreed a price for their assistance. We could not help thinking that the Sudanese would almost certainly have refused to take money for helping us in like conditions, even if it had been offered.

By the end of our first year in Ghana we had decided that we would not return at the end of my contractual eighteen months, and that the time had definitely come for a return to England if only I could get a job. I was not yet attracted by the idea of a return to academic life, as I still wanted to get more practical legal experience, but having qualified as a barrister rather than a solicitor there were few openings available to me. Eventually I was offered a job in the government legal service, starting in June 1961, and in April we left Ghana for good.

7 Back in England

We returned to England in April 1961, shortly after the birth of our third son, Simon. My wife and I had made a deal that she would have another child, and I should travel alone for a short break, on our departure from Ghana, so while she flew back to England with our three sons, I flew to Beirut for a brief holiday and family reunion. I very much enjoyed the chance to see my aunt Najla and her family, as well as Beirut itself. It was to be my last visit to Beirut for many years, because, of course, since the troubles began in that unhappy land, it has not been a place for the casual visitor. In fact it was many years before I saw my aunt again. In 1984 she and her husband escaped from Lebanon for a few weeks to spend a holiday in England, and they spent a week with us, and a week with each of my brothers. But in 1961 Beirut was still the cheerful centre of a happy and prosperous country and I am glad that I saw it again before the terrible wars began. After a few days there, and a quick stopover in Athens on the way home, I rejoined my wife in England. We lived for a while in my mother's house, where she had converted part of her house into a self-contained flat, and embarked on our first experience of house-hunting. We had saved a good deal of money (by the standards of the time) during our African years, and we eventually bought a modest, but pleasant house in St John's, Woking, for £4,750, of which we had to borrow £2,900 on mortgage. Our repayments were, I think, £29 per month.

I began work at the Board of Trade as a legal assistant in June 1961, and remained there for the next three years. At first I found the work quite interesting and not unstimulating. Our main routine work in this department was to advise the administrators on points of law arising from their activities, principally company law and bankruptcy law. There were real legal problems to deal with, and I learned a good deal about working as a solicitor. I was exceptionally fortunate in working for someone of very real abilities. My immediate superior was Michael Kerry who eventually (though not until I had left) became Solicitor (that is, head of the legal section) of the Department of Trade and Industry and after that, Treasury Solicitor, which is the top post in the government legal service, for which services he became a KCB. Michael Kerry taught me a lot about care and accuracy in legal research, something which the ordinary academic is perhaps surprisingly not always very good at. I was glad to be able to repay my debt to him many years later, when I was a fellow at St John's College, Oxford, (which had been Kerry's own college) by nominating him for an honorary fellowship, an honour to which his distinguished career had plainly entitled him.

One of the chief disadvantages of academic life is that the average academic does not receive sufficient criticism from others, most of whom are too busy with their own research to devote enough time to detailed scrutiny of the work of their colleagues. These days academics all seem so busy writing that nobody appears to have enough time to read. As a result some academics tend to become slapdash and lazy in their writing, and do not develop adequate habits of self-criticism. I rather think I suffered from these tendencies myself when I joined the Board of Trade, and it was thanks to Kerry that I learnt greater care and a respect for more scrupulous accuracy in my research. He also taught me a lot in the technique of legal research itself.

Academic legal research is rather different from practical legal research in a variety of ways. The academic is more concerned with theory, with ideas, with ways of thought and analysis. He often scorns legal practitioners' works, with their massive coverage and tendency to exhaustive citations of authoritative precedents, and so on. But the solicitor – and government legal departments function very like solicitors' offices – is of course far more concerned with legal authority, and less concerned with theories and ideas. Virtually any legal precedent is good enough for a government lawyer (at least if it has not been overruled by a higher authority), no matter how silly it may seem. The beautiful thing about precedents is that they save the lawyer from the need to think the problem out afresh. He relies on someone else having done that before, which is what the system of precedent is all about. I once heard a Harvard professor say that there was no Nobel Prize for law because it was a subject in which originality was disapproved of – it was in fact the only subject in which you could actually criticise your opponent's ideas by pointing out that nobody had ever thought of them before, that there was no precedent for them. This is not of course true for academic lawyers but there is a grain of truth in it so far as practising barristers and judges go, and it is even more true of the civil servant. With his desire always to have some justification for any form of action or inaction, precedents are far safer than any other form of justification.

I became a member of a small team working on a minor government Bill, which was passed by Parliament in 1963 and became the Protection of

Depositors Act. It was not a Bill of much public interest and those of us who worked on it were amused at the press reaction when it was first published. After months of hard work, the Bill was ready for publication when we were told that a new government directive required us to provide an estimate as to the public cost of administering the Bill in the explanatory memorandum which accompanied it on publication. A few rough estimates was the best anybody could provide, and so the memorandum declared that the Bill was expected to cost about £150,000 annually. The next day we all saw newspaper headlines declaring, "New Government Controls to Cost £150,000", this being apparently the most important thing about the Bill.

The Bill was a rather technical measure of company law, but it was not an untypical piece of British legislation, a competent and prosaic attempt to protect investors by ensuring that companies published more regular and up-to-date accounts if they solicited deposits from the public. Even such a technical Bill as this involved a great deal of hard work by civil servants, and legal departments, and in this case the burden fell particularly heavily on the government lawyers because even the administrative departments found the legal technicalities hard to master. Working on this Bill was a good piece of training for me, as I learned a lot about how Bills are produced and drafted, and processed through Parliament. All this stood me in good stead a couple of years later when I became involved in a much more important piece of legislation.

Another interesting piece of work I became involved in arose out of some Board of Trade inquiries into a number of insolvent companies which had been the victims of various malpractices. It was decided to exercise the Board's statutory power to petition the court for an order to wind up one of these companies, but the only evidence which we proposed to adduce was the Report of the Board of Trade inspectors. The Report certainly gave ample ground for thinking it was desirable to wind up the company, but unfortunately the Companies Act then in force did not make the Report admissible in evidence as to the truth of its findings. I therefore suggested to my senior colleagues that the Report would technically be hearsay evidence which would be inadmissible, but they laughed at my fears and insisted that several previous petitions had been made on this basis, though it was true that none of them had been contested. At first all seemed to go well. The company resisted our petition by filing an affidavit sworn by its principal shareholder and director, who we thought was the villain of the piece, and we had plenty of evidence to discredit his affidavit, especially the answers he had given the inspectors when cross-examined by them. I culled the transcript of his evidence for examples of these inconsistencies and we passed them on to our counsel as ammunition. However, at the last minute we heard from our counsel that the company had changed tack, after taking new advice. They now wanted to defend the petition by arguing that the Report was indeed inadmissible as hearsay. To do this, they first had to get rid of their own affidavit, and they applied to remove this from the file. When we had our conference with our counsel I asked if we could not resist this application, but he simply asserted in that lofty and maddening way which barristers sometimes have that he did not think it would be "proper". As I was the most junior member of the Board of Trade legal team I did not feel able to press the point though I would certainly have liked to do so. An affidavit, after all, was equivalent to oral evidence, and I did not see why a witness should be entitled to "withdraw" his evidence when he realises that he is about to be cross-examined and that this will probably reveal the evidence to be full of lies. However, our counsel of course was in charge of our case, and we had to go into court ultimately to argue the purely legal point about the inadmissibility of the Report as evidence. Naturally we lost on this point, though my own satisfaction at being proved right on the law was at first swallowed up by indignation at the thought that our fish was going to escape from our hook. Fortunately this did not happen, because although our petition was dismissed the same judge promptly ordered the company to be wound up, on a petition from the Inland Revenue on the much more mundane ground that the company had not paid its taxes.

This was all interesting enough, but unfortunately, after some months of this kind of work I found myself with very little to do. Even when work was available, it had been made clear to me by my colleagues when I first arrived that the nominal lunch hour was, by common consent, stretched to an hour and forty-five minutes. If lunch took an hour, one was permitted to (and indeed, expected to) take a stroll in the park for forty-five minutes afterwards. Furthermore, although the nominal working day was at that time from 9.30 am to 6 pm, nobody would complain if one got in at 9.45 am or 9.50 am (after all what could they expect, given the way British Rail trains were always late?) or left at 5.45 pm or so. So in practice, the working day was usually whittled down to two three-hour periods, which were understood by everyone to run from about 10 am to 1 pm, and then from 2.45 pm to 5.45 pm. The truth was that the legal department appeared to me grossly overstaffed, although my colleagues all denied this, and tried to justify the position by arguing that the civil service had to have a sort of reserve or pool of staff who could be called on to meet sudden crises. It was also suggested by some of my friends that the position in 1962 and early 1963 was atypical, being the last years of a long period of Conservative government, when everybody had run out of ideas, and no new initiatives were being implemented or even planned.

Whatever the explanation, and whatever the justification, the fact was that from the beginning of 1962 until well into 1963 I found myself with very little work. Days and weeks went by in which no files came in my direction at all. After a while, I began, in desperation, to ransack the Board of Trade library for something to read. Being still of a relatively academic turn of mind, I was not too dismayed to discover that the library, as might be expected, was largely confined to books on economics and business and such like. I began to read some economics, and though I had no tutors, and perhaps read rather unintelligently, I probably read almost as much economics during the next eighteen months as the average economics undergraduate at Oxford reads during his three years (though I never mastered the more mathematical side of the subject).

This was all very well, but I could not see myself sitting at my desk reading through the rest of the Board of Trade library even if the government was willing to pay my salary for doing so, and I began to get pretty bored and restless. All this had a sequel which my colleagues found less than amusing, because shortly after I had left the Board of Trade and returned to Oxford in 1964 I saw a letter in *The Financial Times* suggesting that the civil service was understaffed; I fired off an angry letter in reply, based on my own experiences, though I was tactful enough not actually to name the Board of Trade.[1] I later discovered from Kerry that someone in the Treasury had spotted my letter, traced my department, and sent a copy of my letter to the Board of Trade's Solicitor with a somewhat embarrassing demand for an explanation. Needless to say (as all followers of *Yes Minister* could have predicted), an explanation was concocted which pulled the wool over the Treasury's eyes, and nothing more was heard of the matter.

1 Atiyah's letter (29 September 1966) reads:

> "Sir, – I could not help being mildly amused by your article on shortage of staff in the civil service. Two years ago I left the civil service after a three year spell as a legal assistant in one of the major departments of state. For the first two and a half years of that time I estimate that I did, on average, about one day's work in three. This was simply due to gross over-staffing in the section in which I was employed. I cannot speak for the rest of the civil service without any first hand knowledge, but what I did see certainly did not suggest that my situation was in any way unusual."

But all this was still some way off, and luckily for me, some excitement awaited me, even in Her Majesty's Civil Service. I suddenly got caught up in a minor way in a major political battle during 1964. My last six months in the Board of Trade proved in fact exceptionally hectic and exciting. I have often thought of writing a record of those events which may one day supply a historian with a footnote or two, and rather regret that I have waited twenty-five years to do it, so that my recollection can now hardly be completely accurate. But still, some of the events I am about to relate remain very vivid in my memory.

8 Excitement at the Board of Trade

To the best of my recollection, it all began towards the end of 1963, or the beginning of 1964. A Labour MP (who I believe was John Stonehouse, of later ill fame and ignominy) had won a place in the ballot for private members' Bills, and had determined to introduce a Bill to prohibit the practice of resale price maintenance, which was at that time still operated with iron control by British manufacturers and retailers. This Bill was destined to place the government on the rack. Political opinion was at that time bitterly divided about resale price maintenance, but on a free vote it was not impossible that the Stonehouse Bill would be carried. The government clearly had to make up its mind what it intended to do.

Hitherto the Conservative government had remained cautiously in favour of resale price maintenance, or at least had been unwilling to take action against it; and the practice was extremely popular with small shopkeepers who were terrified of what would happen to them if larger shops and discount houses were free to undercut them. These small shopkeepers were traditionally Tory supporters, and they were vociferous in letting the politicians know their views. But within the government machine itself, opinion had increasingly hardened in favour of prohibiting the practice altogether. A small departmental committee had been appointed at the Board of Trade to inquire into the arguments for and against resale price maintenance, and had concluded that the practice was against the public interest, and kept prices unnecessarily high, as well as freezing patterns of retail distribution. But the government had refused to accept the recommendations of this committee, whose report was therefore kept very secret, even though the fact of the committee's existence had been known to the informed press. When I first joined the Board of Trade, opinion among the civil servants was becoming more and more hostile to the practice, and I remember hearing a prominent civil servant (who subsequently became Permanent Secretary) declaiming in the canteen at lunch one day that he had never met an intelligent person who defended the practice.

It so happened that when Mr Stonehouse introduced his private member's Bill, Mr Heath was President of the Board of Trade, having just been appointed to that office – which was his first major ministerial appointment – when Sir Alec Douglas Home succeeded Harold Macmillan as Prime Minister in October 1963. (Strictly, Mr Heath's new title was Secretary of State for Trade, Industry and Regional Development, but that was such a mouthful that nobody ever called him that, and the department itself was still then called the Board of Trade.) The story as I heard it from senior Board of Trade officials was that Mr Heath came into office determined to make a name for himself as a radical and reforming minister. He inquired of his civil servants what crusades he could lead, and his officials delightedly found that he was willing to take on the small shopkeepers in the interests of modernity and reform. Mr Heath was persuaded that resale price maintenance should be outlawed. I did not personally know anything of this. But early in 1964 (I think it was) I was summoned by the head of my department, the Board of Trade Solicitor, Mr Gerard Ryder, and found him in consultation with a Mr Emlyn Davies, who was the Assistant Solicitor to whom I was nominally responsible. Ryder told us that it was possible that, as a result of the Stonehouse Bill, the government would be compelled to decide to introduce its own Bill to outlaw resale price maintenance, and that if they did so, there would be a need for urgency in getting the Bill drafted. Indeed, matters were so urgent, it seemed, that immediate action was needed to prepare some instructions to parliamentary counsel to draft the necessary Bill. As I had worked in a junior capacity on another Bill the previous year, I knew the ropes pretty well. I knew that Parliamentary Counsel were a separate and small government department of legal draftsmen, who drafted all government Bills, and I knew that the civil service lawyers were expected to draw up pretty thorough and extensive instructions to Parliamentary Counsel. I also had a fairly good knowledge of the style of such instructions, as well as of the general law relating to restrictive trade practices. So I volunteered to have a go at home that evening in knocking out a first draft of instructions.

It was, I think, the first time I had ever had to work at home since I had joined the civil service, but I rather enjoyed the experience. It looked as if we were in for a fairly exciting time. I was also personally delighted at the prospect that resale price maintenance might be prohibited. It had always seemed to me to be an utterly pernicious practice which restricted the freedom of consumers. Of course my own views were hardly relevant, but they gave an edge to my interest in the job. I set to with a will that evening, and returned to the office the next morning with a first draft of the instructions already typed out on my own machine, and duly delivered it to my superiors.

I cannot now remember the precise course of events, but I think it was only a day or two afterwards that I was summoned to Ryder's office again to find him in conference with a Miss Moira Dennehey. Miss Dennehey was the Assistant Secretary in charge of the resale prices proposal. She was something of a termagant, who carried around with her wherever she went a box of fifty Turkish cigarettes, which she smoked in profusion. Ryder himself invariably smoked cigars. I came into the smoky atmosphere in his room to find them both plunged in gloom. The Cabinet, it seemed, had only been persuaded by Mr Heath to accept the proposed prohibition of resale price maintenance after a stormy battle in which they had insisted that some system of judicial appeal should be granted to those who wished to continue to maintain prices. Whatever Mr Heath's own reactions, which I never heard in person, Ryder and Miss Dennehey were dismayed by this. They had hoped for and expected approval for a short and simple Bill to outlaw resale price maintenance. Now a far more complex Bill would be needed. Besides, neither of them had any faith whatever in the idea of a judicial appeal against the prohibition. They could not see how such an appeal system would work, since they were both so convinced that resale price maintenance was against the public interest that they could not envisage any sensible grounds on which appeals could be permitted.

I had just been reading the report of the internal Board of Trade Committee, and this Report had carefully and accurately, in the best civil service fashion, set out the general arguments in favour of resale price maintenance which its proponents had relied upon. In broad terms the arguments were that the system of resale price maintenance gave the retailer a sufficient margin to enable him to provide various services to consumers, such as advice on safety (for instance in relation to pharmaceuticals), and general after-sales services, and so on. Of course the argument against was that many consumers did not want or need these services anyhow, and that resale price maintenance enabled inefficient retailers to remain lazily in business and gave no incentive to more efficient ones to cut their costs. But even though we in the civil service had little faith in the arguments in favour of resale price maintenance, this Report did at least set the arguments out in a precise and careful fashion. Of course they were set out in general terms, in relation to all varieties of goods and suppliers, but it immediately occurred to me that these very arguments could be used as the basis for the grounds of appeal which we were now required to write into the Bill. Manufacturers and retailers had for years been arguing the case for resale price maintenance on these grounds. Why should we not now simply require them to prove their case in relation to specific goods before a court of law? I was glad to see, when the Bill was eventually published, a percipient leader in *The Times* comment approvingly on the Bill's approach on this very point.

There was one preliminary point to be settled, as I saw it. It would clearly be out of the question to allow every shopkeeper in the country to appeal against the prohibition on the use of resale price maintenance, so the number of appeals must be kept within bounds. This could only be done by confining appeals to manufacturers, but one key question had first to be settled. Were the appeals to be based on classes of goods, or on groups of manufacturers? I put the question to Ryder, and after a brief pause he said that the appeals should relate to classes of goods. I then told Ryder that I thought it would not be difficult to draw up a set of grounds of appeal, and returning to my room, I got out my copy of the departmental report, and simply put down the arguments in favour of the whole practice, as though they were grounds of appeal in particular cases. The exercise only took me an hour or two, and covered a single sheet of paper.

As soon as I could get it typed I returned to Ryder and showed him what I had done. His eyes immediately lit up, and seizing a pen, he went through my draft, amended it in a number of minor respects, but otherwise accepted it. It became the foundation of the appeal provisions in our instructions to counsel, and was incorporated by him, in his own words of course, in the Bill. From beginning to end, no basic changes were made in these grounds of appeal.

From now on things moved fast. On the political stage, the government announced their decision when Mr Stonehouse's Bill came up for second reading, and that of course killed off the Stonehouse Bill. It also produced a tremendous political uproar, as the Conservative backbenchers were bombarded with complaints from small retailers, and in their turn, warned the government, and Mr Heath in particular, that he could not afford to alienate his own supporters too far. For days the papers were full of RPM as it was called, in the headlines, until some engineer wrote a letter to *The Times* pointing out the RPM stood for "revolutions per minute" and what were the papers talking about? But he was fighting a losing battle. For several months in 1964 RPM meant resale price maintenance and nothing else. Meanwhile we were working flat out to get our instructions to parliamentary counsel finished. And not long after they were delivered, we began to get some drafts back. The Bill was drafted by Sir Noel Hutton, who was the

First Parliamentary Counsel, and as he had also drafted the Bill on which I had worked the previous year, I already knew him quite well. Usually Bills are drafted by counsel working in pairs, but on this occasion there was such a shortage of time, and the Bill (though much complicated by the appeal provisions) not as long and difficult as many major Bills, so it was in fact produced by Sir Noel working alone. After the customary four or five drafts had been produced and we had worked through them word by word and clause by clause, the Bill was finally published about (I think) the middle of February 1964, and a date fixed for the second reading debate in the House of Commons.

This was an important occasion for Mr Heath. It was his first major Bill as a Minister, and it was still expected that he would have a rough ride from many of his backbenchers who were bitterly hostile to the Bill. It is today hard to understand the passions that the subject aroused until one remembers that many people thought it would hit their pockets very hard. Heath had come into office with quite a reputation as a tough Chief Whip who was clearly on the make. Many people thought him abrasive and insensitive to opposition and criticism. In fact that was not the reputation he had among his civil servants at all. My chief Ryder was later to complain that Heath had no backbone, and behaved like jelly in the face of backbencher opposition. The reason for this – so far as it was true – may have been partly that the appeal provisions meant that the effective operation of the Bill had been put back by two or three years. It was Ryder himself who told me that Heath had thought that the Bill might have an immediate impact in cutting the prices of many goods in the shops – something any politician would like to achieve especially in an election year – but that when Heath realised that it was going to be several years before that could possibly happen, he lost interest in the Bill.

The day of the second reading debate was the first occasion I had myself met Heath. He was eating a light meal at his desk, while a team of civil servants was sitting round a table in his room. He fired off a set of instructions: he wanted this and he wanted that. Then there was a chuckle. "I'm afraid this means you won't have time for any lunch", he said as he ate his own lunch. It did not seem very funny at the time, though I rather think it proved incorrect anyhow. We crowded into the "Official Box" in a corner of the House of Commons behind the Speaker's chair, which is set aside for civil servants, to hear the second reading debate. It was of course our job to keep careful track of what was said. The Minister needed to answer points made by other members, especially those on the Conservative side; and for this purpose he might need our help and advice. He might also undertake from time to time to look into some point made by another member, and we then had to make sure that he did look into it, and perhaps write an explanatory letter to his backbencher. These letters were a good way of making members feel that their points were not being ignored, and that the Minister was not too remote from his backbenchers. In addition, of course, genuine points might be made in the debate indicating where pressure would arise in the coming committee stage, and we needed to be ready for that.

I was not enormously impressed by Heath's second reading speech. It was moderately competent, but not (I thought) nearly forceful enough. Nor was he a very effective speaker in debating manner and style. I remember being astonished that at the end of his speech he did not even use the time-hallowed formula, "Mr Speaker, I beg to move that this Bill be read a second time". What he said instead was, "I move the second reading of the Bill". Fortunately the Hansard reporters knew the official ropes better than the Minister and they silently corrected his error. But if Heath himself was not very impressive, most of the other speakers were, I thought, abysmal. The general level of the debate was extremely low. Both in content and in debating skill and speaking ability, the debate was very disappointing. I was really impressed by only one speaker – Anthony Crosland, the Labour member who later became President of the Board of Trade himself, and died tragically while Foreign Secretary in the Callaghan government – seemed to me to stand head and shoulders above the other speakers. I came back from the debate convinced that Crosland would be the next Prime Minister, but I was of course proved wrong in 1977.

The second reading debate did, however, show one thing – the virulence of the opposition to the Bill, even on the Conservative side of the House. The day after the debate, a meeting was summoned at the House of Commons at which Heath, and the Board of Trade Minister of State, Edward du Cann, were both present, together with the civil service team, including myself. Heath opened the discussion by saying, ironically, "We only have one problem now, which is how on earth are we going to get this bloody Bill through committee!" du Cann replied soothingly, saying that he did not think things were as difficult as they appeared, and he was, in fact, proved quite right. But they looked very difficult indeed. Heath had a private party meeting with his backbenchers after the second reading debate at which (we heard) loud and insistent demands were made that major amendments to the Bill must be made. The appeal provisions must be recast. I myself did not have much to do with this side of things, as I was furiously engaged in preparing a variety of other documents for the committee stage of the Bill. But I knew from Ryder that meetings had been held between Heath, Ryder and Hutton at which instructions had been given for the drafting of amendments to be tabled at the committee stage, and these amendments were actually to be shown to the backbenchers' committee. Ryder told me that Heath had personally called at the Office of Parliamentary Counsel, and waited for the draft amendments to be finished, much to the fury of the civil servants who were not used to such treatment. Indeed, Ryder protested (though not officially) that Heath had breached government security in himself entering the Office of Parliamentary Counsel.

Eventually the amendments were produced and they satisfied most of the backbenchers, but when I saw them I was astonished. They appeared to me to be little more than cosmetic changes. The appeal provisions had been recast so as to give them a little more prominence in the Bill – they now appeared at an earlier point – but there had been no change in substance at all. I put this to Ryder and he agreed entirely. When I thought of all the sound and fury being generated by the Conservative backbenchers, I could hardly believe that they would be so easily satisfied; and indeed, many were not, as later events proved. But enough of them were.

At this stage my job was to prepare, or help in preparing, two sets of papers. The first was the Notes on Clauses which every Bill required, in which we set out in simple language which Ministers and members of parliament could understand, the purpose of every section and paragraph in the Bill, how they interrelated, and how the Bill would work in general. And then there were the Notes on Amendments. Once the Bill had passed its second reading and was listed for committee, the proposed amendments began to pour in – dozens and dozens of them. I think there were over a hundred in the end even though the Bill was quite short as Bills go. Every proposed amendment had to be studied to see what its purposes were, and some reasoned answer given to show why the amendment would not be acceptable – or alternatively we had to be ready to advise the Minister that we ought to draft our own amendments to do the job. Strictly, all this work should have fallen to the departmental officials. Miss Dennehey's subordinate, a civil servant Principal, was a Miss Elizabeth Llewellyn Smith, and in the ordinary course of events, these tasks would have been hers. But she was not experienced in the work, she was not a lawyer, and had not worked on a Bill before. So the work fell largely to me. (In 1977 when I returned to Oxford as a Professor and Fellow of St John's College, I found a Chris Llewellyn Smith who was a fellow of the college in nuclear physics: he was

Miss Llewellyn Smith's brother. In 1989 she herself was elected Principal of St Hilda's College at Oxford.)

As the time for the committee stage of the Bill approached, things became more and more hectic. I found myself working very late hours, and for the first time discovered that a civil servant who was working late was entitled to telephone his home at government expense. On one occasion the whole team turned up for work on a Saturday, something I had never known to happen before. I was exhilarated rather than exhausted by these long hours, and although I had been at my desk till 9 pm the previous night, I was still the first in on the Saturday morning. The Board of Trade building was oppressively silent and empty when I got there, and I was rather surprised at how easy it was to penetrate all parts of the building. Ryder's office was open when I arrived, though he was not yet there. On his desk there stood the scrambler telephone with which I promptly tried to phone Parliamentary Counsel, but he too was not yet in his office. I dare say security is a good deal tighter nowadays than it was then.

As the amendments flowed in, we picked one out that we knew was going to be the centre of the coming political battle with the backbenchers. The Bill itself – in accordance with our instructions – had drawn the grounds of appeal very tightly. There were three specific and limited grounds of appeal which required the claimants to prove that resale price maintenance was in the public interest for their goods for one or other of these strictly defined reasons. But the Bill contained no general ground of appeal, enabling claimants to argue that there might be other reasons why the practice was in the public interest; and it was here that battle was going to be joined. The Conservative backbenchers wanted to write in a general ground of appeal, and they had what appeared to be a precedent on their side. In the Restrictive Trade Practices Act of 1956, also the work of a Conservative government, which had first created the Restrictive Practices Court and enabled that Court to declare various restrictive practices to be illegal, there *was* a general ground of exemption to which manufacturers and retailers could appeal. They could, under that Act, simply argue that there were specific grounds on which the practice was in the public interest. But we in the civil service did not regard this as a true parallel. The 1956 Act had attacked a very wide range of restrictive practices, and there was a good case for saying that some of these practices might have public benefits which could not be foreseen when the Bill was drafted. But resale price maintenance was one particular type of restrictive practice, and we contended that the government decision to introduce the Bill itself amounted to a decision that the practice was prima facie illegal and contrary to the public interest. We could not see how the very same issue could then be left in general terms to be decided by the Restrictive Practices Court all over again. We were also convinced as a practical matter that an open and general ground of appeal of the kind being sought by the backbenchers was a serious threat to the working of the Bill. We thought the grounds of exemption were so tight that very few goods would ever get through them – and we were right – but we greatly feared that a general ground of exemption for vague reasons of public interest would gravely weaken the Bill in practice. Many goods might escape under such a clause, and the more cases that were fought before the Restrictive Practices Court, the more long-winded the whole process would be. Instead of resale price maintenance largely disappearing within a couple of years, which was what we hoped for, and what in fact happened, we thought that the amendment sought by the backbenchers created a real risk that the process would stretch out for a decade or more.

So we in the civil service were convinced that this amendment must be resisted to the end; and that no matter what concessions Mr Heath made to his backbenchers he had to hold firm on this particular amendment. It was his reaction to this issue which made my chief Ryder condemn Heath as weak, and lacking in backbone. Mr Heath had several meetings with his backbenchers at which he was subjected to great pressure, and he kept warning the civil servants that he was going to have give way. They fought hard. Indeed, Ryder told me that they had actually used an almost unheard of procedure for instilling more fight into Mr Heath. The Permanent Secretary of the Board of Trade had written to the Prime Minister's secretary suggesting that a letter from the Prime Minister to Mr Heath, opposing the amendment, might be a good idea, and such a letter was, I believe, written. Whether this did the trick, or whether Mr Heath was otherwise persuaded I don't know; but he did eventually decide to fight; and the amendment was in fact quite easily defeated in the end.

Some readers may be surprised by my description of the way in which senior civil servants fought for particular policies in this story. In their public pronouncements civil servants as well as ministers happily agree in minimising the degree of power which civil servants exercise. Ministers, being politicians, want to claim that the power is all theirs; and civil servants, not being politicians, are happy to hide under the skirts of Ministers, while still in practice exercising considerable power. Of course, the constitutional theory that Ministers actually decide on policy and civil servants merely carry it out is true with regard to those matters which are clearly put before Ministers for their decisions. But Ministers obviously cannot decide everything; and in any event nobody in practice has ever succeeded in drawing a precise distinction between deciding on a policy and carrying out a policy. Plainly, as any schoolboy can see, carrying out policies decided by Ministers often requires all sorts of further (and not always very minor) policy questions to be decided, and these often have to be decided by civil servants, acting within the general remit which they think they have from Ministers. None of this is designed to support the "conspiracy theories" which are popular with some politicians, to the effect that civil servants actually work to *subvert* policies decided by Ministers. Most, if not all, senior civil servants do loyally and scrupulously try to make their own policy decisions within the general framework of the policy that has been decided by Ministers, in such a way as to give effect to Ministerial policy.

At the same time I was quite surprised myself at the way in which civil servants sometimes treated Ministers. On one occasion, when the Resale Prices team was under great pressure, and Mr du Cann, the Minister of State, asked for some civil service assistance in connection with a speech he had to make on the Bill, I remember several senior civil servants simply telling du Cann's private office that they were far too busy to help him. In the end, when he pressed again for assistance, I – the most junior member of the team – was despatched to help him.

The government decided to take the Committee stage of the Bill before the whole House of Commons, rather than one of the standing committees, because so many members wanted to take part in the debates; and three full days, Monday, Tuesday and Wednesday, were set apart one week for the start.

The first day a long session was anticipated, and as we (the civil service team) hung around in the corridor waiting our turn to enter the official civil servants' "box" in the chamber, Harold Wilson strolled by and jokingly asked us if we had brought our pyjamas. During the first day's hearings I retreated from the official box for a quiet cigarette at one point (a habit I have long since kicked) and ran into my old Magdalen friend, Bill Rodgers, then a Labour member, and later one of the founders of the SDP. He greeted me, and we had a friendly chat, though of course he was much freer to talk than I could be. He told me that the Labour Party was convinced that the government had decided to introduce a guillotine motion on the Thursday because no business had yet been announced for that day. I knew this was nonsense, because the one thing that had been agreed on the government side was that no guillotine would be tolerated on the Bill, but of course I kept my mouth shut. It was an interesting example of how paranoid politicians can get, because even such a sane fellow as Bill Rodgers had convinced himself that diabolical government machinations were at work.

For almost the whole of the committee stage debates, each of which lasted until late into the evening, I was present in the Official Box behind the Speaker's Chair in the House of Commons. I followed the debates with great interest, observing the more famous figures here and there. Once I saw Sir Winston Churchill walk slowly into the Chamber and sit for a few moments on what may well have been his very last visit to the House of Commons. He was nearly ninety, and very unsteady on his feet – indeed he tripped and fell on his way out and had to be immediately supported by members rushing to his aid.

Usually there were several of us present in the Official Box; but on one occasion I found myself holding the fort on behalf of the Board of Trade and this led to a difficult moment for me. The question was raised during that day's debate whether it would be possible for the Registrar of Restrictive Trading Agreements (who represented the public interest before the Restrictive Practices Court) to *concede* a case before the Court. The point behind the question was all to do with books and the famous Net Book Agreement under which resale price maintenance operated in the case of books. Under the 1956 Act the Net Book Agreement had already been before the Court which had in substance found that the Agreement did operate in the public interest; and members of Parliament sympathetic to publishing interests wanted an assurance that the Net Book Agreement would not be dragged through the Court again under the new Bill. However, the Bill as drafted required that the Court should be "satisfied" that resale price maintenance operated in the public interest in the case of the goods in question before they could be exempted under the Bill. Did this mean that the Court would have to hear the defence of the Net Book Agreement all over again? Sir Noel Hutton, the Bill's draftsman, who was sitting next to me in the Official Box, thought that it did, and was about to pass a note to this effect to Mr Heath. I did not agree with Hutton because, as it seemed to me, the Registrar could concede a case under the Bill. Since he was in charge of presenting the case before the Court I did not see how anyone could force him to argue that the Net Book Agreement was contrary to the public interest, if he was satisfied that the previous judgment of the Court was correct. Given Hutton's very senior status, and my own extremely junior one, I was in a somewhat embarrassing situation, but I did whisper my disagreement to him. I had hardly expected that he would pay any attention to my view, but he obviously regarded me as representing the Board of Trade position, so he sent a note down to the Attorney-General (Sir John Hobson), and we all trooped into the corridor for a hasty consultation. Hutton and I put our views briefly, and the Attorney-General adopted a sort of compromise position, (though one which was in substance what I had argued) saying that the Court would have to be "satisfied" but on the other hand, if the Registrar conceded the case the Court presumably could be satisfied with the concession, and the case would not need to be reheard. In the event this was exactly what happened after the Bill had been passed. The Net Book Agreement was cleared through the Court, without a full defence having to be made, and books were thus exempted from the ban on resale price maintenance – virtually the only goods which were exempt, and remained so for many years.

One of the government's most difficult moments came on a proposed amendment to exempt pharmaceutical products from the Bill. A great argument was developed to the effect that chemists provided a useful service to the public on the sale of simple (non-prescribed) pharmaceuticals such as aspirins, throat lozenges and such like. It was said that if resale price maintenance was abolished, supermarkets and other shops without registered pharmacists would sell these products more cheaply, thus under-cutting the chemists' shops, and that this would be at grave risk to the public who would be endangered by the lack of the chemists' advice when they bought such products. The argument was completely phony, because the truth simply was that the chemists, like everybody else, did not wish to see their profits slashed by more competitive businesses, and there never was the slightest risk to the public in the prohibition of resale price maintenance on these goods. Indeed, in an earlier case under the 1956 Act, where a similar argument had been presented to the Restrictive Practices Court, the Court had found that not a single example of danger to the public health had been produced as a result of the sale of non-prescription pharmaceuticals by shops without a registered chemist. I would dearly have loved to have some copies of the relevant pages of the Court's judgment photocopied and scattered around the House of Commons, but nobody in the debate referred to the Court's findings, and the government only succeeded in having the amendment rejected by one vote. On this occasion Mr Heath rose to the occasion, saying that Winston Churchill had once told him that a majority of one was enough, and he proposed to continue with the Bill.

After the first three days of the Committee Stage, it was apparent that the battle was won. All the other amendments to which the government was opposed were defeated easily enough, and the Committee Stage was eventually completed. I attended the last debate in the House of Commons late at night when Mr Harold Lever, a Labour MP with some reputation as an economist and also a wit, detained the House with a long and passionate speech in which he protested at a formal clause which exempted from the Bill any goods sold under a scheme sponsored by any other Act of Parliament. The debate came to a good-humoured conclusion when we were able to tell the Minister, and he was able to tell the House, that there were in fact no such schemes known to us, so the clause would actually have no practical application. This debate finished about 1 am and for the first and only time in my career as a civil servant I had a government car to take me home.

After that, my own part in the Bill was pretty well over. Nearly all the while the Bill was being drafted, I had a personal interest in the workings of the drafting process, and in the personality of Sir Noel Hutton. This was because I had applied for a transfer to the Office of Parliamentary Counsel, where a vacancy had now arisen. I had long had an interest in the workings of this Office, partly because of my friendship from Ghana days, with Francis Bennion, who was himself a member of the Office, and had encouraged me to apply. It was just about the time when the Resale Prices Bill completed its committee stage that I was told that my application had been accepted, and that I would in the first instance be seconded to the Treasury, the department then responsible for the Office, with the possibility of permanence after a probationary year. I received a very warm letter from Hutton, welcoming me to the Office, and saying that it would have been pleasant if I could simply have been transferred from one side of the table to the other among those working on the Resale Prices Bill; but he had other ideas for me in the Parliamentary Counsel's Office.

I transferred accordingly from the Board of Trade in the Spring of 1964 but in the event my stay in the Parliamentary Counsel's Office was relatively short. I am not sure how much I would have liked the Office if I had stayed, but there were certainly things about it which I soon found rather uncongenial. It was a very lonely place. The counsel worked in pairs on a Bill; but mostly one worked alone. The research and the drafting were necessarily solitary occupations, and the occasions for criticism and discussion with one's colleague were few. This did not wholly suit me. Although even an academic career involves much private research and writing, it also involves more contact with colleagues as well as students. I like to talk about my work, and to some extent, I think aloud in the process of doing so. Thinking aloud was not something that anyone did in the Chambers of the Parliamentary Counsel.

Long hours were also required as a matter of course, often in the preparation of Bills, and also in attendance at the House of Commons. While I had no objection to hard work – in fact I relished it – I began to be more aware of the difficulties of such long hours for a family man. Our family now consisted of four boys, and living in Woking already meant that I left home at 8 am and returned at 7 pm even on a normal day.

It may also be that I joined the Office at too late an age. Although I was still only thirty-three I was already getting on a bit to accept the role of junior dogsbody which is everybody's lot on entering that Office. The first few years there are inevitably years of learning and gaining experience, and I did not find it easy to work with my new chief, John Fiennes, later Hutton's successor as First Parliamentary Counsel. Fiennes had a reputation as the outstanding intellect in the Office, but he did not suffer fools gladly, nor indeed was he too tolerant of his junior assistants. On one occasion, when we had a mild disagreement about something, he proceeded to lay down the law, and asked me if I accepted what he had said. I replied, unwisely, "I suppose so", to which he responded loudly and angrily, "It is not a question of supposing so at all; that is a logically unanswerable proposition".

However, I must, I think, have made some sort of impression on Fiennes, because when he heard that I was thinking of leaving the Office without waiting to complete my probationary year, he was clearly somewhat disturbed, and, speaking with great difficulty, he told me: "I wouldn't want you to suppose that your work has been found unacceptable here". That was probably as near as Fiennes ever came to paying a compliment, and he then hastily brushed his own words aside, insisting that of course the decision must be my own, and that he had no desire to influence me.

In fact, although I had begun to have some worries about my new work, I had not myself had any thought of quitting. Quite apart from my reluctance to acknowledge so soon that I might have made a mistake in my choice of job, we had recently moved to a new house, still in the Woking district, and I had no thoughts then of yet another upheaval. But one day in June 1964, quite out of the blue, I received a letter from the Warden of New College, Oxford, asking me whether I was interested in a law fellowship at the college, and inviting me to visit the college and dine with the fellows. The letter did not actually offer me the fellowship, for which I had not of course applied, but I knew enough of the ways of Oxford colleges to be pretty sure that the letter was all but a formal offer, and that I only had to meet the fellows and avoid blotting my copy book over dinner, to be sure of being offered the fellowship. A few days later, my brother Michael, who was himself a fellow of New College (but who had absented himself from the college meeting at which I had been invited) telephoned to confirm that he thought the fellowship was mine if I wanted it.

I was certainly flattered to receive the invitation; and since I had made up my mind after several rejections that I would apply for no more Oxford fellowships, I was especially gratified that the invitation had come without an application on my part. But my first inclination was to turn it down. However, I thought it would be pleasant to dine at New College and meet the fellows, so I did so one Sunday in July, shortly before most of the fellows dispersed for the summer. I enjoyed the company of the fellows; and I enjoyed the atmosphere of Oxford again. Tossing and turning in bed that night I made up my mind to accept the offer.

9 Back in Oxford

Our return to Oxford was overshadowed by the death of both my parents within a few weeks of each other. My mother was the first to go. She took her own life by taking a huge number of aspirin tablets. It was no surprise as she had already twice attempted suicide within the past few years, but it was sad for me who remembered her as a vigorous and active person only a few years back. In the last few years of her life she had been suffering from severe depression and when she died she was only a shadow of the person she had been up to the age of fifty.

A few weeks later my father died, as he had lived, in rather dramatic and public fashion. He had been invited to speak in a debate at the Oxford Union – the first time he had been asked to speak "on the paper" since the invitation forty-two years earlier which had led to his meeting with my mother. By this time my father had been suffering for some years from a bad heart, and we all knew that he might not have long to live. The debate at the Union that night was on some aspect of Arab–Israeli relations; it was somewhat rowdy and tensions ran high. My father could never keep his emotions in check on such occasions, and shortly after he began to speak, he collapsed and died instantly from a massive heart attack.[1] Christine and I were watching the debate from the public gallery, and we immediately ran down, but there was nothing that we, or anyone, could do. He was removed to the Radcliffe Infirmary where he was pronounced dead on arrival.

Earlier that summer, and before we had actually moved to Oxford I myself had begun to develop some ominous symptoms of heart disease. I was very like my father in build and appearance, and when I began to get some severe chest pains in the summer of 1964 I was packed off by my doctor to see the same consultant who was looking after my father – a Scot called Dr Macmillan, at St Luke's Hospital, Guildford. Dr Macmillan had become quite friendly with my father, who had told him something of his family, and when he had given me the usual ECG tests and found something abnormal there he told me genially that I would have to lose weight. "You come of poor physical stock", he added, "good intellectual stock, but poor

1 Details are provided in *The Times* (London, 23 October 1964) 17.

physical stock!" Dr Macmillan was only too accurate. Not only did I inherit my father's heart problems, but I (and my sister, and later a nephew) also inherited my mother's tendency to depressive illness, though that did not manifest itself for some years.

At the time it was the heart problems which were worrying, though they did not at first appear too serious. Diagnostic techniques were of course much less sophisticated at that time, and it was nearly twenty years before I learned that I had inherited from my father (and passed on to three of my four sons) the dread familial hypercholesterolemia condition, which causes an abnormally high cholesterol level, and almost always leads to atheroma, the furring up of the coronary arteries. It was also twenty-five years before anybody realised I had actually had at this time a minor heart attack with some slight damage to my heart. In fact, after following Dr Macmillan's advice and shedding some weight, I had no further symptoms for many years, but all the same, it seemed at the time a good thing that I was returning to the academic world, which appeared to offer the prospect of a less strenuous life.

After this sad beginning, life for us soon settled down at a new level. In every way, the move to Oxford was a change for the better. We were, for a start, much better off. We now lived in a large five-bedroomed college house in North Oxford (this was before the days when it seemed madness to get out of the housing market) for which we paid a very modest rent – which was also tax deductible under some special arrangement negotiated by the colleges with the tax authorities. The college had already arranged to install oil-fired central heating in the house which to us in those days seemed the very last word in luxury. (A tank full of oil cost us £25!) They also completely redecorated the house and were responsible for all maintenance, so many of those daily household worries became a mere memory for us. In addition, we now had a couple of thousand pounds in savings, having sold our Surrey house, so we were able to buy a new car and indulge in a long summer holiday the following year in Spain, with our four boys. Then there was the end of the commuting nightmare. I could now leave home at a civilised hour, and still get home in time to see my children before they went to bed. True, I dined in college twice a week in those days, but that was hardly to be compared with the usual commuter reasons for being late home.

It was too, a great pleasure to find myself at last a fellow of an Oxford college. The intellectual and social environment of New College was immensely satisfying after my years as a very minor official in the civil service. I much enjoyed getting to know my colleagues at New College, taking part in the meetings of the governing body, dining in hall and so on. The college had its share of Oxford characters, some of whom later became celebrities in other spheres. Apart from my brother Michael, then Savilian Professor of Geometry, of whom I have written earlier, there was, for instance, Tony Quinton, later Lord Quinton and President of Trinity College, Oxford (where my youngest son went in 1981). Quinton became something of a TV celebrity later, but at that time his ponderous but wonderfully Johnsonian manner of expression was unknown outside Oxford.

There was AJ Ayer (always known to everybody as Freddy) who had shaken the philosophic establishment (and even the wider world) with his book, *Language, Truth and Logic*,[2] published when he was twenty-four, in which he had "eliminated" metaphysics as not worth study because it was literally "meaningless" (though it turned out later that this conclusion depended on his definition of "meaningless"). At this time philosophy was largely a closed book to me personally, and I had never heard of *Language, Truth and Logic*, but one day, at a lunchtime discussion at New College with Ayer, David Wiggins, the New College philosophy fellow and one or two others I gathered enough about the book to make me feel ashamed of my ignorance. After lunch I stole off to Blackwells and bought myself a copy. After that I began to read a lot more philosophy, especially when I began my studies into the theory of contract when I first discovered how fascinated philosophers had been down the ages about the nature of promissory obligations.

I recall another common room discussion with Ayer, shortly after the death of Sir Winston Churchill in which he told us that he had been asked by a foreign friend to suggest who was now the greatest living Englishman, a question he had had great difficulty in answering. My suggestion of Bertrand Russell as the chief contender was generally agreed.

Rudolf Peierls, the Professor of Physics, who had played a key role in the development of the atom bomb, was also a fellow. It was he who had first proved in 1940 that the bomb was a real possibility, and it was largely his work which induced the Americans to embark on it. At a common room discussion one day, when the subject came round to the beginnings of the bomb I suggested that the first test must have been a terrifying experience for the scientists because they presumably could not have known how devastating it would be. "Oh no", said Peierls, "we were able

2 AJ Ayer, *Language, Truth and Logic* (1936).

to calculate the amount of energy to be released pretty accurately." I never was much of a scientist.

Then there was Lord David Cecil, grandson of the Lord Salisbury who had been Prime Minister three times at the end of the last century, who always spoke in a breathless, jerky sort of way, like a machine-gun with a silencer attached to it. Another fellow was the college chaplain, Garry Bennett, who much later took his own life after his identity as author of the notorious Crockford's Preface was revealed. One does not like to speak ill of the dead but I must confess I did not like Bennett, who I found self-serving and devious, a view which I think was shared by many of my colleagues. Another fellow who later became prominent as a minor "celebrity" was John Bayley, husband of Iris Murdoch, and author of the sad memoir of his wife simply entitled *Iris*[3] which was later made into a film. After John met my wife at a number of college events, he said she reminded him of Jane Austin's Emma so much that he took to calling her Emma.

When I was first elected a fellow in 1964 New College was in the middle of some turmoil as a result of a preliminary decision, made the previous year, to admit women to the college, both as students and as fellows. At that time, of course, all the undergraduate colleges in Oxford were single-sex colleges, and this had always been the case. New College itself was nearly 600 years old in 1964 and had never had a woman fellow or student. Indeed, the monastic tradition was so strong that as late as the 1950s most men's colleges would not permit women to be brought into dinner except on special guest nights. When Magdalen had appointed a woman as a part-time tutor in law (not of course a position carrying a fellowship) she had not been permitted to lunch in the senior common room, and John Morris had been obliged to give her lunch privately in his rooms on the days when she was teaching. So the proposal to go co-educational was pretty revolutionary stuff by Oxford standards. Naturally, it gave rise to strong feelings. The chief motive for the change was the belief among many tutorial fellows that many able women students were being turned away from Oxford colleges in favour of less able men, and as there were about five or six times as many men as women students, this was obviously pretty plausible. But some of the more traditional-minded fellows were outraged at the proposed change, and no other college had so much as considered it. Indeed, I was told that when the subject had first been mooted the previous year it had been done so in a somewhat light-hearted and not entirely serious frame of mind.

3 J Bayley, *Iris* (1999).

But the idea, once broached, had eventually been taken more seriously and the college governing body had tentatively voted in favour of the change. However, a further vote, to change the college statutes was still required, and this vote required a two-thirds majority. During my first year as a fellow this vote was taken, and the reformers (amongst whom, I counted myself) failed to secure the necessary majority. But New College had at least put the subject on the agenda at Oxford, and very soon afterwards, several other colleges actually made the change. This started an avalanche, and within a decade, virtually all the colleges – including this time, New College – had changed their statutes, and begun to admit both men and women. In retrospect, it is extraordinary how easily the change was made in practice. All the agonising at college meetings, about the need for more bathrooms, and the risk of illicit sex, and so on, turned out to have been very largely pointless. Within a few short years, we were all completely accustomed to the sight of men and women dining together in hall, or having tutorials together, and an effort of mind was needed to remember how it had been different at one time. Indeed, the colleges soon took in their stride the occasional pregnant students some of whom succeeded in turning in excellent academic performances. Few social revolutions have ever been accomplished more easily in the long history of Oxford University.

College social life was all very pleasant, but of course, a tutorial fellow also has a job to do. I now threw myself into academic work with greatly renewed zeal and interest. My years out of academic life had been invaluable years of learning and experience, and maturing. I was now full of ideas for research and writing, and for a few years I even enjoyed tutorial teaching, though that did pall all too soon. I began to write extensively for legal journals, and some of my articles later proved to have been of some value as pioneering pieces. I also threw myself into an ambitious new book on the law of vicarious liability[4] – that part of the law concerning the circumstances in which a company or other employer is legally liable for the actions of its subordinates. It was a massive task which had never been seriously attempted before. The case law was enormous and for months and months I read and took careful notes of hundreds of cases. The book was completed by 1966 and published

4 PS Atiyah, *Vicarious Liability in the Law of Torts* (1967).

in 1967. It was very well reviewed,[5] and added to my reputation, although it never reached a second edition, or even a reprint.[6]

But it was quite widely used, even by legal practitioners, as I discovered some years later. Harry Fisher, then at the Bar, and later a judge, told me that not long after the book was published he was engaged in a case in court which raised issues discussed in the book. Some junior counsel drew attention to the book, and before long all the barristers as well as the judge were surreptitiously reading it – surreptitiously because it was then still regarded as somewhat unacceptable for barristers and judges to acknowledge that they had derived any assistance from legal textbooks. In the 1960s judges very rarely mentioned academic writings by name or attribution, even where it was manifest that ideas had been borrowed from some academic source. Indeed, my book on vicarious liability contains several passages which bear a striking resemblance to passages in the speeches of the judges in a case in the House of Lords decided several years afterwards – but there is no mention of the author by name. The idea that academic lawyers could teach barristers and judges anything of importance was then still regarded as highly suspect – an absurd tradition which I criticised many years afterwards in my Hamlyn Lectures which were published under the title *Pragmatism and Theory in English Law* in 1987.[7] Although the tradition is not yet dead, it is at least now quite acceptable and commonplace for barristers and judges to cite academic works, and some of my own works have since been cited in judgments in the House of Lords, the High Court of Australia, the Supreme Court of Canada, and even some American courts.

This divorce of the practising and the academic legal profession (which would barely be intelligible to lawyers on the Continent, or even in the United States) gave rise to an amusing moment at New College one night. I had invited John Morris as my guest at the annual St Thomas' dinner at New College, and after dinner we found ourselves talking to Lord Wilberforce, an

5 See, e.g., JA Jolowicz, "Book review: Vicarious Liability in the Law of Torts by PS Atiyah" (1968) 26 CLJ 150; H Silberberg, "Book review: Vicarious Liability in the Law of Torts by PS Atiyah" (1969) 2 *Comparative and International Law Journal of Southern Africa* 357; PD McKenzie, "Book review: Vicarious Liability in the Law of Torts by PS Atiyah" (1968–1970) 5 *Victoria University of Wellington Law Review* 272; cf. the mixed review in H Street, "Book review: Vicarious Liability in the Law of Torts by PS Atiyah" (1968) 13 *Society of Public Teachers of Law* 57.

6 The book remains relevant. Despite its having been published in 1967, it has in the present century been described as being "still the leading text on vicarious liability": R Stevens, *Torts and Rights* (2007) 259.

7 PS Atiyah, *Pragmatism and Theory in English Law* (1987).

honorary fellow of the college, and then recently appointed as a Law Lord. There was then pending before the House of Lords an important legal case (referred to by lawyers as *Chaplin v Boys*)[8] which involved a problem in that esoteric field known to lawyers as the conflict of laws. The problem in a nutshell was what law should be applied to decide a case involving a traffic accident in Malta when both parties were British servicemen temporarily resident in Malta, but now back in England. Should the court apply Maltese law, or English law? Precedents suggested that such cases should be decided according to some rather rigid and not very appropriate rules; but John Morris – one of the world's leading experts in the conflict of laws – had written an article[9] some years before arguing for a more flexible approach, in which the court should choose the most appropriate "proper law of the tort" according to all the circumstances of the case, in much the same way was done in the law of contract. This article had made a considerable stir, and Morris' ideas had actually been adopted by some American courts (which are much more receptive to academic arguments) but Lord Wilberforce evidently did not know that the idea of a "proper law of the tort" had originated with Morris. "I don't think we want to adopt this idea of the 'proper law of the tort'", he said, and then, looking at Morris, inquired, rather doubtfully, "You've heard about the 'proper law of the tort' idea, I suppose?" There was a brief, uneasy silence, before Morris broke out in a huge chuckle. "Heard of it?", he said, "I invented it!"

One of the advantages of being an Oxford College fellow is that one often has the opportunity to meet and get to know people who visit Oxford in one capacity or another. Among lawyers, the tradition of making judges honorary fellows was particularly helpful in this respect. I was especially fortunate in that Lord Wilberforce was elected an honorary fellow at about the same time I became a tutorial fellow, and I got to know him very well. By the 1970s he had taken to inquiring of my wife, every time we met, whether I had yet been elected an honorary Bencher of my Inn of Court,[10] and protesting that it was a scandal when he heard that I had not. (I still have not.)

New College had, at the time I joined it, an exceptionally strong legal tradition. Indeed, in 1964 it could in theory have sported a full panel of five judges in the House of Lords. A recently retired Lord Chancellor, Lord Simmonds, told Sir William Hayter, then Warden of New College, who

8 [1971] AC 356 (HL).
9 JHC Morris, "The Proper Law of a Tort" (1951) 64 *Harvard Law Review* 881.
10 Atiyah had been called to the Bar by the Inner Temple in 1956.

told me, that he thought Wilberforce would make an outstanding Lord of Appeal. I came to agree with this conclusion as I read more of Wilberforce's legal judgments. I thought he displayed exceptional acumen and sensitivity, not merely to the legal problems themselves, but to the difficulties of deciding on the appropriate role for the judiciary. It is probably not widely appreciated that one of the most important (though unrecognised) functions of judges in the highest courts is to decide when a problem is one which it is appropriate for the judges to solve, and when it is best left to politicians and legislators. I became convinced that Wilberforce always understood the nature of this problem, and I nearly always agreed with his solutions to it; I thought that other judges often failed to appreciate the problem, and when they did, I found their solutions less satisfying.

Wilberforce actually owed his promotion to the House of Lords to Lord Dilhorne who had been Lord Chancellor at the time, but who lost office ten days later, when the Labour Party won the election of 1964, and replaced him with Lord Gardiner. These two Lord Chancellors, both Magdalen men, posed something of a problem for my old college which would in the normal course of events have delightedly elected both of them to honorary fellowships. But unhappily one of them (I forget which) had been sent down from Magdalen, without taking his degree, and the other had obtained only fourth class honours in Jurisprudence (long since abolished, as something of a contradiction in terms). The result was that for many years Magdalen refused to elect either of them to an honorary fellowship, presumably under John Morris's influence. I met Lord Dilhorne at a dinner at Oxford not long after the 1964 election, and found myself pinned into a corner by him, while he complained at great length at the way in which Magdalen had overlooked his claims to an honorary fellowship. I was extremely embarrassed at these undignified complaints, and could not help wondering that anybody who had held office as Lord Chancellor should care about such a trifle as an honorary fellowship. But Magdalen eventually relented, and elected both Gardiner and Dilhorne to honorary fellowships in the 1980s.

I crossed swords with Lord Dilhorne a year or two later. The Labour government's Prices and Incomes Act 1966 contained a Part IV which was stated to come into force when an Order was made under that Part of the Act. After such an Order was made, some legal doubts had been raised about the validity of the process. In the House of Lords Lord Dilhorne had argued that an Order could not be made under a Part of an Act which was not yet in force, even though the whole purpose of the Order was to bring it into force. Although this was obviously a partisan political point,

Lord Dilhorne was a former Lord Chancellor, and was speaking with the full weight of having held that office. But his point was a silly one because, as a matter of law, it was obvious that the relevant section must by implication be treated as in force for the purpose of giving validity to the necessary order. But in addition Lord Dilhorne had entirely overlooked the fact that the Interpretation Act 1889 (which governs all Acts of Parliaments) contained an express provision dealing with this very possibility, and clearly validated the procedure adopted. I wrote to *The Times* drawing attention to the Interpretation Act and saying (in deference to my former colleagues) that although Parliamentary Counsel sometimes made mistakes, they rarely made elementary blunders.[11] A colleague told me that he had been lunching at his Inn of Court the day the letter appeared, and the discussion at his table having got round to the letter, someone asked, "Who is this fellow Atiyah, anyhow?" Somebody else replied, "Oh, he writes books and things". It could make a reasonable epitaph.

Among the other academic jobs which came my way during my time at New College, was an invitation to serve on the editorial team (mostly Oxford lawyers) who produced new editions from time to time of that ancient classic, *Chitty on Contract*, a massive two-volume work designed for legal practitioners. I took part in the next three editions of this work. The second of these (actually the twenty-fourth edition of the work itself) led to an incident which illustrates how far removed academic lawyers sometimes are from reality. That twenty-fourth edition was first planned in 1974, and the publishers as customary offered the editors a lump sum, to be paid on publication. The arrangements regarding payment were extremely casual, consisting merely of letters passed between the publishers and the general editor who communicated them to the other editors. Nothing in the nature of a formal contract was ever drawn up. But 1974–77 was a period of great inflation, when Michael Foot, as Secretary of State for Employment, presided benignly over wage claims of 20, 30 and eventually 40 per cent. By the time the twenty-fourth edition of *Chitty* was published the lump sum named three years earlier by the publishers had fallen to about half

11 Atiyah's letter (26 October 1966) reads:

> "Sir, – Lord Dilhorne asks today how Part IV of the Prices and Incomes Act could have been brought into operation by an Order in Council made under Part IV itself. The answer is to be found in section 37 of the Interpretation Act, 1889, which provides that an Order in Council may be made under an Act not yet in force in so far as it is necessary to do so for the purpose of bringing the Act into operation. Parliamentary counsel sometimes make mistakes, but they rarely make elementary blunders."

its previous value. Of course, legally speaking, the editors (who all knew the law of contract reasonably well) did not have a leg to stand on. They had contracted to produce the new edition for the agreed sum, and had simply failed to demand that the sum should be index-linked. All the same, the result seemed pretty inequitable to me, and I suggested to the general editor that the publishers should be approached and asked to increase the promised sum. They were, and they did, without a murmur. So much for the law of contract!

Sometime in 1967 I received a visit from an old friend, William Twining, then Professor of Jurisprudence at Belfast University. William and I had first met at Khartoum, where he had joined the Law Faculty a couple of years after I did. Like me, he was an Oxford graduate, with an African background – his father had been Governor of Tanganyika, so he knew East Africa well. He and his wife were about the same age as Christine and me, so we had become good friends in Khartoum, and had watched each other's families grow up from their earliest years.

William was keenly interested in various problems of legal education and, together with another Oxford friend, who had migrated to Yale, Robert Stevens, he had persuaded the publishers Weidenfeld & Nicolson to launch a new series of legal books. These were designed to be law books with a difference – instead of just concentrating on explaining what the law actually is, they were intended to include discussions of the law in its context. The context could be historical, social, economic, political or a combination of all these, but the essential point was to provide some link between the world of law itself, and the world beyond it. Educationally this was a very desirable objective. For too long legal education had tended to be very narrow in England. Although at Oxford a course in law did involve papers in legal history, Roman law and legal philosophy (or jurisprudence as it was usually called), so that it appeared to be a broad-based sort of course, in fact it was, in many respects, just as narrow as most other law courses. The problem was that even the legal history, Roman law and legal philosophy courses were studied in rather a narrow technical legal way: there was no serious attempt (for instance) to link the study of legal history with non-legal history, nor to connect the study of Roman law with the way in which it subsequently came to be adopted as the basis of modern European legal systems. The legal history course at Oxford was entirely concerned with the history of legal doctrine, and proceeded through several centuries of development and change without any reference to what was happening in the country or the social and political changes which were taking place. Very little attempt was usually made to explain legal change in terms of changes in social or political or economic conditions. What was more, the legal history course was heavily slanted towards the mediaeval period, and there was very little about the eighteenth and nineteenth centuries, which were of course those periods with which most undergraduates might have had some familiarity from their general studies of history. Similarly, the study of ordinary legal subjects was extremely narrow and technical, involving little contact with the world outside the law itself.

When William came to see me in 1967 I had begun to develop a keen interest in the contextual study of one particular area of law – what lawyers call the law of tort, that is the law of civil liability. All lawyers knew in a vague and general sort of way that by the 1960s most awards of damages in ordinary tort actions (for instance, actions arising out of road accidents) were paid for by insurance companies, and not by those who were legally responsible for the damage; and law students were beginning to be told by their teachers that this fact of insurance explained many things which were otherwise puzzling about tort liability decisions. But nobody had yet made a serious study of the relationship between legal liability in tort and insurance, and this was something which was increasingly taking my attention. I had first begun to look at this subject when doing my book on vicarious liability, but it was clear to me then that the subject was a large one, and demanded far more attention than could be devoted to it in that particular book. So when William invited me to write a book on contract law for the new *Law in Context* series of legal books I immediately replied by saying that I would like to do a book on tort law for the series. This took William by surprise,[12] but eventually my proposal was accepted.

For the next two or three years I devoted my energies to research on this question. I found that the Americans were far ahead of us in England in studying the relationship between insurance and legal liability. Indeed, there had already been several American studies, and also one Canadian survey, into the effectiveness of tort law and liability insurance. These studies had shown that this was a pretty unsatisfactory way of compensating injured people. In the first place, only those who were able to prove that someone else's fault had caused their injuries were able to recover any compensation at all. That meant that probably half or more of all accident victims never

12 Twining writes in his memoir that he had invited Atiyah to produce a book about regulation or commercial law, to which Atiyah responded that "he was bored with contract and commerce . . . [and that he] wanted to do a number on Torts": Twining, *Jurist in Context: A Memoir* (2019) 154.

received any compensation in the form of damages. But in addition, it transpired that this method of insurance was very slow in operation as well as very costly, because a large part of the insurance premium was swallowed up by legal and administrative costs. This kind of third-party insurance was much more expensive than ordinary insurance, such as householders' or life insurance, where legal and administrative costs were far lower. So Americans had started wondering whether it would not be more sensible to try to shift the emphasis of the system from third-party to ordinary (or first-party) insurance. This meant getting rid of legal liability, either wholly or anyhow partly. At first sight this seems a very drastic thing to do, because most people feel instinctively that the right to sue someone who does them an injury is an absolutely fundamental legal right. But in some cases, at any rate, especially perhaps in road accident cases, it seems to make good sense, because the present system of compulsory third-party insurance means that the person who is responsible for the accident never actually pays for the damage anyhow. So the right to sue him is really the right to claim from his insurance company; and if the accident victim is going to be given an insurance claim, it seems sensible that the kind of insurance provided should be efficient and speedy in operation. So there has been much pressure in many countries to introduce a system of insurance for road accidents under which an injured person would claim compensation from his *own* insurance company rather than from the other party's. After all, is not it more sensible that we should all insure ourselves, rather than each other? For these reasons, many American States now provide for this kind of insurance, and limit the right to sue the other party responsible for a road accident.

Another major aspect to the problem I now began to study in earnest was that there were so many different avenues by which an accident victim could recover compensation. Apart from the possibility of suing another person, the victim might have a claim against his own insurance company in some cases, he might have a claim to a wide range of social security benefits, or he might have a claim against the State under the Criminal Injuries Compensation Scheme, which had been set up in 1964. In addition, of course, he might receive limited compensation or (which came to the same thing) have some of his bills taken care of in other ways – the NHS, for instance, looked after his medical costs in most cases, and if his injuries were relatively short-lived (as most were) his employers might continue to pay his salary or wages. Now it had not been customary to look at all these methods of compensation together, as part of one whole legal system; and when they were looked at as a whole, the total picture began to look amazingly anomalous and haphazard. Whether an injured accident victim received any compensation, and if so, how much, and by what methods, all began to seem to me increasingly arbitrary and irrational. In theory the right to sue was different from these other methods of compensation because it depended on being able to prove that the accident was due to the fault of the person being sued. But once it came to be seen that it was an insurance company which was going to pay, then the difference between the right to sue, and other forms of compensation tended to melt away. They were, in effect, all based on the principle of insurance. But then it began to seem much less obvious why the question of fault should matter. When a person insures his house against fire he does not expect to be denied a claim merely because a fire starts which was partly his fault. What was more, looking at all the different methods of compensation as a whole brought to light the fact that many accident victims received very little compensation while others were compensated several times over.

It so happened that a case raising an important point of law, and involving some of these complications, came before the House of Lords while I was working on my book. In this case (*Parry v Cleaver*)[13] a policeman injured in a road accident was claiming damages from the other driver involved, and the question concerned the amount of damages to which he was entitled. He had had to retire from the police force as a result of his injuries but had been given a police pension by way of compensation. The question that arose before the courts was whether the value of this pension should be taken into account in reducing the damages. Traditionally, it had been argued that such payments should not reduce the damages, because the damages were payable by the person who was to blame for the accident, and there seemed no reason why he should benefit from the police pension. I found myself challenging this sort of argument on the ground that it was unreal and artificial to treat the damages as though they would be paid by the negligent driver. In fact everyone knew they would be paid by his insurance company, and the insurance is really paid by the public through their premiums in very much the same way as a tax. But the public were also paying for the police pension, so I argued that it was absurd for the injured person to be able to claim two lots of compensation for the one injury. When *Parry v Cleaver* reached the House of Lords I happened to see Lord Wilberforce at a New College dinner, and I asked him about the case. He told me that the other four Law Lords had already written their speeches, and that two were in favour of

13 [1970] AC 1 (HL).

allowing the appeal, and two for dismissing it, so that his would be the deciding vote. I thought this would be my chance to influence the development of the law, so I gave Lord Wilberforce the benefit of my views. It would be agreeable to record that I persuaded Lord Wilberforce to decide against the injured plaintiff, but in fact he decided the other way. (However, I did have the satisfaction of seeing the House of Lords move somewhat away from the majority decision in *Parry v Cleaver* in two cases in the 1980s,[14] in which the reasoning of the judges appeared much closer to that for which I had argued.)

This was a small part of the story I was getting to grips with in 1969. And my work on that aspect of the problem remains, I believe, relevant today though in England very little reform has occurred. But another aspect of the problem was (I now think) seen by many people, including myself, from a particular perspective in the 1960s – and the perspective was a rather liberal-left-wing perspective in which we saw accidents as not being *really* the fault of those who caused them, and we also saw the State as a kind of universal insurer. These two ideas led many academics in the 1960s to think that all claims for damages for personal injuries could be abolished, and the State could run a general accident insurance system, so that anybody injured in an accident could recover compensation on the same lines. In New Zealand, which had already developed a far more elaborate and extensive welfare state than England, a compensation system along these lines was eventually introduced,[15] as a result of a very far-reaching report by a judge called Sir Owen Woodhouse.[16] In essence, it meant that actions for damages for personal injuries were abolished, and replaced by State compensation. The compensation was not as generous as damages at law were, but they were much more generous than ordinary social security benefits. What was more – and this was the key point – they were available to *all* accident victims, not just those whose injuries were somebody else's fault. Today, a scheme of that kind probably looks rather left-wing and bureaucratic, and plainly the tide of movement is against this kind of massive social welfare scheme. But in the 1960s, when the welfare system was constantly being expanded in all directions, it did seem that this was the ultimate goal

14 *Westwood v Secretary of State for Employment* [1985] AC 20 (HL); *Dews v National Coal Board* [1988] AC 1 (HL).

15 *Accident Compensation Act 1972* (NZ). The current statute is the *Accident Compensation Act 2001* (NZ).

16 *Compensation for Personal Injury in New Zealand: Report of the Royal Commission of Inquiry* (Wellington, 1967).

to which everything else was gradually moving. Of course I was an academic writer, not a law reformer; my task was not to advocate a particular type of change, but to discuss, analyse and review the way the law worked, so that anomalies and inconsistencies could be brought to light. All this might point to some need for reform, and I was at that time broadly in favour of a New Zealand type of scheme, but that was not my essential purpose.

I began to plan out my new book for the *Law in Context* series, with the intention of covering all the different ways by which an accident might be compensated. But I first wanted to visit the United States and Canada, to meet some of the people who had been most active in research and writing on these issues. With the aid of Robert Stevens, William Twining's co-editor in the *Law in Context* series, I secured an invitation to spend a semester at Yale in the Spring of 1968. I was offered a very modest salary for teaching a single course during the semester, and though I obtained sabbatical leave from New College, so that I was still paid my Oxford salary, it cost me a great deal of money to transport my wife and family (now four sons) to America. Nevertheless, I decided that it would be a useful experience for them, and we resolved to combine the trip with an extensive holiday after the semester was over. I flew to America in February and found a holiday home to rent at the nearby seaside resort of Milton, some twenty minutes down the turnpike from New Haven where Yale University was situated. Christine and the children followed me a few weeks later.

I taught a short advanced course (on contract law) to earn my money, and I had also secured a small grant from an American legal-research foundation to cover my travel costs to a number of other universities where I wanted to visit some leading academics. I visited Robert Keeton, then at Harvard, later to become a federal judge, and co-author of the leading work on no-fault compensation,[17] Harry Kalven at the University of Chicago, Al Conard at the University of Michigan, who had been responsible for the largest survey to date on the effects of road accident compensation, several academics at Temple University in Philadelphia, and, in Toronto, Professor Allen Linden with whom I became very good friends. Linden had done a small survey of road accidents in Toronto,[18] and we discussed its results and methods. On many subsequent visits to Canada, I never failed to visit Toronto (a lovely town for which I acquired a considerable affection) and

17 R Keeton and J O'Connell, *Basic Protection for the Traffic Victim: A Blueprint for Reforming Automobile Insurance* (1965).

18 AM Linden, *The Report of the Osgoode Hall Study on Compensation for Victims of Automobile Accidents* (1965).

my friend Allen. There were to be many attempts to arrange a sabbatical in Toronto (indeed, the Dean at Allen's University had offered me a visiting professorship on the spot when I called on him) but in the event none of them ever came off. Allen Linden was eventually made a judge of the Ontario Supreme Court and later the Court of Appeal (something that can happen to Professors in America and Canada, but not in England)[19] and also served for a term as Chairman of Canada's Law Reform Commission. On one occasion, many years later, when he was visiting England as secretary of an Ontario Legislative Law Reform Committee on road accident compensation, he wanted me to give evidence as an expert to his Committee, but I myself was due to leave England for Canada and the US the day after they arrived in England. He therefore arranged – at the Committee's expense – for me to spend the night (with Christine) at the Churchill Hotel, he took us to dine at the Mirabelle, and in return I talked to his Committee the next morning before catching my plane from Heathrow! After experiences of that kind I began to feel like a Victorian poor relation in my contacts with North American academics.

In Yale itself I was also able to meet Guido Calabresi, a young Professor of Law who was the founder of a completely new "school" of academic lawyers. Calabresi had an economics background as well as a legal training (in fact he had read PPE at Magdalen College when I had been doing law) and he had begun to write a powerful series of articles, culminating in his book, *The Costs of Accidents*,[20] in which he had argued that the law of civil liability was an essential part of the free-market economic system. His idea basically was that most accidents are preventable by a sufficient injection of money – although many accidents may seem unpreventable, that is not necessarily true if they are viewed in a broader time perspective. But the money will not be spent if those who are liable to cause accidents are not held legally liable for the consequences. So it is desirable that legal liability should be maintained in order to ensure that adequate money is spent on safety. What is more (Calabresi's successors, anyhow, have argued) the amount to be invested in safety can also be decided by reference to the law of legal liability. Companies who may be held liable at law for accidents will have an economic incentive to spend money up to the point that the expenditure

19 Things have changed somewhat since Atiyah's time. Although judicial appointments in England are still overwhelmingly drawn from the practising profession, there have been rare but notable appointments from the academy. However, even these appointments have tended to be from among scholars who had a foot in practice.

20 G Calabresi, *The Costs of Accidents: A Legal and Economic Analysis* (1970).

exceeds the amount of their potential liability – or their insurance premiums. Of course all this assumes that the law of liability in tort is the chief way, or even the only way, in which society and the law tries to prevent accidents – which is obviously untrue. There are many other laws for the same purpose, the criminal law, for instance, as well as licensing and regulatory laws. But Calabresi's theories were later seized upon by a new generation of very right-wing academics in the United States, who disliked licensing and regulatory laws as bureaucratic and inefficient, and who wanted, as a matter of ideology, to treat legal liability as the sole way of controlling the levels of expenditure on accident prevention. Of course there are terrible troubles with the extreme versions of this theory, though I have come to think that, within limits, and in some areas, we need to pay attention to the basic idea that legal liability is a kind of market mechanism for controlling the levels of accidents.

But in 1968 I found myself somewhat out of sympathy with these theories, and I thought that England was at that time so far removed from America, in its economic system and in its ideology, that Calabresi's theories had little to offer us of value. I was, however, concerned to learn whether Calabresi thought that his theories were an obstacle to a New Zealand type of national compensation scheme, and I had a number of conversations with him which satisfied me that they were not. In theory, even a national compensation scheme of the New Zealand kind could pay due regard to the economic-deterrence arguments which the economists have developed. To do this it is necessary to ensure that those who cause accidents are liable to pay premiums to the national compensation scheme, just as they now pay premiums to private insurance companies. In fact the New Zealand scheme did make some allowance for the possibility of levying premiums in this way, although in the event this aspect of the scheme was never implemented. At any rate, my concern at this time was to study, to learn, and to think about the possible alternatives, and I learnt much from Calabresi.

My visit to Yale was the first of many visits to the United States, but it was in some ways the least successful. With four small children to accommodate, with Christine separated from her Oxford friends and interests, and with our living several miles out of New Haven, we did not have much social intercourse with the Yale faculty, or anybody else either. I was, of course, still relatively young and unknown myself, so established Yale academics were not exactly queuing up to meet me, or invite me to dinner. Robert Stevens, who had arranged my visit, was unfortunately himself away on a sabbatical while I was there, so I lacked a sponsor who could have introduced me to others. Nevertheless, I was enormously impressed by a number of things which

I began to identify with American law schools – by the energy, and optimism which I saw all round me, as well as by the teaching methods which I had first heard about from John Morris[21] and now saw at first-hand.

American law schools differ very much from English law faculties, and on the whole they are more impressive. They have the great advantage of being graduate institutions, so the students have already done four years of college, doing usually general arts degrees before they start on their law courses. So they are, of course, much older and more mature than English students and it is possible to pitch the level of sophistication in law teaching correspondingly higher. Further, the method of instruction is in many ways vastly superior to English-style lecturing. Most law teaching in America is done with the aid of a casebook which every student must have, and which he brings to class with him, and has open in front of him throughout the class. This book contains extracts from legal cases, articles and other kinds of legal materials, and detailed reference can be made to the contents during the discussion, because everybody has the book in front of him. At its best and most effective, the class hour is spent in Socratic question-and-answer style. The students are expected to, and (at any rate in their first year) they do prepare for class very thoroughly, so that the teacher can ask a series of searching questions, going from one student to another. In this way, answers emerge slowly and – if the exercise is done with real skill – the reasons for them emerge as the answers themselves emerge. What is more, the student is made to see that there are always alternative possible answers, and he is made to examine the advantages and disadvantages of each possible answer. Law is not taught simply as a didactic exercise in which the teacher says, in effect, "This is the Law, don't argue or ask questions".

This method of instruction makes teaching vastly more rewarding for the teacher as well as the student. A class conducted in this fashion is rarely dull, and no one class ever repeats itself. At the same time, the system is very efficient in its use of the teacher's time. A teacher can take a class four or five hours a week for a semester of fifteen or sixteen weeks, so that the class meets for perhaps seventy hours to cover a subject like the law of contract or tort. At Oxford, by contrast, with its much-vaunted tutorial system, the average student got perhaps eight tutorials a term in which he was expected to cover the same quantity of material, and half of that time was often occupied in the student reading out his essay or other written work. It was true

21 Morris had been a visiting professor at Harvard Law School in 1950–1951: P North, "John Humphrey Carlile Morris" (1988) 74 *Proceedings of the British Academy* 443, 451–452.

that the student might also attend some lectures on the same subject, but lectures were largely optional, and were not well integrated into the teaching programme. At the same time the Oxford teacher was expected to teach for anything up to fifteen hours a week (and his teaching involved a highly repetitive process), instead of perhaps four or five hours a week which his American counterpart would be teaching. There was no doubt, in my mind, that the student got far better value for his money out of a course in a top law school like Yale than at Oxford, nor was there any doubt in my mind that teaching in the American style was much more enjoyable for the teacher.

The main failure of the American system was that it involved no teaching in writing, and in order to overcome this problem many American law schools have been forced to include separate courses themselves devoted to teaching writing skills. Unfortunately these courses usually take the form of teaching the students to write American style legal "briefs", a singularly bloodless and tedious form of legal writing, which hardly encourages literary skills. The result is that most American law graduates are far more articulate than English graduates in speaking, but much less able to communicate in writing. These differences may also be noticeable among the teachers. I was very struck, when I attended a Yale faculty meeting, to observe how formally most members spoke on faculty business – they spoke in well-rounded sentences, with a beginning, a middle and an end, with subjects, objects and verbs, all in some sort of reasonable order. By contrast it seemed to me that at Oxford faculty (or college) meetings, many speakers spoke carelessly and casually, without regard to grammar, often leaving their sentences incomplete. Yet in written style, most English academics were much superior to Americans. On the other hand I must in fairness add that the literary weaknesses of American legal academics tended to take the form of verbosity and a uniformly dull and unimaginative style; I rarely encountered the sheer bad grammar and spelling which I sometimes found in the worst effusions of English legal academics, when I was editing the new *Oxford Journal of Legal Studies* between 1981 and 1986.[22]

By the end of the semester at Yale, around the middle of May 1968, I had got what I was looking for, and the family turned to more relaxing matters. We had hired a large car, bought a tent and some camping equipment, and with the boot crammed, and a roof-rack piled high, we set off on a six-week tour of the country. We travelled mostly via the National Parks, truly marvellous places for camping, where the campsites are scrupulously clean, every

22 Atiyah was the foundation editor: see p 171.

site provided with a car park, and a site for the tent, as well as a table with benches attached for eating and preparing food, a tap, and a dustbin; every campsite was well provided with water, toilets and showers. In addition, most of the parks have "trails" or walks, through the woods and natural wildernesses, where nature has been disturbed as little as possible. Information about the trails is provided at the Information Centres, which most parks have, where films are sometimes shown, and where the Park Rangers give talks on the wildlife or other aspects of the park's life. Sometimes these talks would be given out of doors in the evenings, occasionally round a good campfire. Every now and then we would vary our sleeping arrangements by stopping at a motel, having a good scrub, getting our clothes washed in the local laundromats, and, sometimes even getting in a swim, as so many American motels sport a pool.

We went South to Virginia, and Shenandoah National Park at first, then up through Tennessee and Kentucky, West to Arkansas and then Oklahoma, where it rained so torrentially that we pressed ahead without stopping to the Texas panhandle, where we finally found the sun again. From there we went West again through New Mexico and then Arizona where we saw the Petrified Forest and camped at the Grand Canyon. It was while we were there that we heard the news that Robert Kennedy had been shot and later died. This tragedy triggered in my memory a curious event which I had almost forgotten. A month or two earlier I had been visited at Yale by someone who had no connection with the University or the Law School, and who claimed that he wanted to talk to me for reasons I never discovered. He seemed to me to be something of a "nut-case", a prime victim of conspiracy theories, who complained a great deal about a shadowy "they" who were doing or threatening to do all sorts of terrible things. One of the things he claimed "they" were going to do was to shoot Robert Kennedy. I took no notice of this at the time, being convinced that my visitor was a mental case, and I had put the whole thing out of my mind. But after the shooting the incident came back to me, and I did wonder briefly whether it was more than just a coincidence. On reflection, though, I remained convinced that it was not, and I never did anything about it.

We did not unfortunately have time to get all the way to the West Coast, so from the Grand Canyon we turned North to Utah, with its extraordinary sandstone formations in a whole series of fascinating national parks, and from there we went North again to Wyoming where we ended up at Yellowstone National Park, in many ways the high point of our whole tour. Yellowstone was a wonderful place, with its geysers, its scenic beauty and its wildlife (in those days brown bears wandered freely round the park, and one came across them everywhere, but now they have all been driven out again, because the tourists simply failed to read the warning notices and treat them with care and respect). It was still very cold when we arrived in Yellowstone in mid-June. In fact it snowed on our first evening there, but this gave us a wonderful moment when driving round the Park we came across a couple of immense buffaloes by the roadside, looming up out of the dusk, their black fur gradually becoming hidden by the snow that settled on them. The next day, the snow melted and we had a good week of lovely weather there, before we finally turned East again. Four or five days brought us to New York where I left Christine and the two younger boys in a motel, and took the hired car back to New Haven, with Julian and Andrew. We caught the train back to New York and the next day flew home after six memorable weeks.

Back in Oxford I pressed ahead with my book, and completed the first draft by the following year, when I submitted it to William for his comments and criticisms. The book was eventually published in 1970 under the title, *Accidents, Compensation and the Law*,[23] and it launched the new *Law in Context* series, which has now been going successfully for twenty years. Again, the book was well received,[24] and indeed, it set a fashion by enabling some law schools to run new courses on the subject of accident compensation as a whole. I did three editions of the book[25] before handing it over to a young Oxford colleague in 1986 for the fourth edition.[26] By that time I was

23 Twining describes it as "a model of excellence for a 'contextual' work" and adds that although "[t]here is no ideal type for such works . . . anyone wanting to rethink a doctrinal field can learn a great deal from it": Twining, *Jurist in Context: A Memoir* (2019) 154–155. The origins of *Accidents, Compensation and the Law* and the genesis of the *Law in Context* series are explored in W Twining, "Reflections on Law in Context" in P Cane and J Stapleton (eds), *Essays for Patrick Atiyah* (1991).

24 *Accidents, Compensation and the Law* was immediately greeted by considerable acclaim. Bob Hepple wrote that Atiyah had "succeeded in presenting a lucid and comprehensive analysis of a number of fundamental questions about compensation for personal injuries and death . . . consequent upon accidents": BA Hepple, "Book review: Accidents, Compensation and the Law by PS Atiyah" (1971) 29 CLJ 294, 294. Allen Linden remarked that *Accidents, Compensation and the Law* "could trigger a revolution not only in our approach to accident law, but also in legal scholarship and legal education": AM Linden, "Book review: Accidents, Compensation and the Law by PS Atiyah" (1971) 49 *Canadian Bar Review* 146, 146. Another reviewer described the book as "a tour de force": HL Molot, "Book review: Accidents, Compensation and the Law by PS Atiyah" (1972) 10 *Alberta Law Review* 144, 144. Of the third edition, Anthony Ogus wrote that the work "was, and remains, a classic": AI Ogus, "Book review: Accidents, Compensation and the Law (3rd edn) by PS Atiyah" (1981) 1 *International Review of Law and Economics* 118, 119.

25 The second and third editions were published in 1975 and 1980 respectively.

26 Atiyah handed responsibility for the text to Peter Cane, who authored the fourth to eighth editions and co-authored the ninth edition: P Cane, *Atiyah's Accidents, Compensation and the Law*, 4th edn (1987); P Cane, *Atiyah's Accidents, Compensation and the Law*, 5th edn (1993); P Cane,

devoting so much of my energies to the law of contract that I simply had no time to prepare a fourth edition. I was also worried that the book had almost outlived its utility. The revival of the free market ideal, and the withering of the idea that the State could or should run huge bureaucratic welfare schemes meant that the message of the book had become outdated by the late 1980s. Although I still thought that the law of legal liability was full of anomalies, and that it was useful to study compensation systems as a whole, I would not have written the same sort of book in the 1980s as I wrote in the 1960s.

When the book was finished I decided that I would try to see whether an academic could actually achieve anything personally in the way of law reform. I launched a sort of mini-campaign of my own with this end in view. I knew that the issues were too vast and cut across the work of too many government departments to think it possible that the kind of reforms I had in mind could ever be proposed in the routine course of departmental work. Any New Zealand-type reform would have such profound implications for the work of the social security department, the legal profession and the judges that several major departments of the government would be bound to be involved. So I hit on the idea of campaigning for a Royal Commission to take a broad look at the whole field. I opened my campaign with a letter to *The Times* which (rather to my surprise) immediately attracted editorial support.[27] I next drafted a brief memorandum addressed to the Lord

Atiyah's Accidents, Compensation and the Law, 6th edn (1999); P Cane, *Atiyah's Accidents, Compensation and the Law*, 7th edn (2004); P Cane, *Atiyah's Accidents, Compensation and the Law*, 8th edn (2013); P Cane and J Goudkamp, *Atiyah's Accidents, Compensation and the Law*, 9th edn (2018).

27 *The Times* (London, 5 July 1969) editorial reads:

> "The suggestion, mooting for many years, that all injured persons should be compensated under the social security system and that their right of action for damages should be abolished, is being raised again. With distinguished support, Mr. P. S. Atiyah, a lecturer in law, is urging the appointment of a royal commission to undertake a broad review of the law on compensation for personal injuries, whether caused by accident, by criminal assault or by disease.
>
> There is much to be said for such an injury, particularly now that the Government has put forward a new earnings-related scheme for the revision of the social security system, due to become effective in April, 1972. Under that scheme contributions would be channelled into two separate funds, the National Superannuation Fund to be used for pensions, widowhood benefits and death grant, and the Social Insurance Fund for other benefits. The sum devoted to assisting the sick and injured should be distributed much more equitably than at present, and this could be achieved more simply under the White Paper's proposals published earlier this year.
>
> If changes are made to make more adequate benefits available for all, the action for damages could be redundant. Common law damages are now recovered by only about 15 per cent of the industrially injured and 40 per cent of road victims, and, as Mr. Atiyah points out,

Chancellor, Lord Gardiner, urging the appointment of a Royal Commission. I sent this to a number of prominent academic and practising lawyers, and some judges and politicians with some interest in the law or in the social security system, and invited them to sign it. I collected about thirty-five pretty distinguished signatories,[28] the memorandum was itself published in the *New Law Journal*[29] and it was duly despatched to the Lord Chancellor.

The memorandum attracted some publicity in legal circles, and the Industrial Law Society (which was interested because of the implications of my proposals for workmen injured in industrial accidents) organised a public debate in London, at which the Lord Chancellor agreed to preside. Eventually the Lord Chancellor turned my proposal down, though he made it clear to me in a private letter that he was not unsympathetic to the idea of a Royal Commission, but was concerned that the legal profession simply

in most of those cases they are paid not by the 'wrongdoer' but by insurance companies and employers, and in the long run by the public. A person who received damages may also have claimed social security benefit, and subject to a small deduction, he is normally able to receive both forms of compensation, while other less fortunate persons may fail in a claim for damages and be awarded only a niggardly benefit.

In 1946, following the Beveridge report, a departmental committee under Lord Monckton considered the possible abolition of the action for damages for personal injuries, and found much to favour such a change The delays in determining liability and the amount of damages and the costs and uncertainties of litigation referred to by the committee are equally relevant today, and the recommendations of the Winn committee last year would do little to improve the situation. The payment of lump-sum damages, instead of periodical sums, was condemned as unsatisfactory by the Government in 1944 but it still persists.

The Monckton committee commented that none of these drawbacks would attend the recovery of social security benefits, but did not propose any change largely because the level of benefit was so much lower than the damages which could be recovered at law. This argument no longer carries the same force – indeed a person off work because of an industrial injury may now suffer no net financial loss at all. And since litigation is more expensive than the administration of social security, the money now spent on legal aid could be better distributed among many more applicants at social security tribunals. The appointment of the commission proposed should not be delayed."

28 Atiyah was a prolific letter-writer and preserved a large amount of correspondence for posterity's sake. He was evidently successful in his networking efforts. This is apparent from the signatories to his memorandum. They comprised Viscount Radcliffe, Lord Chorley, Professor Lord Lloyd of Hampstead, Sir John Foster KBE QC MP, Geoffrey Howe QC, Morris Finer QC, C Fletcher-Cooke QC MP, David Weitzman QC MP, Professor Richard M Titmuss CBE, Professor Lady Williams CBE, Professor Peter Townsend, Professor HLA Hart, Professor O Kahn-Freund, Professor RFV Houston, Professor Glanville Williams, Professor Geoffrey Sawer, Professor GSA Wheatcroft, Professor KW Wedderburn, DR Harris, Michael Zander, PR Glazebrook, Paul O'Higgins, PM North, Norman St John Stevas MP, ER Luard MP, Jill Knight MBE MP, David Steel MP, Ben Whitaker MP, Alexander W Lyons MP, AR Mackenzie MP, Jack Ashley MP, David Lane MP and Bernard Braine MP.

29 PS Atiyah, "Compensation for Personal Injuries" (1969) 119 *New Law Journal* 653.

could not absorb the massive legal changes already being thrust upon them in those years of Harold Wilson's Labour Government.

In the event, the Royal Commission was established four years later, under the Chairmanship of Lord Pearson, mainly under the impetus of the thalidomide tragedy. The Commission proved an unmitigated disaster, and I came to regret that I had ever advocated it. Its report, published eventually in 1978,[30] was a mass of political compromises with a complete lack of underlying principle, and almost from the beginning it was clear that its proposals were doomed. I met Lord Pearson at a number of discussions and conferences held to consider the report, and it was clear that he was distressed at the hostility shown to it. (At one of these conferences I declared that I had come, not to praise the Pearson report but – I hoped – to bury it.) He even invited me to lunch with him in order to discuss the report, an invitation which caused me some embarrassment. I replied that I would be happy to meet him if I thought that any good purpose would be served, but that I did not really see what good could come from such a meeting. I thought he made a serious mistake in attempting to take part in the discussions following the publication of the report. I could not say that to him, but I did tell him that I thought he had had his say, and the matter was now open to public debate.[31]

30 *Royal Commission on Civil Liability and Compensation for Personal Injury* (1978).

31 The report is analysed in JG Fleming, "The Pearson Report: its 'strategy'" (1979) 42 MLR 250; DK Allen, CJ Bourn and J Holyoak (eds), *Accident Compensation after Pearson* (1979). Atiyah contributed an essay to the latter work entitled "What Now?". He offered the following damming assessment (at 254):

> "As one surveys the battleground at the end of the day, it must be admitted that the scene is not encouraging. The tort action is still to be with us, and its cost and complexity, worse than ever. The forensic lottery will remain as great as ever. The variations in how much compensation is paid, when and how it is paid, whether it is inflation-proofed or not, and many other factors, will remain largely matters to be determined by the cause and place of an accident. In the emotionally-charged atmosphere in which reforms are liable to be debated in these areas, the reformers are likely to be hard-pressed even to hold on to the crumbs of comfort offered by the Royal Commission – the offset of social security benefits, and the three months' threshold for non-pecuniary loss. There is no doubt that a great opportunity has been lost, and five years of effort have been, alas, very nearly wasted. One can only hope to salvage something in the immediate future, and press on in the faith that ultimately rationality must prevail."

Elsewhere Atiyah wrote of the report: "[It] has . . . proved a disappointment. The main proposals . . . are tame and unadventurous and consist chiefly of a large number of relatively minor adjustments to existing institutional arrangements": PS Atiyah, "No-fault Compensation: A Question that Will Not Go Away" (1980) 54 *Tulane Law Review* 271, 274. He did, however, recognise the contribution that the report had made in terms of revealing how the tort "system" worked. He observed that "the Pearson Commission Report . . . has provided an immense fund of information, figures and data on the tort and liability insurance system": PS Atiyah, *Accidents, Compensation and the Law*, 3rd edn (1980) (preface).

While I was running my campaign in 1969 for the establishment of the Royal Commission, I was also trying to run another campaign of a sort. I had returned from Yale convinced, for reasons I have already given, that the teaching system for law students at Oxford was gravely deficient. Although I had no illusions about the possibility of wide-ranging change in Oxford, I did think it might be possible for a group of colleges to get together in such a way as to enable them to modify the traditional tutorial system. I thought that if eight or ten colleges, for instance, could agree, it would be possible for four or five of the main subjects to be taught to the students of all these colleges in large classes, along American lines. In this way, the students could perhaps enjoy forty-eight hours of class teaching on important subject like contract or tort, instead of the usual eight hours. I canvassed my colleagues and suggested that if there was sufficient support, a meeting could be organised at which such a possibility could be discussed. I only received about half a dozen replies to my circular, of which only three or four showed any interest in the idea. I was very depressed by this response, which meant that I had to abandon my ideas, and much as I liked living and working in Oxford, I now began to think seriously of moving elsewhere.

Although many Oxford tutors continue to operate the tutorial system quite happily throughout a career of thirty or forty years I myself was now beginning to find the tutorial system an unbearable grind. Much of the difficulty arose because Oxford tutors were now increasingly seeking to specialise. In earlier days it had been common for Oxford tutors to teach virtually the whole syllabus to the students in their own college, but it was almost impossible to be a serious specialist in one or two subjects and continue to teach six or eight subjects. As a result most Oxford tutors had not been serious specialists, and I am bound to say that until 1950 or so the general level of Oxford law teaching and research was really rather low.[32] By the late 1960s standards were rising but at some cost. In modern times a serious law teacher must read an immense amount of literature which pours out every week if he is to keep abreast of the law generally. A serious specialist must these days also be prepared to keep up with developments in other countries. Nobody in modern times can be a serious academic lawyer in England without some attempt to master American legal writing. But the sheer volume of material from America (as well, of course, of other Commonwealth countries) is such that a person can only specialise in one or

32 This was not an idiosyncratic view. For discussion, see AWB Simpson, *Reflections on "The Concept of Law"* (2011) ch 2.

two subjects, and then only at the expense of breadth of knowledge. In order to cope with the tutorial system and yet to specialise, therefore, it became increasingly the practice for many Oxford tutors to "exchange" pupils with specialists in other colleges. So, for instance, I used to send out many of my students to another tutor to study land law and legal history, while in return I taught his students contract and tort. This solved one problem, but only by creating another. This system meant that term after term I was taking twelve or thirteen tutorials a week in two or three subjects. And when one has heard the twelfth or thirteenth essay in a single week on the same subject it is very hard to maintain one's interest, and give of one's best to the students.

With the growth of my own reputation I was also now reaching the stage at which I could reasonably look for a professorial appointment, but a professorship in Oxford (which would have spared me the burden of tutorial teaching) seemed out of the question in 1969. I was only eligible, by virtue of my interests, for two of the six law Chairs in Oxford, and in 1969 neither of these two seemed likely to fall vacant for a decade.[33] Regretfully, I decided to look elsewhere. I was not attracted by most of the provincial universities in England at that time, but by a series of chances I came to be offered a Chair at the Australian National University (widely referred to as "the ANU") in Canberra. After much heart-searching and many family confabulations, I accepted the offer.[34]

33 Atiyah had in mind the Vinerian Professorship of English Law, which was then held by Rupert Cross, and the Professorship of English Law, which was then held by William Wade. Atiyah would ultimately succeed Wade: see Chapter 11.

34 Dr (later Lord) Alan Rodger succeeded Atiyah at New College.

10 Australian Interlude

We decided to go by sea rather than air; the university was willing to pay first-class fares for myself and my family, and there were decided advantages in being able to take a large quantity of luggage with us. Besides, we thought a few weeks between packing up at one end and starting a new life at the other would give us a breather in which to adjust ourselves to what lay ahead. So we sailed on 23 December 1969 on the P&O liner, *Iberia*. The voyage took nearly five weeks, and it certainly gave us a touch of luxury. Indeed, so lavish were the facilities and the meals that after a few days out it became clear that considerable self-restraint would be needed to avoid gaining much unwanted weight. The *Iberia* boasted every comfort, we had three cabins for the family, all with private shower rooms and loos, and the first class was air-conditioned throughout. But in some ways the world of the P&O liners seemed to have stood still since passengers were Indian civil servants returning from leave in the 1920s, though the waiters and cabin staff were now mostly Indians (many from Goa) rather than English. One day I spied a Goan in a tiny cubby hole off the deck, about the size of sentry box, making rope quoits for deck games. I gathered that he was employed throughout the voyage on this task, replenishing the supply of quoits as those used in the deck games got lost overboard. It seemed a curious use of labour.

We had enjoyable stops, as though on a luxury cruise, in the Canaries, at Dacca, and in South Africa. Here we were able to get off the boat at Cape Town, and again for a swim at Durban beach, observing this problem land, but without getting involved in its problems. Arrival at Sydney was spectacular, and we were treated like VIPs, being met on arrival, whisked through customs and immigration, and driven round for a while, before taking the plane to Canberra that afternoon, leaving our heavy luggage to follow by train.

The university had arranged temporary accommodation for us, pending the arrival of our furniture and other belongings, and they had also agreed to enlarge and adapt one of their houses for us, which we were later able to buy. The first few days were a blur of new impressions, arrangements hastily made for the children's schools – the school year began the day after we arrived – and other necessary activities such as buying a car. Eventually, life settled into an even keel, our things arrived, and we moved into our new house, high in Red Hill, one of Canberra's best suburbs.

Even after almost twenty years I find it difficult to write of our time in Australia, which began in excitement and with keen anticipation, and ended in anger and frustration. I will come to the reasons for this shortly, but I must first try to be objective about our experiences there. Personally I found much to enjoy in Australia, and especially in Canberra. The country was then much more prosperous than England, and the National University in Canberra had benefited from the general policy of the Federal government to be generous to Canberra in terms of facilities and institutions.

The Law Faculty was finely equipped in terms of buildings, and facilities, for instance. When the new Law buildings had gone up a few years earlier, a large and comfortable room for the fourth Professor was already there, well furnished and equipped. This became my room, and I had, for the first time in my life, my own secretary in an adjoining room. (All professors had secretaries, although when not fully engaged for their professor, they were expected to do typing and other work for other members of the faculty.) The Law Faculty was also well served with research assistants, and an excellent administrative staff – indeed the whole university functioned better than any other university I have worked in. The academic staff made the decisions, but were admirably served by able administrators, to whom routine work could be perfectly well delegated. Professors generally sat on the university's most important committees and boards, but relations between professors and other staff always seemed to me very good, at least in the Law Faculty. We had a comfortable faculty lounge in which we had an informal meeting over tea once a week at which the Dean would outline current administrative problems, and keep the junior staff abreast of developments. Each Faculty had a degree of independence, which (though it did not match the status of American law schools) enabled many decisions to be taken directly by the Dean and the professors, without having to get the approval of committees and other bodies. The Dean, for instance, had the power to engage research assistants on his own authority, and every professor was entitled to free air fares to other parts of Australia or New Zealand for research purposes, simply on signing the appropriate chits for himself. The Dean also had a very generous entertainment allowance, which enabled him to take visitors off to a restaurant for an agreeable meal, with wives and other guests, which I was able to take advantage of when I was myself Dean in 1973.

In egalitarian-minded England, universities have never been generously funded with support staff, so that academics spend a large part of their time doing clerical and other minor work which could more efficiently be done by professional administrators and secretaries who are paid half as much. Of course the inevitable result is that academics are not so productive in research, and their teaching probably also suffers. But in the Australian National University at this time (I hope things have not changed for the worse since), I found the arrangements particularly conducive to the pursuit of my own work. I was able to write and pursue research more freely than at any other time in my working life. (Even when I eventually held a Chair at Oxford which left me plenty of time for my own research and writing, I still had far less secretarial and clerical assistance so that I had to type my own letters, for instance.) Whether it was because of these conditions, or whether I was simply reaching my own peak, I was particularly productive during my three years in Canberra.

Canberra had quite a lot to offer in terms of social and domestic life. It was in many ways an attractive town to live in. The climate was superb (though the winters were much colder than Sydney), the autumn especially attractive with many weeks of unbroken sunshine every year. For keen gardeners and outdoor living enthusiasts there was also much pleasure – except for the terrible flies which settled on one by the hundred unless one sprayed oneself with some evil-smelling anti-fly repellent. Christine was able to indulge her passion for riding and she took all the boys with her in turn for some lessons until they became moderately proficient. Our house was well placed in the suburb of Red Hill, which gave us attractive views over the city and the lake. In the autumn early morning mists often surrounded the town below while the sun broke through on the hillside higher up, and steeples and towers could be seen through the mist below. We had a largish garden by English town standards, in which I built a patio protected from the sun by a vine-covered pergola. In our third year we installed a filtered swimming pool, and Andrew and I spent some hard-working days laying a very large paved surround of attractive purple-tinged slabs round the pool. For a few weeks that summer we enjoyed the bliss of sun-bathing and swimming, with the merry chink of glasses of iced drinks interspersed with the noise of splashing.

I also found much to approve of in the legal education offered at the university. Unlike the crammed three-year course in England, law required a minimum of four years' study in Australia, and many students actually did combined arts-law or economics-law courses which required five years. I greatly approved these combined courses which seemed to me to help produce maturer and better-rounded students, as well as enabling some of our law teaching itself to be more sophisticated. Canberra also benefited from a rather unusual situation, in that there were many civil servants there who worked part-time for law degrees, with support from the government, in the form of time off for study and in payment of fees. This kind of part-time work at university level is often very unsatisfactory, but in Canberra some of our best students came from the part-timers in the civil service. This was partly because many of these students were "new Australians", that is migrants from Eastern Europe, who had not had the opportunity of university education in their own countries, and partly because many of them were very highly motivated.

I soon found, also, that academic lawyers enjoyed a better status in Australia than in England. Their academic traditions were different (they borrowed more from Scotland than England) and the relationship between the practising legal profession and judges on the one hand, and the academics, on the other, was closer and based on a greater degree of mutual respect than in England.[1] I soon got to know many judges in Canberra and Sydney, and I never felt that I was patronised by them.

Under these conditions my own work flourished, and I soon found myself receiving invitations to extend my activities. A three-man Law Reform Committee for the Australian Capital Territory was established not long after I started at the ANU, and I was invited to join it as a part-time member.[2] (The Chairman was Dick Blackburn, a judge, who was a graduate of Magdalen College and whom I had been told to look out for by Rupert Cross.) One of the major tasks for this Committee was to make recommendations on the shape of the statute book for the Australian Capital Territory, which involved me in some prolonged research. When the Territory had first been established in 1911 the Constitution simply declared that all the statutes of New South Wales (out of whose lands it was carved) which were of general application should continue to apply, but there had been very little serious attempt to discover what these statutes were, or how they applied in the Canberra of 1973. The preparation of this Report of the Committee largely fell to me, and I spent weeks wading through obsolete statutes in the New South Wales statute book, trying to work out which of them applied to Canberra.

1 John Fleming, another great torts scholar with experience of both Australia and England, held similar sentiments: JG Fleming, "The Pearson Report: Its 'Strategy'" (1979) 42 *Modern Law Review* 249, 268 fn 54.

2 "Reform body named", *The Canberra Times* (Canberra, 10 August 1971) 3. Atiyah seemingly also served on a committee established by the Australian Capital Territory government regarding civil procedure ("Court restaurant plan", *The Canberra Times* (Canberra, 6 February 1973) 1).

In my second year I organised a conference, in conjunction with the Solicitor-General's department, on a topic which then had some interest in commercial circles – namely, the possibility of Australia adhering to some new international Conventions on the law of sale of goods. (In fact the Conventions were not a success and were superseded later by more satisfactory international agreements, but at the time there was some interest in them.) This conference brought together businessmen, commercial lawyers, academics and civil servants from the Solicitor-General's department, and much hard work was involved in the detailed planning and organisation. We gave a dinner to the participants at which the then Minister of Trade, Mr William McMahon, was invited to speak, and I sat next to him. He appeared to me something of a buffoon, whose conversation gave no inkling of any abilities or understanding of commercial problems, and it was with some amazement that a few months later I heard that he had become Prime Minister in succession to Mr Gorton. In fact he *was* little better than a buffoon, but his parliamentary colleagues had never appreciated the fact. They were then to discover it, as McMahon's performances as Prime Minister made every Australian squirm in embarrassment at the thought of their country being represented by this untalented, ignorant and undignified man.

In 1971 I was invited to do a report for the Commonwealth Department of Transport which had launched a massive twenty-five-part study into road accidents. The Department had decided to commission an expert report on every aspect of the subject, from roads to vehicles, and I was asked to do one on insurance. I found this a fascinating exercise, because the Australian States had built up their own system of third-party insurance which was in some ways more efficient than that which existed in England and other countries. I travelled widely throughout the States, meeting many people engaged in the motor insurance business, and learning a great deal about the details of motor insurance. My chief task was to advise the Department whether, in the interests of road safety, the existing third-party system should be revised or reformed, but I took the opportunity to discuss at some length the various proposals then being studied round the world for some form of "no-fault insurance system". My report ran to nearly 250 pages[3] and it was given extensive publicity by the Federal Government.[4] A few years ago I had

3 PS Atiyah, *A Review of Insurance in Relation to Road Safety* (1973).

4 "Motor insurance no-fault plan", *The Canberra Times* (Canberra, 16 August 1972) 15; "'No-fault' insurance plan being examined", *The Canberra Times* (Canberra, 28 October 1972) 3; "Court restaurant plan", *The Canberra Times* (Canberra, 6 February 1973) 1; "Third party scheme for ACT", *The Canberra Times* (Canberra, 4 February 1974) 1.

a letter from an Australian academic who wrote to ask my current views on some aspect of the subject which was again being reviewed, and he told me that for fifteen years all studies of the subject had taken my report as their starting point.

After I had completed this report the Government of New South Wales decided to set up a small committee under the Chairmanship of Mr Justice Meares, to study the possibility of introducing a no-fault insurance scheme for road accidents in that State, and I was invited to join this committee.[5] So for some months I used to take the morning plane from Canberra to Sydney, and return on the late afternoon plane, whenever a meeting of this committee was being held. When Sir Otto Kahn-Freund, the distinguished comparative lawyer from the LSE (who spent his last few years at Oxford) visited Canberra he remarked that these flights looked like the Australian equivalent of the late commuting trains to London, packed with businessmen and civil servants, carrying their briefcases, but (as I pointed out to him) not their umbrellas. This committee never finished its work, because it was eventually superseded by a new committee set up by the Commonwealth government after the Labor Party victory which made Gough Whitlam Prime Minister.

The Labor Party had promised in its manifesto to set up a national committee of inquiry into the question of compensation for accidents, along the lines of the Woodhouse Commission in New Zealand,[6] whose report was at this time still under active consideration in that country, and eventually led to a very wide-ranging and fundamental reform of the law. As my book *Accidents, Compensation and the Law*, had by now been published, and I was becoming accepted as a leading authority on this subject, I was not unduly surprised, shortly after the election, to receive a telephone call from the new Prime Minister who invited me to be one of three members on this commission. (My secretary in her excitement cut the call off, fortunately before the PM was on the line!) I was rather surprised that Whitlam had decided to invite Mr Justice Woodhouse over from New Zealand to chair the national committee, because this meant that the outcome was from the beginning highly predictable, and inevitably the committee was greeted with considerable hostility by the Australian bar. The idea of abolishing all litigation for accident compensation cases – which was what the New Zealand committee had proposed, and was eventually enacted – was not

5 "Compensation inquiry team", *The Canberra Times* (Canberra, 24 January 1973) 1.
6 See p 120.

exactly welcome news to the lawyers who profited from this work in the somewhat litigious States of New South Wales and Victoria. There were also formidable constitutional difficulties in the way of enacting a wide-ranging scheme in Australia because the legislative powers of the federal Parliament of Australia were severely circumscribed by the Constitution, and the traditional methods of interpretation of the Constitution were narrow and literal. I was, however, very excited by the prospect of working with the national committee, and though I had been due to go abroad on a six month sabbatical in 1973–74 I happily gave this up to participate in its work. (The Vice-Chancellor of the ANU was less happy about it – the Labor government had set up a huge number of committees of inquiry, shortly after taking office, and was drawing extensively on the academic staff of the ANU to man these inquiries, but he grudgingly agreed to my serving on the committee.)

The national committee ran into problems almost immediately. So many committees of inquiry had been set up that many of them had overlapping areas of interest, and many of the Labor Party supporters had been drawing up plans for their particular fiefs in total unawareness of the existence of rival plans in other quarters. We had scarcely got going (in fact Woodhouse had not even arrived in Australia yet) when the government announced that it was about to proceed with a dramatic new workers' compensation bill[7] which would clearly cut across the work we had been appointed to do. Our remit was to look into the problems of compensation for *all* accidents, and, following the New Zealand precedent, everyone assumed that this meant that all accident victims were to be compensated equally (with very few exceptions for self-inflicted injuries and the like). This meant that there would be no room for preferential treatment for particular groups of accident victims, such as those injured at work. But the new workers' compensation bill was intended to place injured workers in an almost unbelievably preferential position – the terms to be offered were ludicrously generous, comprising basically full payment of all lost earnings, not only to injured workers, but also to the widows of their dependants, no matter how high the earnings. Furthermore the definition of worker was extended to breaking point, and the concept of an industrial injury likewise was extended to cover practically any injury no matter how remotely related to a person's employment. Under the Bill's proposals, if I had been killed in an aircraft accident while flying from Canberra to Sydney to take part in the work of the national committee, Christine would have been entitled to a pension for her

7 *Compensation (Commonwealth Employees) Bill* 1973 (Cth).

life equal to my full earnings from all sources. It was immediately obvious to me when I saw the proposals that they would pull the rug from under the feet of our own inquiry. It would be quite impossible to match the sort of compensation here proposed for all accident victims, and I felt that the Bill had to be stopped.

This was, however, politically impossible. The Bill's proponent was Clyde Cameron, the new Minister for Labour, who I had met some months before the election when I had seen the way the wind was blowing, and had tried to divert him from this kind of extravaganza. I had suggested politely that his proposals would cost an immense amount of money which could be better spent on other things, but his only reply was that Australia was a rich country which could afford to be generous. Furthermore, this Bill was his special "baby" – he had spent twenty years in opposition waiting for the day when he could introduce it, and he was not easily to be diverted now. I went to Sydney to discuss the difficulties with Mr Justice Meares, the third member of the national committee and we telephoned Woodhouse in New Zealand to warn him of our problems. He drafted a letter to the Prime Minister which we all agreed, pointing out the difficulties, but we got little satisfaction. In the event, it did not matter because the workers' compensation bill became bogged down in a committee of the Senate (where the Labor Party had no majority) and was never in fact passed.

Towards the middle of 1973 the national committee began to get under way. The early stages were slow and frustrating, as Woodhouse was still in New Zealand, and we needed to find premises and recruit staff. However, Woodhouse came on several visits and was more or less established by the middle of 1973 in Sydney. I had first met him on a brief visit to New Zealand a year or two earlier, and I now got to know him quite well, though I never really became intimate with him. Although I was at that time in considerable sympathy with what Woodhouse had proposed in New Zealand – basically the abolition of personal injury litigation and its replacement by a national compensation scheme – I confess that I found him a little difficult to deal with. He was rather proud of his New Zealand achievements, and having considered the matter once for the purposes of the New Zealand inquiry, he had, I thought, a rather closed mind on most of the issues. Moreover, the New Zealand report, though it read very well and carried the argument easily and fluently, was in some ways shallow, or at least one-sided. The conclusions having been once arrived at, all difficulties and doubts were brushed aside. I still had doubts and reservations about some of the issues, and I found it difficult to persuade Woodhouse to reconsider these seriously. I also thought that he preened himself on being a subtle politician. He thought that he had not only solved the problem, but also knew how to sell his ideas. In fact he was inclined to be a little pompous and proud of his status as an intimate of Prime Minister. I do not think he ever appreciated quite how formidable an opposition he was likely to find in the Australian legal profession. In New Zealand, with its strong welfare traditions, the legal profession had eventually accepted the idea of abolishing personal injury litigation; but I could not see the Australians caving in under Woodhouse's persuasive subtleties. And in fact, they did not.

There were early problems arising from the fact that the national committee was originally assigned to the Attorney-General as the responsible Minister. The Attorney was Senator Lionel Murphy, of Irish origins, and a somewhat combative and aggressive politician. Like many members of the Labor Party which had been out of office for over twenty years, he was almost paranoiac about opposition, suspecting plots and conspiracies in every corner. He had not been long in office when he suspected the Security Service (which was nominally his responsibility) of refusing to accept his authority, and he actually descended on their headquarters with a squad of police, and physically took control of the building! Later, when the Labor Party were clearly on the way out, Whitlam appointed Murphy to the High Court Bench, an irresponsible and bad appointment, because Murphy had absolutely no genuine judicial qualities. In fact things went from bad to worse when he was charged, while on the High Court, with having conspired to pervert the course of justice in a shady matter involving some equally shady characters. He was convicted, had his conviction quashed on appeal,[8] and eventually died before the retrial.[9] This was the kind of man the national committee was dealing with, and we ran into difficulties almost immediately. The difficulties became so acute that Woodhouse eventually appealed to Whitlam, and insisted on the national committee being moved from the Attorney-General's responsibilities. We were then placed under the direct responsibility of the Prime Minister.

We recruited a formidable team to staff the national committee. Among these was Geoffrey Palmer, a New Zealander, well known to Woodhouse who had worked on some of the post-Report developments in New Zealand and knew the issues well. Palmer had recently been teaching law in the

8 *R v Murphy* (1985) 4 NSWLR 42 (CA).

9 Atiyah had these details incorrect. Murphy was acquitted following the second trial. For a magisterial account of the trials, see N Cowdery, "Reflections on the Murphy Trials" (2008) 27 *University of Queensland Law Journal* 5.

United States (at the University of Iowa Law School where he was well remembered as I discovered on a brief visit there in 1979). I found him a likeable and impressive man and he was a tower of strength to the committee. Later he returned to New Zealand and went into politics, where he rose rapidly. I next met him in England around 1982 when he was deputy leader of the New Zealand Labor Party, and he came to tea with us at our home in Oxford. I then filled him in on the details of the English political scene – this was the time when the British Labour Party was lurching further and further to the left – and was glad to discover that his political leanings were very far removed from those of the British Left. Later still, in 1990, he became Prime Minister of New Zealand, though he only held that office for a few months. I suspect he was too sane and balanced in his ideas ever to be a successful leader of a left-wing political party.

My own connection with the national committee came to a premature and unhappy end when I decided to leave Australia for reasons which I go into later, and I resigned from the committee in September 1973 before it had really got into its stride.

On the domestic side, our time in Australia was overshadowed by two great problems which extended between them over almost the whole of the three and a half years which we spent there. The first was Christine's health. She had already been worried by some strange and distressing symptoms before we even arrived, and these gradually became worse. She put on weight and seemed perpetually hungry; she had manic periods of over-energy; her face became puffy and her hair fell out. Her GP seemed baffled and tried one thing after another without success, but seemed reluctant to send her to a consultant. Eventually he did so, with immediate results. The consultant, Dr Hammett, took one glance at her when he walked through the waiting room to his own room, and when she saw him, he took a book down from his shelves and read out her own symptoms to her. His diagnosis was instantaneous and entirely correct. Christine was suffering from a very rare disorder known as Cushing's syndrome (after a Yale doctor who first identified it early in the twentieth century), caused by the malfunctioning of the adrenalin glands. The over-production of adrenalin was the cause of all her symptoms, and the excessive and unnatural weight increase had alerted Hammett to the probable cause. The only cure for the disease was a major operation involving removal of the adrenalin glands, so that thereafter Christine would have to take cortisone tablets daily (cortisone and adrenalin are chemically the same thing). She was whisked into hospital immediately for clinical tests to confirm the diagnosis, and the operation was performed within a few days. Although she was home quite soon, given the major nature of the operation, she suffered severely from post-operative depression as a result of the shake-up to her system caused by the sudden reduction in the quantity of adrenalin, and it was some weeks before the beneficial results of the operation became apparent. But in due course they did; the symptoms disappeared, the unnatural weight melted away, and Christine recovered her looks and her figure. It was a miraculous delivery, and we celebrated it by taking a winter holiday in the middle of 1972, driving up to Queensland and spending a few days on Heron Island, one of the Southerly islands of the Great Barrier Reef, a truly wonderful place, the nearest thing to paradise I have ever seen.

Our other problem was of a different nature. It concerned our eldest son Julian, who was now eighteen. He was not an easy adolescent, and at this time his future gave us much anxiety because he was not of an academic character, and had left school at sixteen. He had tried various things, like being apprenticed to a motor mechanic, but without success; and for much of this time he was unemployed, or only doing casual labouring jobs. He had also fallen in with some friends who were rather of his own kind; they seemed to us amiable and harmless enough although it was true that they often looked very rough, in their clothes and appearance. But despite this sort of common enough problem of a difficult adolescent eldest son, nothing in our past experience had prepared us for what now hit us.

It all began with a phone call late one evening from one of Julian's friends with whom he had been out – a lad we knew as Macka. His call had a hysterical edge which communicated itself to me. He told me that Julian had been beaten up and arrested by the police and had been taken off by them to a police station. I immediately telephoned the central police station where I asked to speak to the officer in charge. I told him what we had just heard and said that I wanted to make an official protest at the conduct of the policemen. I also asked where Julian would have been taken after being arrested, and was told that he would have been taken to a small local police station. This was untrue and I am almost sure that it was a deliberate lie designed to ensure that we would be delayed reaching the central police station. When we got there, the officer in charge was already interviewing Julian and we joined him. I was throughout the whole of this interview under the impression that we were the complaining parties; that we were there, and that Julian was being interviewed in connection with our complaint about the policemen in question. Because of this I made no attempt to stop or interrupt the very vigorous cross-examination which then ensued, and which was all taken down by a stenographer. Every effort was made to trip Julian up, to go back over what he had said, to get him to admit inconsistencies; but he stuck to his story throughout. He said that he had simply been out with his friends, that they had been laughing and joking inoffensively, that the two policemen had then come up to them and asked them some question to which they been given a reasonable reply. As the policemen were walking away they thought they heard some offensive remark, turned round, and beckoned Julian over to them. Quite innocently, he went towards them where his friends could not see precisely what was happening. Without further warning, they then leapt on him, flung him to the ground, forced his hands behind his back and put handcuffs on him. The cross-examination continued for about two hours, and by the end I was absolutely convinced that Julian had been telling the truth. When it was over, the officer asked whether we would be happy if the policemen were dealt with informally or whether we wanted to bring proceedings. I said we would be quite happy if the matter was dealt with informally. The officer was then about to leave, when I gathered that, before we had arrived at the police station, Julian had already been charged with some offences – using offensive language, and even (forsooth) resisting arrest. I assumed that these charges would now be dropped, but the officer told me that the matter was not up to him, and he left us.

I was flabbergasted, and immediately felt we had been tricked. It seemed that the whole of the cross-examination had been conducted to show that Julian was in fact guilty of some offence – a totally improper procedure because he had already been charged and such cross-examination after charge is not permitted under Anglo-Australian police procedure. The idea that we were the complaining parties, and the complaint itself, now seemed to have disappeared from the agenda.

I decided that if the police were going to behave in this manner we would have to take the whole thing more seriously; so the next day we consulted a solicitor and instructed him to issue writs claiming damages against the policemen responsible (because Macka had taken their numbers the police authorities were legally obliged to give us their names). It is clear from later events that the police regarded this as a declaration of war; and they decided to fight with every weapon at their disposal. They had quite a few. Canberra was full of policemen and as they did not have a great deal to do in the way of serious crime, they spent much of their time harassing youngsters with petty motoring charges. From now on, every time that Julian went out on his motorcycle he was liable to be stopped by the police – he began to receive numerous summonses for speeding. If he had not been speeding, they stopped him anyhow and went over his motorcycle with a fine toothcomb hoping to catch him in some illegality.

Quite apart from this intolerable activity, I had anyhow been outraged by the violence with which Julian had been treated. Even if he had been guilty of shouting some abusive remark at the police I could not see any reason for the violent nature of the arrest and the use of handcuffs. I did not believe this would have been normal police practice in England, but the more I inquired into Australian practice, the more I discovered how far it differed from English. People were, it seemed, arrested on the most trivial grounds, handcuffed, taken to the police station and treated like serious criminals there – fingerprinted and so on. Young motorists, especially, were even liable to be arrested for minor motoring offences, instead of simply being asked for their name and address and summonsed. I decided to look into the law, and I then discovered that the Canberra laws relating to powers of arrest were in a terrible state. There was a vital ambiguity in the relevant Ordinance, but certainly on one reading of the Ordinance the police had no power to arrest anyhow for the offence of using abusive language, with which Julian had been charged, unless a demand was first made for the offender's name and address, and he either refused to comply or gave an answer which the police had reasonable ground to think was false. And of course, if there was no power of arrest, the trumped-up charge of resisting arrest could not be sustained in law. I also discovered that the routine fingerprinting of all those charged with offences had been held illegal by a Supreme Court judge in Canberra not very long before, but apparently no notice had been taken of this judicial precedent at the Canberra police station.

For some time nothing more was heard about our complaint against the policemen; but when the case against Julian was about to start, we were told, outside the court-room, that if we agreed to drop our actions against the policemen, the charges would be dropped. We were given about five minutes to make up our minds on this, an absolutely outrageous procedure. In effect the police were trying to bargain the public power of prosecution in return for our dropping a wholly private action against two individual policemen. Of course they had absolutely no right to make any such bargain, which would have been an illegal contract. Indeed, if we had agreed to the bargain, and the charges against Julian had then been dropped, we could legally have gone back on the bargain, and continued our actions against the police. They could not, in law, have relied on such an illegal contract as a defence. But when I suggested this to our counsel he said he could not be a party to such a proceeding. I made no complaint about this because I knew that counsel had to live with the system; and if our counsel had behaved as I suggested, he would never have been able to make any bargain again with the police on behalf of a future client. Nevertheless, I think he was wrong, and failed in his duty to us. In any event we had such a short period of time to consider the offer, that we had not really reached any firm decision before it was too late, and the case began.

The hearing was a travesty. The magistrate was incompetent. Everybody knew he was incompetent – even the head of the Attorney-General's department admitted to me that he was so bad that he had no business to be on the bench. That may sound like an exaggerated or even a mythical remark, but it is the literal truth. Even allowing for my partiality as an observer, it seemed to me quite clear that the police evidence against Julian was given in a shifty and unconvincing way. Julian himself gave his evidence clearly and honestly, even though he was vigorously cross-examined with the aid of the transcript taken in the police station after he had been arrested. Four of his friends gave evidence – all said they had seen and heard nothing to justify the police behaviour; the magistrate dismissed their evidence saying that because they had seen and heard nothing their evidence was irrelevant! All our efforts were unavailing, even though at the end the magistrate said he thought the case was trivial and he simply gave Julian a conditional discharge.

We filed a notice of appeal immediately – appeals were by way of full rehearing before a Supreme Court judge and I felt sure we would succeed there. The Supreme Court judges were honourable, decent and competent lawyers in Australia, and they frequently overturned magistrates' court convictions which depended on disputed police evidence in cases of this kind. But before our appeal was due to be heard, things took a more sinister turn.

One evening Julian was out with a friend in Christine's mini. We had encouraged him to use the car in preference to the motorcycle, because he was less easily identified in a car (to such lengths had our freedoms been affected by the campaign of police persecution). On this occasion, a policeman did recognise him in the town, and beckoned him to get out of the car, and walk across the road. Bearing in mind what had happened the last time he had followed such an instruction, Julian declined to follow it, and told the policeman that he could say what he wanted while Julian was still in the car, and his friend was a witness. The policeman then began to threaten Julian, at which, perhaps unwisely, Julian rolled up the windows and locked the car doors. Police re-enforcements were summoned, and they threatened to smash the windows of the car unless the door was opened. Julian's friend at this point became alarmed, and he opened his door, Julian was dragged out of the car, arrested and taken to the police station where he was once again (illegally) fingerprinted, and charged with new trumped-up charges of assaulting a policeman, resisting arrest and so on. His friend, questioned by the police as to what he was "prepared to say" told them he would say exactly what he had seen, whereupon he was sent home without a statement being taken from him. We were called up to come to the police station and offer bail to get Julian released.

By this time I had had enough. I had not personally responded well or perhaps very wisely to what had been happening. I had been so outraged, so shaken to my depths, that I had rather floundered around, complaining to all and sundry about the misbehaviour of the police. The sensible course would simply have been to wait until we got before a Supreme Court judge before getting too agitated; but I had, in truth, been quite shattered by these events. Part of the problem was that I had been under great pressure at work while all this was going on; I had been appointed Dean of the Law Faculty some months before, I was engaged in various projects on behalf of the Law Reform Committee, I had now been appointed to the national committee, and I was simply more exhausted than I had been willing to recognise. In the upshot I had begun to suffer from a serious depression, and had had to seek medical treatment for that. In addition, Christine had begun to pressurise me by suggesting that we return to England.

Partly as a result of these events, I had agreed that we should start planning a return to England, and after one particularly strenuous series of events I had telephoned Michael in England to ask his assistance. I knew that there was a vacant Law Chair at the University of Birmingham and I also asked Michael to contact my old friend William Twining, now at the University of Warwick, to see if there was any possibility of a post there. It turned out that a new Chair had just been authorised at Warwick and my interest in it had been enthusiastically welcomed by William.[10] It was not very long before I also received an invitation to an interview, expenses paid, at Birmingham. So I was able to feel reasonably confident that one or other of these posts would be mine.

When the national committee had got going it had been agreed that each member of the committee would travel to England, Canada and the US in order to study at first hand some aspects of their compensation laws, and by June 1973 it had become convenient for me to make my own visit. I was

10 See further Twining, *Jurist in Context: A Memoir* (2019) 155.

therefore able to visit Birmingham and Warwick universities for interviews, and, at Warwick I spent some time meeting members of the academic staff, and discussing with them the nature of the courses they were teaching. It is possible that, in the event, I would have been happier at Birmingham, but the authorities there, although they had arranged a formal interview for me, were clearly under the impression that I was going to Warwick anyhow, and they did not put themselves out to attract me. In the event I received an offer from Warwick and accepted it.

I also spent some hectic days studying the practical workings of English social security tribunals, and spent a day actually observing the operation of one of these tribunals in action. I had wanted to see a typical series of appeals but chanced on what must have been one of the most unusual cases ever to be heard by such a tribunal. The case concerned an elderly lady who claimed that she had been misled by the Ministry officials as to her entitlements to a pension, as a result of which she had failed to claim her benefits. Eventually her rights were recognised and she claimed back payment of all her lost benefits. Now the relevant statutes allowed back payments for up to twelve months but no further, but the claimant wished to argue that because she had been misled by the Ministry officials this normal twelve-months bar should not be applied – in technical legal language she wanted to claim that the Ministry was "estopped" from setting up the time bar. What was so unusual about the case was not the nature of the claim – thousands of such claims had probably been made over the years and disallowed – but the status of the lady and her representative. She was clearly not a humble working-class widow, because two of her sons drove to the tribunal's premises in their own Rolls-Royces (one each!) and her case was argued for her by her grandson, who was then studying for the bar, and had just taken his bar final examination. Although he was not yet a qualified barrister, the tribunals permitted informal representation and he was allowed to argue her case. What had clearly happened was that the young man had looked into his grandmother's claim, and thought it worth cutting his teeth on it, thus gaining some practical experience as well as challenging what the family evidently thought a serious injustice. The young man had an ingenious argument to make, and he made it very well. The Ministry had for some years been relying on a precedent in cases of this kind, a decision of the National Insurance Commissioner to the effect that the Ministry could not legally be "estopped" because estoppel could not avail against a statutory provision. This precedent was itself based on an earlier decision of Lord Chief Justice Goddard in the High Court, but what the aspiring barrister was able to point out to the tribunal was that Lord Goddard's decision or dictum had been overruled in a later case by the Court of Appeal, in a decision given by Lord Denning.[11] It was an excellent legal argument – but it overlooked the fact that what passes for law in the Court of Appeal is a very different matter from what passes for law in a humble administrative tribunal. Far too many cases had been decided on the basis of this precedent for it to be upset by such a tribunal, and the appeal was inevitably dismissed. It might have stood some chance of success in the Court of Appeal.

I later went on to Toronto and San Francisco where I looked into the workers' compensation system of these two states. In Toronto I looked especially into the insurance system operated by the Ontario Workers' Compensation Board, but I shall write of this further in my next chapter. On my return to Canberra I wrote an extensive report on these visits for the benefit of my colleagues on the national committee.

When I got back to Canberra I told Woodhouse and Meares that I was planning to return to England after the committee's work was finished, and we discussed the timetable. Woodhouse was anyhow anxious to wind things up by Christmas, so that he could get back to New Zealand, and although this looked somewhat over optimistic to me, I told Warwick University that I would start in January 1974.

But the situation concerning Julian was now becoming acute, and Christine and I had already agreed that she and the boys should return to England around September, we would sell our house, and I would find somewhere to stay in Sydney to finish off my work on the national committee. Now that I had a secure job to go to, there seemed no reason why Christine should not be able to go ahead of me, find a house and start the process of settling down again in England. However, these plans were shattered by the latest incident between Julian and the police shortly after my return to Canberra. I decided that it was not safe for him to remain in Australia, because there was a grave risk of his ending up in jail on some trumped-up charge. So the day after the last incident I bought him a ticket for England and the next day I took him to Sydney and put him on the flight for London. Christine's parents arranged to meet him and put him up for a while, and we brought forward our own plans for the departure of Christine and the other boys. A few days later a couple of policemen came round to our house claiming to have a warrant for Julian's arrest because he had not responded to his bail. I told them he was not there, and when they began to question me, I said that I had nothing

11 *Lever Finance Ltd v Westminster London Borough Council* [1971] 1 QB 222 (CA).

Figure 10.1 Australian National University. Credit: Australian National University Archives.

further to say to them. Although I was tempted to tell them that he was by then 12,000 miles outside their jurisdiction, I confess that after what we had gone through I saw no reason to make their work any easier. (I was later told by a barrister friend that the police had been given the clearest instructions by the Attorney-General not to execute the arrest warrant, but by this time I was not surprised at anything that the police did.)

At the last moment we changed our plans again. I decided that I would fly to England with Christine and our other three boys, though at this stage I still hoped to return to finish my work on the national committee. I toyed with the idea of issuing a press statement explaining why I had sent Julian out of the country, and I even consulted a number of friends about this, including the present Chief Justice of the High Court of Australia.[12] In the end I decided that a private letter to Whitlam would be more likely to achieve some results, though it was probably unrealistic of me to think that any real results were ever probable. However, I wrote the letter, and posted it at the airport on our way out of Canberra. The next day we were back in England. In the event I never returned to Australia. I had told Whitlam that if he preferred to take no action on my letter he could treat it as an offer of my resignation from the national committee, and that is what he did.

12 Sir Garfield Barwick.

11 Warwick University

I arrived back in England in the summer of 1973, somewhat shell-shocked by the traumatic events which had led to our precipitate departure from Australia. For a while, also, I hoped that some response from the Prime Minister would enable me to return to resume my work on the national committee. I was deeply troubled, and often unable to sleep. One night I got up about 2 am and telephoned Woodhouse in Sydney to find out if the Prime Minister had consulted him, but he could tell me nothing. Eventually the letter arrived, and my resignation from the committee was accepted.[1] I turned to my new job as Professor at the University of Warwick, where my commencement was brought forward to the beginning of the autumn term.

I was in for a rude shock. The University of Warwick was totally different from anything I had anticipated. It was one of the new universities, established in the 1960s, and there were a great many things about it which I did not like at all. What had initially attracted me to the university was the rather special ethos of the Law Department, which was pioneering a law degree of a much more overtly social character. The idea was that law should be taught "in its context", so almost every course had a significant non-legal component. Courses were thus highly "relevant", and not just in a gimmicky way. I approved of the whole idea, and indeed my own writings, and especially my book *Accidents, Compensation and the Law*, had been based on similar ideals about the desirability of treating legal education as a social science. I did feel some scepticism about the degree to which the interest in "sociology" had spread among the law lecturers, but I was at first willing to be tolerant about this. I had never seriously studied the subject, and what I had read had always looked impressive and mysterious, with its almost impenetrable

1 The national committee reported in 1974: National Committee of Inquiry on Compensation and Rehabilitation in Australia, *Report of the National Committee of Inquiry on Compensat ion and Rehabilitation in Australia* (1974). For discussion, see H Luntz, *Compensation and Rehabilitation: A Survey of the Report of the National Committee of Inquiry into Compensation and Rehabilitation in Australia and the National Compensation Bill 1974* (1975) and H Luntz, "Looking Back at Accident Compensation: An Australian Perspective" (2003) 34 *Victoria University of Wellington Law Review* 279.

jargon, and at first I accepted it on trust, assuming that it was a respectable academic discipline. So intellectually I was generally in tune with what was being attempted in the Law Department. But alas there were many other aspects of the university that I did not take to.

For a start the university campus was exceptionally unattractive. A whole mass of white-tiled buildings, closely resembling public lavatories (or modern airports) had been run up in the shortest possible time, and new buildings were going up everywhere all the time. Things were not assisted by the fact that the white tiles soon started falling off many of the buildings which had to be festooned with scaffolding while repairs were made. So the campus constantly resembled a giant building site, muddy and messy. Landscaping had scarcely begun and even on a pleasant summer's day there was hardly anywhere to sit out and enjoy a sandwich or a glass of beer. Then the buildings themselves were at that time extremely deficient in the facilities they offered. There was no staff lounge or club or lunchroom. Egalitarianism ruled everywhere, so staff shared toilets with the students and joined them in the queues for lunch at student cafeterias or lunch counters. The Law Department had no building of its own at that time, simply a cluster of offices in a corridor which might have been in Whitehall (except that in that case the quality of the fittings and furnishings would have been much higher).

I soon discovered too that, by comparison with the Australian National University, Warwick had a shoestring sort of budget, or at least the Law Department did, though I suspected that some other departments simply were more successful at extracting funds from the university administration than we were. When I first arrived the Law Department had one secretary and no other administrative personnel of any kind (in Canberra for a Faculty perhaps twice as large, the ANU had had a graduate Faculty Secretary, a graduate assistant to the Faculty Secretary, four secretaries for the professoriate, a couple of other typists and a general odd-job man). When my books arrived from Australia I had personally to carry box after heavy box from my car upstairs to my own room and shelve them. (In Canberra that had been done for me by porters.) I was given a miserable room in a most unattractive building, where the telephone shared a number with another room. For the first few weeks after I arrived, every phone call which came through was meant for my remote colleague who shared the number. Since he rarely appeared to be in, I was forced either to try to work through the piercing din of a ringing phone, or answer it, and then find myself taking messages or running round passages looking for my colleague.

Something else which I soon discovered was that the organisation of the university was entirely different from that at more traditional universities, like older English (non-Oxbridge) universities as well as the ANU. In those universities it was traditionally assumed that more senior staff, like professors, would sit on the committees and boards and make most of the decisions. In the new egalitarian mood of the 1960s when the University of Warwick had been set up, this was thought quite unacceptable. Professors had no "privileges", but shared "chores" and all decision-making with other staff. There was no "Dean" to the law school. There was not even a "head" of department. There was merely a chairman who became (after I had left) a "Chair". Most committees seemed to consist of university administrators and a handful of junior lecturers. This totally failed to achieve its aims – which were of course to make the junior staff feel that they had a say in the management of the institution. Because they tended to be younger and inexperienced, and because their membership of committees rotated rapidly, the administrative staff simply ran rings round them at committee meetings and tended to make the real decisions themselves. Academics, both senior and junior, felt shunted into the sidelines. Indeed, most of the junior staff, in whose supposed interests the university organisation had taken this form, felt far more alienated from the real centres of power than they did in any other university I had ever been involved in. Conspiracy theories were rife, and it was widely believed by the junior lecturers that the university was simply run by a small clique led by the Vice-Chancellor and the Registrar. While I did not share these conspiracy theories, I too soon began to feel alienated from the university as a whole. After my experiences as Dean at the ANU I had looked forward to making a worthwhile contribution at Warwick, not merely in academic work in the law school, but in the university as a whole. In fact I never had any opportunity to do this, as I was never asked to sit on a university committee which had the smallest power or authority.

There were other respects in which I was somewhat shocked by what I found at Warwick, though this may have been more my own fault in simply being unprepared for the obvious. I had gone to Australia only four years earlier, with something of a reputation in academic legal circles as a radical, a reformer and even perhaps an "angry young man". Now on my return I suddenly discovered that I was a member of the "establishment", the old guard. Although I was barely conscious of having aged over these four years, I found the new department of law at Warwick staffed by a generation of junior lecturers who wore jeans and sweaters, did not wear ties or jackets, put their feet up on the tables at meetings and behaved (and looked) almost exactly like the students themselves. Their geniality and freshness hardly made up for their inexperience as administrators or indeed their general irresponsibility. On one occasion, shortly after I arrived, I found myself at a meeting at which arrangements had to be made for a student to resit a paper he had failed in the last examinations. Because law at Warwick was merely a department of the Faculty of Social Sciences, the decision to require the student to resit the paper had been made by the Faculty Board, and was actually contrary to the recommendations of the Law Department itself. At this meeting I was astounded to hear it suggested (perhaps not entirely seriously) that the Law Department might actually "fake" an examination and simply pass on to the Board a piece of paper saying the student had passed a non-existent resit. I quickly made it clear that I could not be a party to anything of that kind, which probably resulted in my being immediately classified as stuffy and old-fashioned. On another occasion, I was asked to chair a committee to decide how to spend a recent special grant of £15,000 which had been allocated for law books in the library. My young colleagues, sprawling around me, with their feet up on the table, made it clear to me that they could not possibly approve the expenditure of a single pound until a number of fundamental issues had been cleared up. As I recollect, these began by being questions about the nature of the law school, what its long-term aims should be and so on, which were perhaps reasonable enough; but they rapidly moved on to further questions such as what were the purposes of the university as a whole (or indeed, any university), what was the role of the universities in society; and anyhow what was society, and so on and so on. After a three-hour meeting, we had not decided on any of the proposed list of books, or law reports I had put before my colleagues. After that I disbanded the committee and made all the decisions myself, in consultation with the librarian. It was symptomatic of the attitude of my colleagues that I never heard a word of complaint or any suggestion that things ought to be done differently. The trouble simply was that they did not know how to make practical decisions.

It was not only the conditions at the university which troubled me. Political and public affairs, especially during that first year after our return, seemed to me equally depressing. This was the winter of 1973–74, the year of the miners' strike which led to the election of February 1974 which forced the Conservatives out of office. I had for some years been slowly moving to the right myself, and I viewed with horror the return of a Labour Government so deeply in hock to the unions. I had good cause to do so. Over the next two or three years, my standard of living as a university professor fell by perhaps twenty-five per cent, as inflation roared away under the Labour Government, and university salaries (especially those of the senior staff) fell behind every year. With our four growing sons, and my wife and I all dependent on one salary, I viewed with cynicism the calls for greater equality of income which seemed to come principally (at least among my acquaintances) from families who had two salaries and no children. Then another blow fell, in that same winter, when the Arab-Israeli war led to the huge increase in oil prices, and for a time, a serious shortage of oil. Our new house had oil-fired central heating, and for a while I could get no deliveries at all. The company which had supplied our predecessors in the house at first refused to supply any new customers, and no-one else would take us on either. When they did eventually agree to supply us, they would only deliver oil in the same quantities as our predecessors had used – and they had not had four children using their bedrooms for evening study.

Many of the problems of that year and many of the things which I disliked at Warwick University may seem, in retrospect, to have been petty irritants, and had I been in a more robust state of mind, I could probably have borne them more easily. But as it was, my condition worsened, and I became very deeply depressed. I consulted doctors who prescribed anti-depressants; these certainly helped, but they also tended to have a somewhat stupefying effect, so that I became more lethargic and felt desperately tired the whole time. On many occasions it was only with the utmost difficulty that I succeeded in teaching my classes, and at home, it was not uncommon for me actually to find myself shedding tears over absurd trifles. This deep depression lasted for the whole of my first year, and only lifted in the autumn of my second year. And for the next four or five years I remained highly vulnerable to renewed attacks of depression, which could descend on me with terrifying suddenness, and often alternated with equally unhealthy manic periods during which I had alarming and almost superhuman bursts of energy.

Fortunately, things were not gloom and depression the whole time. There were other sides to life, even during that first year. We had been very fortunate in selling our Canberra home at a huge profit, so we were able to buy an enormous Victorian house in one of the finest streets in Leamington which comfortably housed our growing family. It was very conveniently situated, a couple of hundred yards from the Boys' grammar school where three of our sons were being educated together at one stage. While our eldest son, Julian, continued to give us much cause for worry (though he never had any serious problems with the English police, as he had with the Australian), our other three sons appeared to be developing well. During our years in Leamington

Andrew secured a place at Leeds University, and our third and fourth sons, Simon and Jeremy, both went to the grammar school, and showed considerable academic promise. Jeremy was a great reader, and spent many hours reading *The Lord of the Rings* aloud to my wife while she painted the hall and stairways in our new home.

We also re-established old friendships, especially with the Twinings, who we had known well in Khartoum days, and made new ones. While I did not become intimate with any of the younger English lecturers at the law school, we did make good friendships with an American and an Australian couple. The American was Tom Hervey, an interesting and unusual character. A Harvard Law School graduate, he had a fine sharp mind, and was an excellent lawyer, as well as a very good and conscientious teacher. His main interests coincided with mine, so we shared courses and students, and had many happy hours discussing the latest cases and problems in the law of contract and tort. But despite his abilities, Tom simply had no creative talents as an academic. Some years after I had left Warwick when I was editing the *Oxford Journal of Legal Studies*, I sent a number of books to Tom and asked him to do a review essay on them, which I thought well within his powers. After discussing it with me, he agreed to do this, but some months later, he returned the whole lot to me, confessing shamefacedly that he simply had nothing to say. As modern academics are expected to write and publish, this was a great handicap to him, and he was never able to secure promotion. Another strange thing about Tom was that, although he appeared to have decided to settle in England, and eventually saw his children growing up as English as ours, he himself was very American in his ways and ideas. Aggressively and vigorously entrepreneurial, Tom's orientation fitted ill in the England of the Harold Wilson era. But his entrepreneurial spirit eventually came into its own because he began to work on computer programmes for lawyers, and became so successful at this that he set up his own company and finally left Warwick University.

The Australian couple we first got to know at Warwick were John and Joan Dwyer, both at that time barristers from Melbourne. I had actually met John at a conference at Melbourne, but only got to know him well when he came to Warwick for a sabbatical term during my second year there, accompanied by Joan and a couple of young daughters. We became close friends and colleagues and John provided an admirable foil for me at Warwick when he spent another year there in 1976–77 while I was doing a major piece of writing. After that we saw them less frequently but they came to England every second year or so, and we have always maintained contact with them.

Another, happier side to our domestic life after our return to England, was the ready accessibility of France. Long one of our favourite holiday haunts, Christine and I spent holidays there in 1974 and again in 1975 with our two younger boys (the older ones by this time preferred to make their own holiday arrangements). In 1974 we were in the Dordogne, an area we fell in love with, and some years later we were able to buy our own holiday home there. In 1975 we went to the Loire valley which we had also previously visited on several occasions.

Despite my acute depression during my first year at Warwick University I had managed to do a certain amount of writing. I had done a new edition of *Accidents, Compensation and the Law*[2] which had sold sufficiently well to get the *Law in Context* series off the ground and encourage the publishers who at one time had been inclined to cancel the whole venture. I had also done a serious piece of research developing out of my work for the Australian compensation committee, concerning the relationship between accident rates and insurance premiums.[3] Some academic legal literature had for some years been suggesting that the widespread practice of insurance tended to weaken the deterrent effect of the law of civil liability, because employers and motorists and others who were heavily at risk never in practice paid out the damages awarded against them – they were nearly always paid by insurance companies. On the other hand, other academics, especially those associated with the new law-and-economics school, argued that even though the damages were paid by insurance companies, the persons liable had to pay the premiums, and premiums could be varied up and down to reflect bad and good accident records. In this way, it was sometimes suggested, insurance did not necessarily weaken the deterrent effect of the law. There had been much writing on the general subject, not only in England, but more specifically in America and Canada, but I was conscious that nobody had ever made a serious study of the statistics which were available on this question.

In Toronto, on behalf of the Australian national compensation committee, I had spent three days studying at first hand the workings of the Ontario Workers' Compensation Board, which had a high reputation for fairness and efficiency in handling this one major type of accident. This Board had adopted a fairly sophisticated system of varying the levies they charged to

2 PS Atiyah, *Accidents, Compensation and the Law*, 2nd edn (1975).

3 PS Atiyah, "Accident Prevention and Variable Premium Rates for Work-Connected Accidents" – I (1975) 4 *Industrial Law Journal* 1; PS Atiyah, "Accident Prevention and Variable Premium Rates for Work-Connected Accidents" – II (1975) 4 *Industrial Law Journal* 89.

employers in accordance with their accident experience, and I had looked at this system particularly closely. The Toronto officials who I had spoken to were all convinced that their system operated to reduce accident rates but when I questioned them closely about the way it worked they admitted that they had never actually sought to monitor it, by (for instance) comparing the accident rates of those subject to penalty levies and those companies not so subject. At my suggestion they had made a limited inquiry into the efficacy of these rates by examining the statistical record of a small number of companies, and they had sent me the results of this inquiry.

During my first year at Warwick I subjected these figures to a close examination which made me very dubious of the efficacy of the whole system of penalty-rating adopted by the Ontario Board. I published these results in an academic journal[4] and sent a copy to the British Royal Commission on accidents and compensation (which had been set up while I was in Australia, and was still sitting). Lord Pearson, the Chairman of the Commission, invited me to lunch at the House of Lords, a novel experience for me, but the peer's lunchroom looked distinctly un-aristocratic. Indeed, I noticed a very unlordly tin can on the carpet designed to collect the raindrops percolating through the roof!

Later I received an invitation to give "evidence" to the Royal Commission and did so,[5] though it was a somewhat depressing experience. Lord Pearson made it evident that the Commission took a very narrow view of their terms of reference, and he also explained to me that the trade unions (who at that time seemed almost as strong as the Government) had told the Royal Commission that they expected to surrender nothing in the way of privileges or special benefits available for industrial accident victims, though they certainly expected to improve the position of accident victims generally. Their attitude, as well as Lord Pearson's view of the Commission's terms of reference, appeared to preclude any general solution to the problem of compensation for accident victims. I carried on a desultory correspondence with the Commission's statistical staff on one or two points, and I also corresponded with Professor Prest, the only economist on the Commission, over a few issues, but I do not think I had much influence on their deliberations, though I can at least claim to have put the whole subject on the agenda.

4 ibid.

5 The evidence that Atiyah gave is discussed in "Compensation for Industrial Injury: Memorandum of Evidence submitted to the Royal Commission on Civil Liability and Compensation for Personal Injury by the Industrial Law Society" (1975) 4 *Industrial Law Journal* 195.

I have already written of the failure of the Royal Commission to arouse any enthusiasm for the reforms proposed in its report.[6]

I thus managed to keep myself busy during that first year at Warwick though my depression was severe enough to prevent me doing any truly original or novel work. William Twining was constantly encouraging me to do a major book on the law of contract, perhaps for the *Law in Context* series, but I simply did not see how this could be done. My only response was a three-page note explaining why I thought a *Law in Context* book on contract law could not be written. But early in my second year, the depression began to lift, and I suddenly found myself deeply, and indeed passionately excited by a new project. The catalyst was the appearance of a new short book on contract law by an American Professor, named Grant Gilmore, called provocatively, *The Death of Contract*.[7] Gilmore referred in this book to some casual remarks which I had tossed out in my own *Introduction to the Law of Contract*, suggesting that the nineteenth-century foundations of English contract law had been profoundly affected by the economic theories generally known as "classical economics" widely taken to have been founded by Adam Smith. At the time I had written this, the thought had no originality, and was not based on my own research. It was, in my student days, a cliche to say that English contract law was influenced by the laissez-faire ideas of the classical economists. But Grant Gilmore's little book reminded me that I had at one time thought seriously of pursuing this relationship, and I began, tentatively and cautiously at first, to browse in the library on the economic origins of the law of contract in the eighteenth and nineteenth centuries.

I rapidly became deeply engrossed in this subject, and soon discovered that I had all unknowingly, hit upon a gold mine for legal research. There was a huge mass of material of every kind about the historical relationships between law and economics (and even more, law and economic thought) in the last two centuries, most of it totally unknown to legal historians or contemporary academic lawyers. I soon realised that what I was studying was the whole history of a massive intellectual movement – the movement known as freedom of contract, or more broadly, laissez-faire – which had its foundations in post-Reformation England, but developed only slowly until the time of Adam Smith. In a sense, indeed, what I was studying was the historical foundations of the idea of the free market, and its association with

6 See p 130.
7 G Gilmore, *The Death of Contract* (1974).

the law. My work seemed particularly timely because 1974–75, when I first began to get involved seriously in this research, appeared to mark the absolute nadir in England of the whole concept of the free market. The return to office of Harold Wilson's second administration in 1974 had led, even among Conservatives, to a rather despairing belief that the days of the free market appeared over. Planning – by Government and Unions – appeared to control all economic activity. At the same time, the legal concept of freedom of contract was at its lowest point. Almost every kind of contract was subject to legal and statutory intervention which overrode the freedom of the parties on scores of vital issues. Indeed, whole areas of contract law had disappeared altogether, and were replaced by administrative mechanisms. All this meant that I was faced with a fascinating piece of history – the rise and fall of freedom of contract, a remarkable swing of a remarkable pendulum. Subsequent events indeed confirmed that this was a particularly good moment for this study, because after Mrs Thatcher's election win in 1979, it soon became clear that the same pendulum was beginning to swing rapidly in the opposite direction again. As I watched the political events of the 1980s, I was often amused to recollect how closely the renewed upward swing of the pendulum matched the earlier swing of the period from about 1750 to 1850. This meant that I had caught the movement precisely at the moment of its changing direction, and thus had a neat historical story to tell – the story of the rise and later the decline and fall of freedom of contract as an economic ideal and a legal concept.

Much to my relief I now found that Warwick University was actually a very good place for this research. Unlike most universities which have separate law libraries, Warwick had taken the deliberate policy decision of integrating the law library with the rest of the social sciences material. This was an enormous advantage to me, because it meant that I often stumbled across non-legal material on the shelves which would otherwise have remained unknown to me. I began to look at the shelves more closely in certain areas, and found all sorts of fascinating material about the history of economic thought, and its relationship to contract law. What was particularly exciting – as it always is to the academic – was the feeling that I was treading such virgin soil. Lawyers had simply never studied this material at all, and even English legal historians (with one or two isolated and uninfluential exceptions) had never shown any interest in the relationship between legal development and its social and economic environment. Indeed, English legal historians were far more interested in the mediaeval history of legal doctrine than they were in the nineteenth century. In this respect I found

Warwick a congenial place to work,[8] and I am glad to be able to make some amends for the rather critical and sour comments I have previously made about the University of Warwick – especially as the university later heaped coals of fire on my head by awarding me an honorary LLD degree[9] in 1989.[10]

I soon realised that I had a major project on hand, and began to sketch out the bones of a very wide-ranging book. I had at first intended to study the relationship of economics to contract law, as a contemporary theoretical matter, as well as in its historical context, and my reading was designed to produce a two-part book, the first historical and the second, contemporary. I actually read and collected enough material for this two-part study, but when eventually I started to write I soon realised that the historical side would absorb all my energies in the first instance. In the event, the second part of the study was never written, and though my notes remain intact, they are increasingly indecipherable, and I am afraid Part II will now never be written.

Part I was, in all conscience, enough. The research alone was a massive exercise. Because I was primarily interested in studying the relationship between economics (or economic thought) and the law, much of the material I sought was buried deep in historical literature which often had very little about the law. I found myself searching for needles in haystacks. I often had to read a whole book for single worthwhile reference, and became adept at skimming a book in the course of an evening. As the research progressed, my depression lifted, and was replaced by a prolonged burst of manic energy. I threw away my antidepressant pills and had instead to ask my doctor to prescribe me sleeping pills to enable my restless mind to get some sleep. I worked as I had never worked before. I brought home books to read every evening and every weekend. I carried around with me little reference cards on which I jotted down my notes, and for a year or two, I am afraid I neglected my family and virtually all other interests. I was obsessed with the work, and begrudged time spent in any other activity. Doing the

8 Atiyah clearly made an impact on his colleagues at Warwick. Avrom Sherr writes (A Sherr, "Editorial" (2011) 18 *International Journal of the Legal Profession* 1, 1):

> "[T]here were giants walking Warwick [in] . . . 1974 . . . Patrick Atiyah would buy a couple of jam doughnuts at about 11.00 in the morning, go into the Law School common room, feed up on a bit of the sugar and then let loose. It could have been a case decided the day before in the Court of Appeal or the House of Lords but it was equally likely to be the tennis, some element of politics or – anything. It was always unbelievably entertaining, the clearness of thought, the amazing perception and the humour both obvious and unacknowledged."

9 Warwick's higher doctoral degree in law.

10 See further p xxiii.

work in this obsessive way was probably an advantage in the end, because it was so concentrated in time, and I was so engrossed in it, that I carried much of the material and the ideas in my head during this period. This was invaluable, because the most interesting and most original part of what I sought to do was to relate these disparate sources of material into an integral whole. I needed to keep the material and the ideas continuously in the forefront of my mind so that I could constantly make mental notes of how the different pieces of my gigantic jigsaw all fitted together. Had I spent ten years over the task – which one could easily have done – and kept all my notes on computer-retrievable discs, I am quite certain that I would never have noticed many of the detailed relationships between my sources which kept obtruding on my mind because of the way I worked.

I was very interested to hear from a mutual friend some years later that my brother Michael's unique mathematical gifts appeared to consist also of a rare ability to relate phenomena across traditional boundaries, to see patterns in relationships where others had seen none. Although I never compared my abilities with his, I was struck by this apparently strange example of the influence of heredity.

Despite this renewed interest in my work there were still many things I found deeply unsatisfying about Warwick University, and I began to explore possibilities of escape. I approached an old Oxford friend, Don Harris, now Director of the new Socio-Legal Centre at Oxford, to see if there were any possibilities there. He regretfully explained to me that the Centre was financed by the SSRC (the Social Science Research Council, whose name Margaret Thatcher later insisted on changing to the Economic and Social Science Research Council) and that they were very short of funds themselves. He suggested that I contact the SSRC myself, so I did so, and discovered for the first time that the Council operated a scheme of personal research grants which paid an academic's salary for a year and enabled him to take a year off his normal teaching duties and devote himself full-time to a piece of research or writing. I was encouraged to apply for one of these grants, and to assist my application I sat down for the first time to sketch out a thirty-five-page synopsis of the work I was engaged in. I sent off an application for a grant for the academic year 1976–77 and early in 1976 I was told that I was one of the successful candidates. Not very long after this I opened my *Times* one morning to read that Professor HWR Wade had been appointed Master of Gonville and Caius College, Cambridge. That announcement was full of significance for me, because it meant that the Chair which Wade held at Oxford would now be vacant, and this was one of the only two Chairs at Oxford for which my interests made me eligible. The other Chair was held by Rupert Cross, my old tutor, and I knew he was due to retire in another two or three years' time. Until now I had assumed that that would be the earliest date when an opportunity might arise for me to return to Oxford. Now, suddenly, the opportunity presented itself at once.

Of course I knew that the competition for such a Chair would be intense but I also felt I would probably be one of the strongest candidates. I expected my chief rival to be Guenter Treitel, an old colleague, and also a Magdalen man, whose election to a fellowship at Magdalen had taken place the night on which I attended the BCL dinner at the end of my four-year stay at Oxford as a student. Treitel had thus been an Oxford fellow for over twenty years, and indeed had been promoted to the position of All Souls Reader in English Law the year I had arrived as a mere fellow at New College.[11] In one sense, therefore, he was the obvious and natural candidate. He was also a "safe" if rather conservative scholar, for whom I had a healthy respect – indeed we had once collaborated on an academic article in the 1960s.[12] But it did seem to me that Treitel's kind of scholarship was a little *too* safe and, indeed, was dated. His sole interest appeared to be in doctrinal analysis of contract legal questions, with the minimum of attention to policy issues. He never dabbled in broader policy issues, he would not touch economics, he appeared uninterested in history, and indeed, he hardly ever wrote on any subject except contract law. The question, of course, was whether Oxford would prefer a "safe" appointment, or a rather less conventional one. I did not have very long to wait. Contrary to its usual practice, the university made its decision with unusual rapidity, and only a few weeks after the closing date for applications for the Chair, I received a letter offering me the appointment. I learnt later that most of the internal Oxford members of the electoral committee had at first favoured Treitel,[13] but that the decision had been swung in my favour by the strong views expressed by the two external assessors, one from Cambridge and one from Manchester.[14] I must admit

11 Atiyah appears to have been mistaken about the chronology. Atiyah started at New College in 1964. Treitel was not appointed All Souls Reader in English Law until 1974: see FMB Reynolds, "Guenter Heinz Treitel 26 October 1928–14 June 2019" (2021) 19 *Biographical Memoirs of Fellows of the British Academy* 129, 140.

12 PS Atiyah and GH Treitel, "Misrepresentation Act 1967" (1967) 30 MLR 369.

13 The Oxford members of the committee included Tony Honoré, who had been Atiyah's colleague at New College: see p xiv. One suspects that he would have been in Atiyah's favour.

14 Unfortunately, efforts to determine the full composition of the committee have been unsuccessful. However, the minutes of the relevant meeting of St John's Governing Body record that Mark Freedland served as the College's representative on the panel. I am grateful to Mr Michael Riordan, the College's Archivist, for retrieving this detail.

that reading the letter of appointment from the University Registrar was one of the greatest moments of my life. A university professorship is probably not, to most people, a particularly exciting appointment, but to a person who has committed himself to an academic life, a professorship at Oxford does look close to the top of the greasy pole.

My appointment was announced in *The Times*,[15] and the following day I received an invitation to allow my name to appear in *Who's Who*. My children were much more impressed by this than by the appointment itself.

Because I had already secured my grant from the SSRC for the academic year 1976–77 the commencement of my appointment was deferred until 1 October 1977. So by the time the summer examinations were over at Warwick in 1976 I was able to look forward to some fourteen months free of normal teaching chores. By the autumn of 1976 I expected to be ready to start writing, but first I had an interesting few weeks in the United States. My work on the theoretical foundations of contract law had brought me into close contact with American writings in this area, and I was by now familiar with many of the leading names in the field working in American universities. Some of these I had corresponded with, and a few of them I had personally met. Amongst these was one who later became a close friend and an academic collaborator, Professor Robert Summers of Cornell University, or Bob as he was universally known. Bob was a man of many enthusiasms, indeed his whole approach to his life and his work was brimful of enthusiasm – "fantastic" was his favourite word, uttered as no mere cliche but with fervent belief. One of Bob's many enthusiasms was a love of Oxford. He had first visited Oxford to study legal theory informally under the guidance of Professor Herbert Hart, Oxford's distinguished legal theorist who had revivified the study of legal philosophy in England after almost a century of stagnation. Later Bob spent every sabbatical in Oxford, and eventually he acquired a small flat on the Woodstock Road to ease these visits, and facilitate further shorter visits. I had met him briefly when I was a fellow of New College in the 1960s, but it was on one of his sabbaticals in 1976 that I first got to know him closely. His wife Dorothy accompanied him on most visits, and Christine and I got to know them both very well. They had five children, and we had four, so we had much in common as families.

My SSRC grant included a generous expense allowance to enable me to visit a number of scholars in the United States who I wanted to meet and talk to before I settled down to my write my book, and Bob gave me helpful

15 *The Times* (London, 17 June 1976).

advice as to where I should go and who I should meet. I planned a three-week visit which took me to Yale, Harvard, Madison, Cornell, the University of Texas at Austin and a number of other law schools where I had particular friends or acquaintances. This was my first academic visit to the United States since 1968,[16] when I had been completely unknown there, and I was rather surprised to discover that I now had something of a reputation. At Yale I was invited to give a lecture to the first-year students, and to everyone's astonishment (including mine) the response was so great that the *venue* had to be changed twice to accommodate the audience. At Harvard I had been invited to present a paper to a group of social and legal historians, and had written a rough account of some of the main themes I intended to work into my book. This too went down very well and my sponsors, Professors Morton Horwitz and Duncan Kennedy were especially enthusiastic.

Both Horwitz and Kennedy were keenly interested in the nineteenth-century history of contract law,[17] and its relationship with social and economic conditions and ideals, though both of them took positions with which I was not myself much in sympathy. Horwitz adopted a more or classic Marxist analysis of the history of contract law, and attempted to demonstrate in his writings that, at least in America, the lawyers and judges had pursued a conscious policy of subsidising industry by externalising many costs onto the shoulders of workers or other third parties. While there may have been truth in this analysis in America, conditions in nineteenth-century England were very different and I was convinced that the story was much more complex than this. Apart from anything else, it was apparent to me that English nineteenth-century judges did not simply associate themselves as members of the "governing classes" against the labouring class. They saw themselves rather as arbitrators, mediating between the industrialists and commercial classes, and the rest of society – which included both the labourers and also the aristocratic landowners.

Duncan Kennedy wrote less than Horwitz, and his position was often difficult to grasp, but he was a wonderful person to listen to. His ideas poured out of him like the waters of Niagara Falls, and listening to him was very much like being under those Falls! The waters surged out, submerging rocks and difficulties, sweeping aside obstructions, sparkling with aphorisms, gems and quotations or references to writers and theorists, many of them unknown to me. On one occasion I spent an evening with Kennedy

16 See pp 123–125.
17 See, e.g., MJ Horwitz, *The Transformation of American Law, 1780–1860* (1977) ch 6.

and a young visitor to Harvard, called Richard Danzig who attempted for a couple of hours to stem the tide of Kennedy's brilliant talk, much more successfully than I could. It was an extraordinary evening of academic talk, such as I had never previously encountered, and I confess that I felt overwhelmed by it. For the first time in my life, I also felt I was growing old – I simply did not have the speed of mind to keep up with these two able and nimble intellects. Kennedy was one of the founders of a movement which became known as "Critical Legal Studies" and I got to know him, and the movement better when I spent a year at Harvard in 1982–83. At the appropriate place I shall say something more about this movement.[18]

I returned from America, excited, invigorated, and full of energy for the task ahead of me. I collected my notes, I arranged my desk, and a table by the side of it, so that I had plenty of room to work, and I settled down to write. It was all done on a manual typewriter – this was before word processors became commonplace amongst academics – and I typed with two or three fingers. But the work soon surged ahead. I often wrote as much as 8,000 words in a day. I wrote very fast, partly because I had sketched out the general story in my mind already, and partly because, as I had written my notes, I had often written them in a form which enabled me to incorporate them bodily in my text. Indeed, I had often kept even mental notes of the way I wanted to express things, and such was the speed at which I had been working that my mind was brimming over with all this material. I was also going through one of my "manic" phases, so that my mind raced ahead of my writing, and my nights were once again often restless as I composed sentences and paragraphs of my next chapters in the early hours of the morning, while still lying in bed.

By Christmas I had already written a large part of the book, and by the Spring of 1977 the back of the whole work had been broken. I had soon realised that my original idea of the two-part work, embracing both the historical and the contemporary studies, could not possibly be realised within the one volume. I concentrated therefore on my historical material, and the book took shape under the title *The Rise and Fall of Freedom of Contract*.

Throughout these months, Christine and I had spent some leisure hours house-hunting in and around Oxford, preparatory to our move there for the next academic year. We eventually found an old rectory, being disposed of by the Church authorities, in the village of Middleton Stoney, some ten miles north of Oxford, near Bicester. It was not (alas) one of those lovely

18 See pp 185–188.

old Georgian rectories in which Oxford seems to abound – we could never have afforded such a house – but it did all the same have much to offer. It was large enough to accommodate our four sons, even though two of them were now adults and did not make their homes with us all the time. It had a large garden of nearly an acre, which included a splendid old orchard, and a huge area of lawn which (we discovered later) had originally been laid out as a tennis court. But it was all in a pretty dreadful condition, and a great deal of work had to be done to the house and the garden. The rectory was empty and, as soon as we exchanged contracts around February or March, we were given access to start work on it. The more serious work – installation of a new bathroom, and extension of the central heating, etc – obviously had to be professionally done, but the redecoration of the house, and various other do-it-yourself repairs and renovations I resolved to do myself; the roof of the large garden "shed" or "tennis-room" as it proclaimed itself needed to be recovered and this was largely done by Julian. The garden, too, I tackled with assistance from the family, even to the extent of restoring the old tennis court. For some three or four months, from March until July when we finally moved in, I combined the intellectual effort of working on my book, with bursts of physical energy, working on the house. My "manic" phase reached an extraordinary peak during these months, extending both to the intellectual and the physical. It was probably not very healthy, but it served a very useful purpose, because it enabled me to redecorate the entire house, generally renovate it in other ways, and at the same time, get the garden under control. By July I had virtually finished the book, and very nearly exhausted myself as well. Indeed, the physical work had affected the muscles in my hands and I had to consult a doctor who was somewhat bemused to be told that I was a university professor; at the same time he sternly warned me to rest my hands or else they would be severely damaged.

This extreme "manic" phase of my depressive condition inevitably had its reaction, and in my first term at Oxford the depression returned. But it was never so acute again, and though I had to resort to my anti-depressants for another year I was finally able to give them up for good not long after.

12 Oxford Again

So in the summer of 1977 the family moved once again back to Oxford, or at least its environs, and I took up my Chair in October. One of our first problems was the education of our two younger sons, Simon and Jeremy. By this time Julian was twenty-three, and Andrew was well settled at Leeds University, but Simon and Jeremy were still at school. The nearest secondary school to us in Middleton Stoney was the Bicester Comprehensive, and although we were not, at this time, opposed to the Comprehensive schools in principle, what we heard about this school filled us with some foreboding. On the other hand, Simon had just taken his O-levels with considerable success at Leamington College; university education, perhaps even at Oxford, seemed well within his grasp, and we felt that two years at Bicester would not destroy his prospects. Jeremy, however, still had four or five years at school, and as he showed great promise and interest in classics, we decided to send him to Magdalen College School, a direct grant day school (as it was in those days), although the cost was heavy.

But after a few weeks it became apparent that things at the Bicester school were just not working well. Simon's A-level mathematics class actually included students who had failed O-level maths. and for the whole of the first half of the autumn term he did nothing which he had not previously done for his O-levels. The lack of inspiration was also deadening in its effects, and Simon was almost ceasing to be his usual cheery self. By half-term matters were becoming urgent, and we decided to transfer him also to Magdalen College School. The cost was very heavy, and we would have had great difficulty in affording it – I was already paying Andrew the maximum parental contribution while he was at university, and this was a time when after several years of Labour Governments, university salaries were distinctly depressed. If necessary I would have raised further money on our mortgage, but in the event help came from the family. Michael generously offered to lend us what we needed, and shortly afterwards Christine's parents sold their house in Surrey and bought a small bungalow in Bicester in order to live near us. With what they saved by this exchange they paid Simon's school fees for the remainder of his two years at Magdalen. We could not but be struck by the fact that Christine's parents, working class as they would have been the first to admit, long-standing Labour voters, and by now the traditional "old age pensioners" who, according to Labour mythology were the downtrodden poor, should have been able to render this assistance to us, a middle-class family, who could not afford to educate our own children.

Despite this financial assistance we were for several years quite hard up after our move – I had actually had to take a cut in salary when I took up my Oxford Chair. Country life, with two children having to be ferried to and from school every day necessitated two cars which stretched our resources to the utmost. Christine's parents again came to her help, assisting her to buy a modest second-hand Fiat 127, while I disposed of my old Ford Cortina and bought a tiny two-cylinder Fiat 126. For the next two years I drove Simon and Jeremy to and from school in this car six days a week, even though there was barely room for the three of us – Simon was by this time ten or eleven stone, and Jeremy was about six foot tall. The extreme modesty of my car occasionally caused me some embarrassment, as when I had to give a lift to a distinguished American visiting professor, who was no doubt more used to driving around in a land battleship. On one occasion, after I had attended one of the college's annual black-tie dinners I left the college in company with a distinguished honorary fellow. As we separated in the college carpark, I saw him head for his elegant Jaguar, while I climbed into my 126. I was out first, heading North, and my colleague followed me. For some moments I suspect he felt too embarrassed to overtake me, but eventually he did so, practically sweeping my 126 into the ditch as he roared past!

The problem of schools and cars solved, we were now able to settle down to our new life. My first year or two were quiet ones. My statutory obligations as a Professor at Oxford required of me only thirty-six hours teaching a year, so I was able to devote much more time to writing and research. This certainly suited me because I was far more interested in my own research, and I was not a particularly gifted teacher. Though I had never really enjoyed tutorial work,[1] I did not dislike lecturing, and all my teaching now took the form of lecturing, though with occasional seminars. I was, of course, able to choose the subjects on which I wanted to lecture and in my first year I gave a course of lectures on the Foundations of Contractual Liability which became sufficiently popular to be worth repeating every year I was at Oxford. Of course, as always at Oxford, lectures were voluntary for the students, and although one often began the course with over

1 See p 131.

a hundred students, a lecturer was doing quite well if he retained twenty throughout his course. Another course I gave in my first year proved less popular – indeed my audience faded away almost entirely. This was on Law and Society in the Nineteenth Century, but at Oxford legal history concentrated heavily on the mediaeval period, and nineteenth-century history hardly figured at all in the Legal History paper in Schools. So most students found it too extra-curricular to be worth attending. I was disappointed that one of my main interests, stemming from my work on the history of freedom of contract, did not figure sufficiently in the syllabus to enable me to maintain this course of lectures, but I felt reluctantly compelled to drop it after the first year.

The great growth of academic interest in the relationship between law and economics had, at this stage, made virtually no ripple on the placid waters of Oxford, but not long after I took up my Chair, Don Harris at the Socio-Legal Centre took the initiative in planning a new BCL course on Remedies in Contract and Tort, which was intended to have a modest element of introductory economics. This subject was particularly well suited for introducing economics to law students because there was a considerable and reasonably intelligible literature on it in the United States, and it was also a subject in which economic considerations were often very visible, even in the judgments of English judges who rarely explicitly adverted to them. A small team of about half a dozen Oxford fellows planned this new course, taking considerable trouble over the teaching arrangements. A proposed new BCL optional subject, supported in this way, normally had no difficulty in being approved by the Law Board but unfortunately we ran into considerable opposition from Professor Treitel, ostensibly on the ground that the new course would overlap with the established course on Restitution which he was engaged in teaching, and that this would involve a loss of students from that course.

Treitel had by this time succeeded Rupert Cross in the Vinerian Chair,[2] but he had returned to Oxford after a long spell in America in an apparently

2 Francis Reynolds writes in FMB Reynolds, "Guenter Treitel" (2020) 19 *Biographical Memoirs of Fellows of the British Academy* 129, 141:

> "In 1978 the Vinerian Chair of English Law fell vacant with the retirement of Professor Sir Rupert Cross and was advertised. Guenter did not apply: he records that it seemed pointless in view of his unsuccessful application for the St John's Chair two years earlier, and that he did not want to trouble his referees a second time. However, the electors resolved in April 1978 to invite him to accept election, and this he did (though not in an entirely straightforward way, the resolution of which was complicated by the fact that the Registrar took it on himself

hostile mood. Whether he harboured resentment against me for having secured my professorial appointment before him I know not, but he certainly behaved in a very strange way on this occasion. When he had first returned from America to take up the Vinerian Chair, the Board had recently made its decision about launching the *Oxford Journal of Legal Studies*, and I had written a friendly letter to Treitel, bringing him up to date on what had happened, inviting his general support for the journal, and in particular, offering to publish his inaugural lecture which was then pending. Treitel had at first responded sympathetically, and had promised to let us have the lecture for publication, so that we had announced it as one of our first batch of articles in our pre-launch publicity material. But after the Law Board had voted to establish the new Remedies course over Treitel's opposition he reacted furiously, and wrote me an angry letter demanding his lecture back and refusing to let us publish it. This was a side of Treitel that I had never seen before, and I was somewhat astonished by it. I thought perhaps he had reacted in a brief moment of anger, and might think better of it later, so I wrote a mollifying reply, suggesting that he might prefer to think the matter over for a day or two and saying that in the meantime I would keep his manuscript which we were still anxious to publish. I thought that its non-appearance after it had been announced in our preliminary publicity material might actually cause him some embarrassment. Again I had an angry reply, demanding the return of his manuscript, and an insistence that he would not be embarrassed by its non-appearance. So I returned the lecture to him.[3] Treitel resigned from the Law Board (to which he had just been elected) and also from the team teaching the Restitution course – which, as it happened, was not significantly affected by the new Remedies course. After that I scarcely exchanged two words with Treitel for the whole of the rest of my tenure of my Chair – during which he also refused to rejoin the Law Board, an almost unheard of proceeding for the Vinerian Professor.

We began teaching the new course in 1981, and it was immediately apparent that we had a considerable success on our hands. It was popular with the BCL students, and we regularly had twenty or even thirty students taking it. We distributed the lecturing responsibility among the several interested parties and all joined together in a series of seminars at which we tried to pull

to negotiate with him without consulting the Faculty Board). In the result his appointment ran from October 1979, no doubt partly because of his existing commitments in the United States."

3 The lecture was published as G Treitel, *Doctrine and Discretion in the Law of Contract* (1981).

the subject together. Of course, by some standards the economic element was rather elementary if not jejune, but most of our students had not done economics before university at all, so this was probably inevitable. I myself wrote a completely original course of lectures on Remedies for Nuisance in which I introduced economic arguments very extensively, and I also took responsibility for two or three of the seminars every year.

I had, of course, also to play my role as an administrator, though fortunately my duties on this side were never too heavy. I was immediately elected to the Law Board and played a fairly vigorous role on that Board and its committees throughout my tenure of the Chair. I was also, as is the custom at Oxford, attached to a college, and was duly elected to my fellowship at St John's. I played a modest part in college activities, and for some years at least I took seriously my duties as a member of the governing body. I was given a small room in St John's, though of course (as is also the custom at Oxford) secretarial services and other facilities for professors were severely lacking. I never had my own secretary, though I was entitled to the services of the secretarial office in the Law Faculty building at the magnificent Oxford Law Library. This lack of secretarial assistance was only a minor irritant, however, and in general I greatly enjoyed being back in Oxford. Indeed, I enjoyed the quiet of those first two years when I was able to get on with my own work, and in particular, to finish off my *magnum opus*, *The Rise and Fall of Freedom of Contract*, and see it through the press – it was published, as were nearly all my new books, by the Oxford University Press.

Later, as I became better known, and my reputation grew overseas, the demands on my time grew correspondingly. I began to get invitations to give lectures, and papers, to attend conferences, to evaluate books for publication, to sit on professorial selection committees and so forth. One of the professorial selection committees I was called upon to attend a few years later was at Cambridge where I was put up for the night. I was sorry to be away from home that particular night because it was the night that Simon's results in the Law Society's final examinations were due to appear. At that time the results were published in *The Daily Telegraph* and *The Times* and the articled clerks (as they used to be called) streamed down to Fleet Street late the previous night to get hold of the early editions as they came off the presses about midnight. But that year the newspapers were on strike (this was before Rupert Murdoch smashed the print unions by moving *The Times* to Wapping) and the candidates did not know when or how they would get their results. Simon later told us that they went down to Fleet Street to be greeted by pickets who swore that they would never get their results that night, and who prevented their entering the offices at *The Daily Telegraph* where the results had been posted up; however, at *The Times* the results were actually read out to them by somebody in the road, and Simon did not have long to wait before hearing his own name. Luckily, he was able to phone Christine and she phoned me in my Cambridge hotel around midnight.

After a while I began to get a stream of overseas visitors, who were attracted to Oxford like filings to a magnet. Scholars from all over the world would write to me, telling me they proposed to visit Oxford and asking if they could meet me. Oxford also made increasing demands on my time, after the first year or two, although in the politest possible way. Indeed mostly, these were requests rather than demands, but as they were the kind of thing a university professor was expected to do, I naturally did them.

Shortly after my return the Law Faculty began to explore the possibility of sponsoring the publication of a law journal, in conjunction with the Oxford University Press. I was asked to participate in these discussions, and when the decision was made to go ahead, I was invited by the Law Board to be the first general editor of the journal, which was christened the *Oxford Journal of Legal Studies*. This Journal appeared three times a year, and I remained general editor for the first six years, so I was responsible for seeing eighteen numbers through the press. It was a very demanding task, and this time the lack of secretarial assistance was rather more than a minor irritant, because I had to do a great part of the thing on my own. I had colleagues to assist me with notes and with book reviews, and members of the Oxford Faculty were very generous in evaluating much of the material submitted, but I made myself responsible for most of the editorial decisions, and a great deal of the basic organisation and the work of proof-reading fell to me. When I visited American law schools, which I did very frequently from 1979 onwards, I marvelled at the equipment and financial and secretarial assistance with which they produced their own law journals. In most cases, they had a large room of their own (at Harvard a whole building!) equipped with half a dozen word processors, and a like number of secretaries. These journals were edited by the students, and in most cases the editorial committee amongst whom the work was divided numbered perhaps twenty or more students. I flattered myself that the quality of academic law journals was not proportionate to their cost of production. Our *Journal* rapidly established itself in the academic community, and I soon began to receive contributions from round the world.

My relative freedom from academic chores at this time left me plenty of time for diversionary activities and I was a regular letter-writer to *The Times*, which usually published my letters. On one occasion I wrote an immensely long letter[4] about a decision of the House of Lords[5] in a case involving a large-scale steel strike which had provoked much interest and publicity. My letter was provoked by the bland insistence of the judges in the House of Lords that they had nothing to do with policy issues, and were merely enforcing the law. I wanted the sophisticated readers of *The Times* to understand that it was not wholly true to say that judges were never involved in policy issues, because major appellate decisions often required some selection among the policies available, even if it was only to insist that certain kinds of policy decision were actually less objectionable in coming from the judiciary than others. My letter stirred up quite a response, and I also received a private (and handwritten) letter from Lord Denning, at that time Master of the Rolls. Lord Denning had taken a much more active or interventionist view of the judicial role in these strike cases, but he rather misunderstood the gist of my letter which he appeared to regard as supporting his position. I was, however, somewhat amused by his letter which recounted that he had received letters of support for his decisions from trade unionists of many years standing, while one of the Law Lords who had reversed his decision, Lord Diplock, "received nothing but letters of abuse"!

A letter of support from an active member of the judiciary was rather unusual; but on another occasion I received a letter from Lord Simon of Glaisdale about an academic note I had published in the *Law Quarterly Review*.[6] This was also a letter of support which I found particularly useful when another academic wrote a reply to my note,[7] and with Lord Simon's consent, I was able to quote from his letter to me in a final and crushing rejoinder.[8] It is not often that academics can actually quote a letter of

4 *The Times* (London, 12 February 1980).

5 *Express Newspapers v McShane* [1980] AC 672 (HL).

6 PS Atiyah, "Economic Duress and 'The Overborne Will'" (1982) 98 LQR 197.

7 D Tiplady, "Concepts of Duress" (1983) 99 LQR 188.

8 PS Atiyah, "Duress and the Overborne Will Again" (1983) 99 LQR 353. In his original note, Atiyah had argued that the case of *Lynch v DPP of Northern Ireland* [1975] AC 653 (HL) involved a "unanimous and authoritative rejection of the 'overborne will theory' of duress": (n 8 at 200). In his reply, Tiplady contended that *Lynch* involved no such rejection. To support this, Tiplady cited Lord Simon to the effect that the words "will" and "wish" are often used interchangeably (n 9 at 193). Atiyah's response reads (n 10 at 354):

> "Perhaps I may be permitted to quote (with permission) the following from a letter to me by Lord Simon himself:
>
> > 'I was astonished that the writer of the L.Q.R. should have quoted me to the effect that *will* and *wish*, etc., etc., have frequently been used interchangeably, as if I myself thought they were juridically (or even psychologically) interchangeable. It should have been obvious that I was protesting against the confusion. I used "wish" advisedly when I had a shot at definition.'"

support from the judge in question when they have written about a judicial decision of that judge, so this was a rather satisfying occasion.

As I became better known in the academic world I began to get occasional inquiries from the media about legal issues. These usually took the form of telephone calls in which I was told that somebody was considering making a radio or television programme about some legal question that might interest me, with a fairly clear hint that I might be invited to take part in the programme and I was asked a few preliminary questions. At first I responded generously with my time and knowledge to these calls, and they often went on for half an hour or more; but as I never heard anything more of the proposed programmes afterwards, I began to become more suspicious and cynical. Indeed, I soon realised that this was a cheap and easy way for programme producers to obtain information, and the time came when I responded to such a call by announcing in advance that if I was going to be asked to give a substantial amount of time to their inquiries I would expect a fee for my assistance even if the programme came to nothing. Surprisingly enough this did not deter the callers, and I did in fact collect a few fees from this sort of thing.

On two occasions it seemed that I was actually going to take part in a television programme. Once I was approached by Thames Television about a programme they planned concerning the law of negligence and its bearing on those injured or affected by defective drugs. This was, of course, one of my special interests, and after we had discussed this for some time the company said they would like me to give them a few minutes of my time answering questions for their programme. They came round to my study at St John's College, with their equipment, and we had an interesting question-and-answer session for thirty or forty minutes. I was intrigued to discover that the filming of the questions and of the answers was done entirely separately – I was first asked the questions and was filmed while I responded; the camera was then turned on my interviewer who was filmed posing all the questions in succession. It was much easier to splice the questions into the answers, I was told, than to keep turning the camera round from the interviewer to the speaker. Anyhow, all appeared to go well, and I was duly thanked and told that they would let me know when the programme was to be televised. On the day in question I and my family all trooped into the television room only to discover that the programme had been replaced at the last minute by another. A few days later I had rather an embarrassed phone call from a member of the programme-team who told me that there had been some legal problems about the film, and an injunction had been granted against the company which prevented them from showing it. They assured me, however, that they would appeal. Some months later I was reading the law report in *The Times* about a case in the Court of Appeal when it gradually dawned on me that this was the very case concerning the programme for which I had been filmed. The Court of Appeal, by a majority, dismissed the appeal, but Lord Denning dissented and would have allowed it. (For interested lawyers the case was *Schering Chemicals Ltd v Falkman Ltd* [1981] 2 All ER 321 (CA)). I did not relish being censored by order of the Court of Appeal and, partial though I may have been, I felt Lord Denning was right on this, as well as on numerous other occasions when he dissented.

My next venture into television proved no more successful. I was approached by Granada Television who ran the very successful series of programmes built around hypothetical problems. For those who have not seen any of these programmes, they consist of a moderator who asks a number of visiting experts and professionals a series of questions about how they would behave in a given hypothetical situation, often involving difficult moral dilemmas. The questions are often varied by posing small alterations in the hypothetical situation to see how people would respond to these changes. With an interesting subject, a wide and varied "cast" and a skilful moderator, the programmes were sometimes very successful. Curiously enough, these programmes were originally based on the style of teaching for which the Harvard Law School had become famous. The so-called Socratic method of teaching at Harvard consisted of taking a case from the Law Reports, and questioning the students about possible fact-variations to test their powers of analysing relevance, and to see how consistently they could maintain a position. Many of the Harvard law faculty were highly proficient at this method of teaching which was undoubtedly an excellent teaching instrument, as well as a possible entertainment. (But as an entertainment it eventually ran into trouble as students began to complain that it held them up to ridicule and exposed their weaknesses.)

When Granada launched their series of hypotheticals they often recruited Harvard Law School professors as their moderators, but somebody obviously wondered whether English law professors might not be able to do the job, and one day I got a telephone call from Brian Lapping who directed the programmes, asking whether I would be interested in taking part. I am afraid I reacted at first with some caution, indeed suspicion, after my earlier experiences with television companies. But it gradually became clearer to me that I was being offered a chance of "star billing" in a major programme. I soon began to realise what star billing meant in the television world.

When I discovered that the programme was due to be filmed at some fabulous castle in the north of England, starting on a Friday evening (to which my family were invited) I protested that I had a seminar at Oxford on Fridays which lasted until 6.30 pm. No problem, I was assured. I would be picked up by car, driven to the airport and flown north by private plane with my family. Not surprisingly I accepted the invitation and over the summer I spent many hours working with the Granada producers over a possible programme. This was a programme without (in the first instance) a script or a theme. It was my task, working with the producer, to conjure up a theme and some sort of script. Of course, the essence of the programme was that it was largely spontaneous; so the "script" consisted more of a scenario in which I dreamt up a series of questions to be put to the various "experts". The theme we were working on was a political one: it concerned the ways in which politicians would pressure their colleagues in favour of a policy – using expert reports, leaks, arm-twisting and so on, to push a favoured project. Everything seemed to be going quite well, and we had a couple of rehearsals, the second of which at Brown's Hotel was quite an elaborate affair at which a number of ex-Labour ministers were present like Peter Shore, Merlyn Rees and others. There were three moderators on this occasion: Benno Schmidt from Columbia Law School, another man who had previously done one of the most successful of the programmes, and me. I thought I had done reasonably well on this occasion, especially as I got Peter Shore to admit that if he commissioned a report which supported his project he would present it to the Cabinet, while if it opposed the project he would probably have suppressed it. But my performance did not satisfy the producers and I was politely but firmly told that they did not after all want me on the programme – though they did pay me off quite handsomely. Thus, ignominiously, ended my television career before it had begun. I returned to my law books.

As time went on, and especially after the publication of my *magnum opus The Rise and Fall of Freedom of Contract*, I began to receive more and more invitations to visit overseas law schools to lecture or (especially in America) to spend a sabbatical term or year. One of the first of these invitations actually caused me considerable personal difficulties as it came from the Hebrew University of Jerusalem. I was invited to deliver the Lionel Cohen lecture in 1979.[9] This lecture was founded by an English judge, and it was organised by an English charitable trust which paid all the expenses. But when I first received the invitation I felt great difficulties about accepting. I could hardly

9 PS Atiyah, "Judges and Policy" (1980) 15 *Israel Law Review* 346.

forget that my father had spent the last twenty years of his life defending the rights of the Palestinian Arabs against Israel; I myself had known at school Arab boys who had lost their homes in Palestine; Israel was still occupying parts of my father's native land, Lebanon. At first, I declined the invitation. But I then had a very persuasive letter from Mr Jonathan Cohen, the Chairman of the Trustees in which he expressed his sadness about the prospects of future peace in the Middle East if people like me felt unable to act as a bridge between Arab and Jew, and so eventually I accepted. I insisted that my hosts should know of my Arab background, and though I went as a legal scholar and not as a political or public figure, I found the visit a sad occasion. On the one hand my hosts in the Hebrew University were welcoming and hospitable. Of course it was impossible not to feel sympathy with the Jewish people, visiting them in their homes and in the university. Most of them, in their own environment, seemed decent enough people, simply trying to live their lives in peace and with security. Indeed, I found that many in the legal profession were among those most concerned to defend and uphold Arab rights. On the other hand I could not escape the feeling that the Arabs in Israel (even in Israel proper, not just the occupied territories) were treated and felt themselves to be treated, as though they were the indigenous inhabitants in an enemy-occupied land. One evening my wife and I took a taxi to some event and we exchanged a word or two with the taxi-driver in Arabic. He was clearly very puzzled as to our identity, and eventually burst out with: "Inta yehudi?" – "Are you a Jew?" I explained my Arab parentage to him, whereupon he began to speak freely and vehemently about the situation of the Arabs. He begged us to visit him in his home, which we would very much like to have done, but unfortunately there was simply no time.

Other invitations proved more enjoyable. During these years I visited Germany, Holland, Canada (several times), Japan, Sweden, Hong Kong and several other places to lecture or give seminars. The visit to Sweden took place in 1988 after I had retired. I went to give the annual Cassel lecture at the University of Stockholm,[10] and Christine and I were treated almost royally. We stayed at the Grand Hotel (where I was told the Nobel prize winners are put up when they come to collect their awards) and were given a magnificent suite of rooms facing the sea and the Royal Palace. On our first evening we were invited to have a quiet meal in the hotel and pressed to order whatever we wanted at the expense of the Cassel foundation. Despite this I could not quite bring myself to order a bottle of Chateau Laffite at dinner

10 PS Atiyah, *Essays on Contract* (1986) ch 12.

when I saw it priced at some £250, but in fact we got our glass of Chateau Laffitte a night or two later at a private dinner given to us by Jan Hellner, Stockholm's most distinguished (and probably richest) law professor.

My invitation to visit Hong Kong proved most timely, as it arrived just a week before my son Simon left for Hong Kong to work for his employers (the legal firm Linklaters and Paines) for a couple of years. Although I was then still recovering from my heart operation I accepted the invitation for the following year and Christine and I spent several enjoyable weeks in Hong Kong over the Christmas period of 1988–89. My visit to Japan proved the most demanding of these overseas excursions. I spent three weeks there in the autumn of 1983, the first lecturing at Tokyo University, the third at Osaka University and the middle week I was allowed to enjoy myself as a tourist. My visit was sponsored by an insurance company, though my immediate host was a Japanese law professor who made all the arrangements. The academic side of the visit proved heavy and demanding. My hosts had set up a number of "teams", rather like task-forces, whose job had been to study my works so that they could contribute seriously to a series of seminars. These seminars were sometimes all-day affairs, with a break for lunch, and even allowing for the fact that everything had to be translated, a prodigious amount of work seemed involved. In England a seminar was usually a fairly leisurely affair, lasting for one-and-a-half or perhaps two hours, but these seminars ran for five or six hours. What was more, I felt as though I was almost "on trial" since the object of the seminars was often to enable my hosts to question me and challenge my ideas. It was not unknown for one of them to ask me to reconcile different things I had said in my writings, and quotations were thrown at me from my own books! At the end of the third week, with a final all-day session eventually winding up at six in the evening I was just about feeling all in when my host announced that he would now call on me to sum up the discussions of the past three weeks! At this point I politely but firmly declined, and suggested that perhaps it was best to leave matters where they were.

By far the greater number of my invitations came from America, and I spent several sabbaticals teaching in America during the next few years, as well as making many shorter visits there for conferences and lectures. My first visit was in 1979 when I spent a semester at the University of Texas at Austin. Christine and I enjoyed Texas very much – contrary to popular image we did not find the people of Texas (or anyhow Austin where we stayed) brash and vulgar but actually rather old-fashioned and courteous. Shortly afterwards I was invited to deliver one of the Oliver Wendell Holmes

Figure 12.1 St John's College, Oxford. Credit: By permission of the President and Fellows of St John's College, Oxford.

Lectures at Harvard Law School in 1981, one of the greatest honours which can be bestowed on a legal scholar in the common law world, and on that occasion Christine and I took the opportunity to visit my sister in California for a week, financed by lectures at Berkeley and Stanford. In fact the publication of *The Rise and Fall of Freedom of Contract* suddenly made me a well-known figure in the American academic legal community and when I casually told an American friend in 1980 that I was contemplating spending another sabbatical term in America I suddenly began to receive phone calls from all over the United States. In one week, in fact, I received phone calls from the Deans of Cornell, Virginia, Boston University and eventually Harvard, inviting me to spend a semester as a visiting professor with them. Because of the time difference between England and America many of these calls came through in the evenings when I was at home, and my wife often answered the phone. As the invitations came flocking in, things got to such a pass that whenever some secretary announced on the phone that Dean so-and-so of the such-and-such Law School wished to speak to Professor Atiyah my wife would say, as she passed me the phone, "Don't accept" (or, very occasionally, "Say yes"!). In the event I spent the academic year of 1982–83 teaching at Harvard.

13 America

I found my visits to America very exciting as well as very rewarding occasions, in all senses. Not only was I paid salaries far in excess of what I earned in England, but I also found myself in great demand as a visitor to other law schools and institutions. Almost every other weekend I would fly to another part of the country to visit some other law school, to give a lecture or a faculty seminar. Every such invitation was made on the basis of all my expenses being paid and in addition I was usually paid an honorarium of several hundred dollars. (Occasionally I was also invited to give endowed lectures designed for publication where the honoraria were much higher.) On these visits I was nearly always entertained at dinner by several members of the faculty, often with their wives, all at law school expense. On many occasions Christine's travel and other expenses were also covered by my hosts. One of the most lavish of these occasions occurred on my visit to Texas in 1979 when Tulane University in New Orleans invited me to give a lecture under a special "Shell" programme. This was a substantial fund held by the law school for the purpose of entertaining visiting guest lecturers, and both Christine and I were royally entertained for three days in the French quarter of New Orleans, being taken to all the best restaurants for lunch and dinner.

During my year at Harvard I travelled extensively around the country, giving lectures and seminars at Yale, Columbia, Cornell, Virginia, Duke University (in North Carolina), Iowa, Indiana, SMU at Dallas and other places. At Harvard itself I taught torts to a first-year class which was one of the most enjoyable teaching experiences I have ever had. The first-year students at Harvard are the cream of the country's college graduates, bursting with the desire to learn and to outshine their contemporaries. In many ways the first semester determines their future, because the best performers during that semester are quickly earmarked as members of the editorial team which will look after the *Harvard Law Review*, and at the end of their first year they are already securing vacation jobs with legal firms who will probably offer them regular employment when they graduate. Once the first year is over, motivation wanes, and indeed, by then many of the brightest students begin to be bored by book-learning. They will by then have done four years of college and one year of law school, and during that year they will have mastered legal techniques sufficiently thoroughly to enable them to get up any other legal subject. So although their knowledge of law is still limited, they begin to have an understandable urge to get to grips with real problems. Indeed, many of them are able to do a certain amount of this after the first year, while still studying, because they get recruited as research assistants to some of the professors with substantial outside practices. But during the first year, and especially the first semester, their enthusiasm is unbounded, and oral discussion in a class of a hundred well-prepared students is a real pleasure. Torts is also one of the subjects best suited to this kind of teaching because the discussion can centre round the fascinating case law of the subject, and then range far and wide. Many of my students were also much older and more mature than the average English undergraduate. At least a third of the class had been out in the world for several years since leaving college, many of them had first-class academic records in other subjects for which they had discovered little demand in the American marketplace, and these students therefore contributed a maturity of knowledge and sophistication to our discussions. I greatly enjoyed this class and I think my enjoyment was reciprocated. Several of my students went out of their way to tell me privately that my class had been the high-mark of their first semester.

In my second semester I found the teaching much harder going. I gave an optional course on no-fault compensation on a comparative basis but I must confess that I failed to rouse a great deal of interest in my students and I found (as I had been warned) that teaching optional courses was much harder work. I also gave a seminar on the theory of contract which attracted quite a large group of advanced students, many of whom had studied economics or philosophy to a much higher level than I had ever done myself. This was the most advanced piece of teaching I have ever done in my life, and I had to work very hard to keep my nose ahead of my students. It was very demanding but also intellectually satisfying and I think most of my students got a good deal of stimulus from the seminars.

One thing made a great impression on me at Harvard, and that was the power and status of an independent institution in the United States. Like most of the great American universities Harvard is a private institution which does not depend on government money in the way all British universities do. Its income comes from fees and its immense endowments; its status and prestige come partly from its wealth, and partly from the number of famous alumni. But it also comes from its independence from the government. During my year at Harvard, this independence was illustrated by an incident, or series of incidents, which I felt demonstrated the immense gulf between the position of a great private university like Harvard and a government-financed university like Oxford. The Harvard students had pressed the university authorities to subscribe to a non-discrimination declaration which committed the university to the principle of non-discrimination (amongst other groups) against homosexuals, and the university had eventually agreed to do this. But the declaration was no mere statement of ideals: it was meant to be acted on, and one way in which the university did act upon it was by refusing facilities to potential employers who visited the university for recruiting staff unless these employers also accepted the same principle of non-discrimination. Most employers complied readily enough but (for perhaps obvious reasons) the United States Navy did not. Harvard stuck to its guns: if the Navy would not subscribe to the declaration, they would be refused access to the university for recruitment. The Navy responded by threatening that in that event they would simply not recruit from Harvard at all. The impasse was not resolved while I was still at Harvard and I do not know the eventual outcome of this battle. But I rejoiced in it. It seemed to me the sign of a healthy society when a private institution was powerful enough to challenge the federal government itself. I could not imagine such a thing happening in England. For this reason I have long felt that a great university like Oxford should stop taking money directly from the government. Oxford should, in my view, simply insist on raising its fees to a level adequate to cover its costs. Students on public grants would continue to have their fees paid as they do now so they should be no worse off. Foreign students would of course find their fees increased, and doubtless the university would need to raise more private endowments to assist needy students with generous grants and loans. I cannot believe that a university with Oxford's name and status could not achieve its independence in this way. I did once try to persuade Sir Rex Richards, when he was Vice-Chancellor, of the desirability of this course, but I got nowhere, and so far as I am aware, no such proposal has ever been seriously entertained in Oxford.

Fortunately for me, some of the troubles which later beset Harvard and American universities in general did not impinge on me too severely. The problem of "politically correct language" had not yet begun to surface seriously, although I did learn that some students thought I treated feminine issues too lightly.

There were, however, deep divisions in the Harvard Faculty which made the place an unhappy one for the permanent faculty in the Law School.

Harvard was the centre of the movement known as "Critical Legal Studies" and a minority of the Law School were active members of this movement. The "crits" as they were often called were fundamentally political radicals who rejected much at the centre of American society and culture. While some were just plain old-fashioned socialists, many were just as hostile to big government as they were to capitalist economics and culture, and it was never too clear to me exactly what they did want or believe in. The one thing that united them was a belief that law as practised in America was largely a fraud in its pretence at being neutral and impartial among all people. They claimed that legal principles were largely indeterminate because it was possible to justify almost any kind of decision with some legal principle or other, and that what actually happened in practice was that decisions were systematically biased in favour of the property classes, the underpinnings of capitalism and so on. To many English people it will seem strange that such beliefs were regarded as somehow relevant to legal education rather than as purely political matters to be fought over at elections. But the crits, though very political animals, did not want to fight elections. Their programme (insofar as they had a positive programme at all) appeared to be designed to enable them to launch a sort of *coup d'état* through the judiciary. Ideally they would have liked a President to appoint a majority of crits to the United States Supreme Court who would thereupon have begun to remould American society. I could not help thinking that America was the only country in the world in which one would plan a *coup d'état* by seizing control of the judiciary.

I never had much sympathy for the crits myself. It seemed to me their sudden appearance in the 1980s was largely due to the fact that America had never had a serious socialist political party with really radical left-wing programmes. Although the crits were by no means all socialists, they were radicals and left-wingers in the broadest sense. I regarded their premises as fundamentally flawed and anyhow largely dominated by peculiarities of the American legal system. I never accepted the basic thesis that legal principles are fundamentally indeterminate and can justify anything at all. This has always seemed to me an absurd exaggeration, though within limits there is truth in it, because in marginal situations, in difficult borderline cases, legal principles may not provide an adequate guide to a decision. It is true that there are many peculiarities of the American legal system which make its law much more uncertain, and its legal principles far more indeterminate than in most other countries – indeed I was working on a book at this time which attempted to explain and document this fact.[1] But even where legal principles are indeterminate I have always been happy to accept that judges and courts must pursue policies in their decision-making and believe that there is in most areas sufficient agreement over what policies should be thus pursued. Of course it is undeniable that in the American context there are some issues like abortion in which there is simply no consensus, and judges cannot seriously pretend that pure legal principle dictates what the Supreme Court is to do with cases of this kind. But it is still possible to argue for principled decision-making in the sense that consistency, workability, and other accepted values and policies can be drawn on to justify a result. The one thing that I find absurd is that judges should try to pursue policies of their own which are manifestly unacceptable to the majority of the American people, simply because the judges feel a sympathy for the downtrodden poor or any other disadvantaged group. Yet this, as it seems to me, is what the crits want.

Unhappily the disagreements between the crits and more conventional lawyers and teachers are not just political disagreements about ends. The crits are such political radicals that they believe that law schools are the places where the current legal system is entrenched by teaching which accepts its basic premisses. Since they reject the fundamental premisses on which their whole legal system (and society) is founded they regard it as essential to get control of law schools in order to teach a far more critical and radical approach to all law. To them this is even more important than scholarly merit, so tremendous battles take place over new appointments, especially when tenure is in issue. In Harvard, as in most American law schools, a tenured appointment must be confirmed by the whole faculty, and may be blackballed by a large minority. The crits usually vote as a block on tenure cases, sometimes even irrespective of academic merit. In all this they are often very short-sighted because even if, by some chance, they ever secured a majority of the faculty for their views, it is wildly improbable that a law school like Harvard would be allowed to pursue its own way to the critical millennium. Inevitably the alumni, with their immense wealth, and the rest of the university, with a keen eye for the reputation of Harvard as a whole, would act so as to deprive the crits of their triumph.

I saw enough of the disagreements at Harvard between the two blocs to appreciate that the law school was often an unhappy place. Faculty meetings

1 This is a reference to the book that would become PS Atiyah and RS Summers, *Form and Substance in Anglo-American Law: A Comparative Study of Legal Reasoning, Legal Theory, and Legal Institutions* (1987).

often lasted for hours while fundamental disagreements were ventilated. Compromise seemed impossible, and all issues could be converted into basic political disagreements. For example, during the year I was there, the law school was riven by a debate over a proposal that students should be allowed to "pass" when asked a question by the instructor in class, that is they should be able simply to refuse to answer, without any adverse comment being permitted, or any adverse effect on a student's record. The crits favoured the proposal because they thought that some professors exploited their knowledge and power over the class to hold up to ridicule students whose answers were thought poor. But classroom discussion was the very heart of the teaching system at Harvard, and if students felt under no obligation to answer when called upon it was naturally feared that the whole system of instruction would gradually disintegrate. I also thought there was a moral point at issue: students who refused to answer were nevertheless learning from the discussion in which the others took open part, and were thus freeriding on the system.

A little while after my year at Harvard I again became involved in a minor way in the battle between the crits and the rest because I was asked to evaluate a tenure paper by an avowed crit. Obviously this was a confidential exercise and I do not wish to be indiscreet, but it is an open secret that this particular case gave rise to a tremendous battle which generated enormous quantities of paper. Virtually every member of the law faculty wrote comments, often at enormous length on the tenure paper of the candidate, and when the candidate's application was first rejected by the Law School an appeal was made to the University President on the ground that the case had not been judged fairly on academic grounds. The President appointed a committee to look further into the case, and a second time I was asked to evaluate the tenure paper, together, this time, with all the comments of other members of the faculty. It was a desperately unhappy situation. I myself felt that the paper was of adequate academic standing to justify a decision to grant tenure, and I was not happy that the candidate had had an altogether fair appraisal. On the other hand I could well appreciate the hostility roused by the crits and the fear of the other faculty members that they were being threatened with a gradual takeover. In truth this was a rare case in which non-academic considerations, in the narrowest sense, might well have been justifiably considered in my opinion in deciding whether to make an appointment. In England I do not think a university would hesitate to take account of fears that a candidate for such a position might, simply because of his opinions, have a disruptive effect on the life and work of the institution but at Harvard this was not openly accepted. In the event the candidate was refused tenure.

Although I was not sympathetic to the crits and their aims, I did find much of their work on the indeterminacy of law especially interesting. Ever since the work of the so-called Realists in the 1920s there has been a strong vein of scepticism in American legal theory which takes the form of denying the certainty or predictability of law, and insisting that legal principles are so malleable and vague that judges and lawyers can justify almost any result without violation of legal principle. I had in earlier days had a good deal of sympathy with this idea, chiefly because I could not take seriously the assertions of English judges and lawyers that the outcome of difficult legal cases was absolutely determined by legal principles even when it was manifest that there was (for instance) a clash of principles which had to be settled by the judges on some other ground. But for most English lawyers and theorists, Professor Hart's work in the 1960s had adequately explained away these difficulties.[2] Hart had argued that indeterminacy affects only a small number of difficult borderline cases in the law, and that in the overwhelming majority of legal disputes the rules and principles of the law are sufficiently determinate to lead to predictable results. While it might be true that legal principles appeared to be unclear in their application in a much larger proportion of cases and disputes than this, this was to overlook the existence of agreed criteria by which most such principles could in fact be applied.

I had long been aware in a vague sort of way that Hart's approach to this problem of indeterminacy in law did not wholly account for American attitudes, and I was also sure that part of the reason for this was that American law was in practice much more uncertain than English law for a large number of reasons, such as (for instance) the use of juries in civil cases. But neither I nor anybody else had ever systematically explored the differences between the English and the American legal systems from this point of view. However, a few months before I went to Harvard my son Simon, who was then studying for his final exams in law at Nottingham University, came home for a few days' quiet revision. He happened to ask me a few questions about American Legal Realism, and I began to explain to him some of the background differences between the two legal systems which helped to account for the Realist movement, and which explained why its tenets were not such absurd exaggeration in the American context as they often seemed to English theorists who knew little of the practical differences

2 HLA Hart, *The Concept of Law* (1961) 124.

between the two legal systems. As I spoke I suddenly became aware that I had stumbled across a rich field which would justify further research. I went into my study and jotted down a few preliminary ideas. At first I thought of writing an article on the subject, but I knew that I would need an American collaborator to do the subject full justice. It so happened that my good friend Bob Summers was then on a sabbatical in Oxford, and I had invited him to dinner at St John's a few days later. So when we met at this dinner I broached the subject to him and suggested we collaborate on it. He immediately saw its potential, but upgraded the project and suggested we write a book on it. We shook hands on the idea there and then. So it was that when I got to Harvard I had a ready-made research project involving a major comparison of Anglo-American law, and I threw myself into this with energy and enthusiasm. For the next three or four years Bob and I worked on the book, with draft chapters going backwards and forwards, and occasional meetings in Oxford or Cornell when we discussed where we were going. For both of us it proved a very worthwhile project from which we learned a great deal, and there is no more rewarding academic research than that from which one learns oneself. The project also encouraged me to return to America for several further visits over the next few years.

Most of these further visits were made to Duke University in North Carolina which I found a very attractive law school situated in a very attractive part of the United States. Harvard was no doubt intellectually pre-eminent and I am glad I spent one year there; but it was not a place I would have wanted to revisit, and when the Dean sounded me discreetly about the possibility of a permanent appointment I made it clear that I was not interested. Apart from the schisms which rent the Law School there were other aspects of the place I did not care for. The Law School was very large (it had about 1,500 students doing the basic law degree), and the Faculty too remote from the students, and indeed from each other. I got to know a small number of the professors quite well – for the most part these were the ones who regularly lunched in the law school faculty lunchroom – but there were many others who I would gladly have got to know better, but who were rarely to be seen. Many of these had substantial legal practices, like Alan Dershowitz (who was later propelled to fame by his defence of Claus von Bülow) and Larry Tribe who was reputed to have a larger Supreme Court practice in constitutional cases than any other lawyer in the country; others (like Arthur Miller) one saw more often on television than in the Law School, though I have no doubt he was a conscientious teacher and certainly a distinguished scholar.

I did try to get to know a few of my students, and when my youngest son Jeremy spent a few weeks of the Easter vacation from Oxford with us, I introduced him to some members of my torts class who showed him around and looked after him. On one occasion also I took some of them to lunch in a small student-frequented restaurant in Harvard Square where we enjoyed a glass of beer by courtesy of Professor Larry Tribe and the United States Supreme Court, to whom we gave thanks with a toast. This restaurant had been denied a liquor licence by the Massachusetts state authorities under a state law which forbade the sale of alcohol in premises situated within (I think) fifty yards of any church without the consent of the church. The restaurant had challenged the state law as unconstitutional on the ground that it violated the separation of church and state by giving the church a veto over the sale of alcohol in proximity to the church. The case had gone all the way to the United States Supreme Court where Professor Tribe had won a victory for the restaurant owner,[3] and so it came about that we were able to enjoy a glass of beer there.

But these social occasions had been rather few and far between, and neither Christine nor I really enjoyed living in what was essentially a suburb of Boston. Boston itself is, of course, a large city and though many Americans appear to think it is attractive as American cities go, it has its usual share of violence and squalor. It was also a rather frightening place to drive a car, and equally frightening, though for different reasons, to travel by subway. On the other hand I found the Southeastern part of the United States a more relaxing place to visit. North Carolina is a much more rural environment than Massachusetts; it has a much warmer climate; it has virtually no really large metropolitan cities like Boston; and it is possible to live and get about in an altogether more relaxed and less frenetic way. After I had been to visit the Law School at Duke for one or two brief periods during my year at Harvard I began to feel much more at home there than in the Northeastern part of the country. I also liked the Faculty and the Law School at Duke. It was much smaller than Harvard, relations between Faculty and students appeared closer and altogether more friendly, and the Faculty themselves, as often happens in smaller communities, socialised a great deal amongst themselves. So it happened that when I received, even before my year at Harvard was up, an invitation to visit Duke on my next sabbatical, I resolved to accept it as soon as my commitments at Oxford permitted.

3 *Larkin v Grendel's Den, Inc* 459 US 116 (1982).

In the event Christine and I spent the winter semester at Duke in 1985, and very enjoyable it proved. I pursued my research into the Anglo-American book with Bob Summers, and visited California for a week in the mid-semester break where we stayed with my sister. I taught a first-year class on contract which was almost as exciting and stimulating as my torts class at Harvard. Although Duke may not be in the same league as Harvard, it is certainly in the top fifteen or twenty American law schools and the best third of the class were almost as good as the students anywhere.

I began now to learn more of the financial basis of law schools and legal education in America, and to understand how tertiary education operates in a truly market-led system. Much has been said in recent years about the desirability of university education in Britain becoming more responsive to the market, but I do not think many people in Britain really understand what a market-led system actually involves. Legal education in the United States illustrates a genuine free-market system. In the first place most of the leading law schools in the country are private universities which depend on fees for their funding. The fees must therefore be high enough to cover virtually the entire costs of the law school, which in American universities is a self-accounting graduate institution. This does not, however, mean that poorer students are debarred from legal education, because every State has one or more state law schools where the fees are much lower. In any event, most of the private universities have very substantial funds from their endowments with which they are able to assist poorer students with grants or loans. American universities are also so organised that there are many opportunities for the students to earn money by doing part-time work in the university itself, such as by serving in the cafeterias, working in the libraries and so on. In addition the federal government has a substantial programme of loans at low interest rates which are available to graduate students. Of course this means that most law students graduate with a large debt but they regard these debts as investments. They know that the practice of law carries large salaries and that they can expect to earn very substantial amounts immediately on graduating, and thus their debts can be paid off in a few years.

But this is not the only impact of the market on legal education. In the market for legal education, quality and price vary as they do in the market for most commodities. There is an immense range in the quality of the institutions offering legal education in the United States – far greater than the comparable range in England. The top twenty law schools in the country are possibly the best institutions of legal education in the world, though even among themselves the quality differs and there is a pecking order.

(A semi-official pecking order in fact exists, and is compiled annually on the basis of questionnaires completed by law teachers themselves who are asked to rank the top law schools according to the best of their judgement.) Below them there is a further very wide range, starting with medium grade private or state law schools, and descending at the bottom to night-schools which have few pretensions. Now the legal firms who recruit from the law schools recognise the pecking order to a greater or lesser degree, and pay starting salaries commensurate with the quality of the law schools. So students who choose better and more expensive law schools (and who satisfy the entrance requirements) may incur higher debts but can confidently expect to earn higher salaries.

In addition, the better law schools compete vigorously for the best candidates for teaching posts. There is no flat-rate salary structure though no doubt in most law schools there is a sort of basic or average salary which most full professors can expect to earn. Even these salaries must be sufficiently competitive with earnings in private practice to attract good-quality professors and they tend therefore to be far higher than salaries in other university departments such as arts or even mathematics. (So, though we have never actually compared notes, I suspect I have earned more in the United States than my famous mathematical brother!) There is also sufficient flexibility to enable good law schools to offer exceptionally high salaries to attract scholars of international distinction. These scholars are valuable because they enhance the status and prestige of the law school in the market, encourage law firms to pay higher salaries to its graduates, and so encourage students to pay the higher fees necessary to pay these salaries. Of course many of these distinguished scholars are able to supplement their salaries very substantially by extra earnings from private practice, giving papers at conferences, outside lectures and so on. It would not be difficult for an American law professor to add 50 per cent or more to his salary from activities of this kind.

Another aspect of the influence of the market is that law school graduates must be, and are, adequately trained to be of immediate use in the practice of the law, so that they can justify the salaries that are paid to them. In England legal education has never professed to equip graduates for immediate practice and graduates require at least another year's training at the professional colleges, plus a further two years' on-the-job training before they qualify as barristers or solicitors. (To some extent this is compensated for by the fact that they graduate much younger than in America, where students must do four years of "College" education before they start at law school.)

All this means that in American law schools many bread-and-butter subjects are taught and probably fewer students do the less "relevant" courses such as legal theory or legal history. This does not mean that these subjects are not taught, however, and there are many law teachers who specialise in one practical or relevant subject and one more theoretical subject.

Because of all this market orientation, American law schools are far more efficient institutions in the strict financial sense than most English universities, that is to say they are very concerned to produce their products at the lowest financial cost compatible with the quality of their products. But their products consist not only of the education given to their students, but also their research in the form of legal articles and books. Since legal academics are relatively highly paid compared with secretaries and other ancillary staff such as library assistants, research assistants and so forth, no good American law school would tolerate the waste involved in expecting their academic staff to spend time doing things which can be done more cheaply by lower paid employees. The result is that all good American law schools are immensely better off than English law schools in these ancillary ways. No self-respecting American law school, for instance, would be without a considerable staff of library research workers who are qualified in law as well as in librarianship, and whose job is to assist the academic staff in finding material relevant to their research projects. Needless to say, from well-qualified assistants of this kind, the assistance is not just a matter of finding the books on the shelves, but of tracking things down, keeping an eye open for new material, and generally acting as a research assistant. In addition there are often funds available to employ students as part-time research assistants on specific projects, which helps the students to pay their way, as well as helping the academics to be more productive.

By the time I went to Duke in 1985 my academic reputation was such that I was paid a salary at the highest level usually reserved for academics of international reputation. As the pound sterling fell during these few months to its lowest point ever against the dollar (approaching within a whisker of parity for a few days) this proved a particularly profitable sabbatical for me. Indeed, when Duke Law School offered me a permanent appointment I was for a while sorely tempted. The inducements were tremendous. I was offered a salary which was more than three times what I earned at Oxford; what was more I was invited to take part in a special programme which meant that by forgoing my right to formal sabbatical leave I could be assured of doing all my teaching in one semester per year for at least the first three or four years of my appointment, and probably indefinitely. Each semester lasts about four months, and I would have been free to spend the rest of the year in England. I was thus being offered the opportunity to triple my salary for about half the amount of work I did in Oxford. In addition the Law School was prepared to offer work to Christine for the time we spent in America, helping with foreign students, acting as a library assistant and so forth.

We returned to England in the Spring of 1985 mulling this offer over, but tempting though it was, in the end we decided against it, and as it turned out, this proved fortunate. What actually decided me against the offer in the end was the belief that dividing our lives between two homes in this way would prove too unsettling. While I would have had far more time for my private research work I was afraid that the constant shifting backwards and forwards would actually make it hard for me to settle to my work. I was, however, still very attracted to Duke and I spent two further periods teaching short courses there in the Spring of 1987[4] and again 1989.

4 In 1987, Atiyah delivered the Currie Lecture at Duke: PS Atiyah, "Tort Law and the Alternatives: Some Anglo-American Comparisons" (1987) 6 *Duke Law Journal* 1002.

14 Winding Down

By the time I reached my fiftieth birthday in 1981 I was, for the first time in my life, reasonably comfortably off. Of course, all things are relative, and my earnings never came anywhere near those of a successful lawyer in private practice. Indeed, virtually all my working life was spent in a period of low incomes and high taxation. Bringing up four children on an academic salary had never been easy financially, but by this stage my visits to America, and the increase in my earnings from my books and other writings, meant that for the first time my income exceeded our expenditure. My year at Harvard had proved particularly profitable financially though that was partly because I worked hard on giving external lectures and visiting other institutions. On one occasion I had to get up at 6 am to catch a plane to North Carolina where I spent a couple of days teaching at Duke University, including a seminar at 9 pm the same night. In addition I virtually crammed one-and-a-half year's teaching into one academic year. Not only did I do a full year's stint at Harvard, but I flew home for a few weeks over Christmas and gave some lectures at Oxford in January. At the end of the second semester at Harvard I returned in time for the summer term at Oxford and gave my usual courses there while marking Harvard examination papers and seminar papers.

The profits from this year enabled us to fulfil a dream we had long entertained, namely, to buy a modest holiday home in the South of France. While I was at home during the Christmas break, we inserted an advertisement in the *Sunday Times* which produced only a few replies, but of these one seemed to offer exactly what we were looking for. As I only had a few days before I was due to return to Harvard, I flew down to Bordeaux one day, visited the house on offer and flew back the next evening. There were no winter evening flights from Bordeaux to London at that time so I had to fly in a tiny six or eight-seater plane from Bergerac to Paris where I picked up a late British Airways flight to Heathrow. Having left my car at the airport, I got home very late in the evening, just as Christine also arrived, bringing with her Simon who was coming home for a few days' rest from Chester where he was spending a year doing the College of Law's professional legal course. I had brought the inevitable bottle of wine with me, and we all sat up very late, drinking the wine while I described the

Figure 14.1 Photograph and portrait by Juliet Wood. All rights reserved. Image reproduced with permission.

house and we mulled over the offer. We decided to take the plunge, and in the summer of 1983, after my exhausting year at Harvard, and the Oxford summer term was finished, Christine and I drove down to spend our first holiday there.

The house is in a tiny village called Fondefière, some six or seven miles south of Sainte-Foy-la-Grande on the Dordogne. In fact it is situated in the Gironde but is within a few hundred metres of the boundaries with the Dordogne and also the Lot-et-Garonne. We have a small garden surrounded by vineyards and open countryside. The peace and quiet is almost indescribable. Since that year we have spent many months in Fondefière. For the first few years I would take my computer and books down with me, and work steadily, during the mornings, leaving the afternoons to more pleasurable activities. Since I retired in 1988 we have been regularly spending three or four months a year there during the Spring and Summer, and the computer, though still in occasional use, has been rather less in evidence. The house has proved a very rewarding investment.

Not surprisingly the years of my tenure of the Chair of English law at Oxford also saw my career reach a peak in a variety of other ways. A number of academic distinctions and honours came my way. The year after I moved back to Oxford I was elected a Fellow of the British Academy,[1] a distinction I confess to being somewhat ambivalent about. It was an honour I was pleased to receive as an indication of the way my senior colleagues felt about me, but I confess that the more I learnt of the British Academy the less I felt able to take the institution itself very seriously. It was, of course, founded as a learned academy for artists and social scientists who had gradually been shouldered out of the Royal Society as that institution came to be reserved purely for scientists, but it never matched the Royal Society in prestige, and one of the main reasons for this was that it actually had so little to do. In fact almost the sole function of the fellows who were members of Section Eight (the Jurisprudence section) was recommending the election of new fellows. It was thus an honour to be a fellow but little else, and an honour furthermore for which a fellow had to pay a significant annual subscription. Other honours came more cheaply, such as election as a foreign member of the American Law Institute which generously waived its subscription for foreign members, an honorary degree at Warwick University[2] which cost me nothing, and being appointed a Queen's Counsel[3] for which I only had to pay the cost of hiring the eccentric clothes required for the occasion. Another honour – the Swiney Prize – actually brought some economic reward in the form of a silver cup and a cheque for £100.[4] This Prize awarded jointly by the Royal Society for Arts and the Royal College of Physicians was founded in the nineteenth century by an otherwise unknown man named Swiney who had simply handed over £5,000 in notes with instructions to provide a prize for works of general or medical jurisprudence, consisting of a silver cup costing a hundred pounds, and a further hundred pounds in cash. When the Prize was first awarded, a hundred pounds bought a very large quantity of silver, and I gather the earliest cups were pretty large. Unhappily for me the Royal Society of Arts and the Royal College of Physicians discharged their obligations to the donor without regard to the ravages of inflation, and my cup is little bigger than an egg cup.

The summer and autumn of 1986 proved a very exhausting one for me. I had worked hard through the summer, completing the latest draft of the Anglo-American book on which Bob Summers and I had been working

1 Atiyah was elected in 1978: *https://www.thebritishacademy.ac.uk/deceased-fellows/?page=4*.
2 See p 161.
3 Atiyah was appointed in 1989: *London Gazette* (issue 51700, 11 April 1989) 4311.
4 "Annual report of the council" (1984) 132 *Journal of the Royal Society of Arts* 583.

intermittently for four years. In September I flew to Cornell (taking in a visit to North Western University in Chicago to give a Faculty seminar) to spend two weeks with Bob to finalise the text of the book. Every morning we spent two or three hours going through one or two chapters, paragraph by paragraph, sometimes word by word. In the afternoons and evenings we would separately reread the next chapter or two so we could come to our meetings the next morning with our memories refreshed. At the end of the fortnight, we had virtually finished agreeing the amendments needed to finalise the text and also agreed the shape of the final chapter which was yet to be written. After leaving Cornell I flew to Toronto for a couple of days to take part in a commercial law workshop, regularly organised by another old friend, Jacob Ziegel, and then returned to Oxford in time for the autumn term – though not without trauma, as my British Airways flight home from Toronto failed to materialise and in common with a couple of hundred other passengers I was beginning to expect a night on the airport floor, when I luckily got transferred to an Air Canada flight.

I returned to Oxford to finish off the Anglo-American book,[5] to get off to the press the last number of the *Oxford Journal of Legal Studies* for which I was to be responsible, and of course to meet my usual lecturing commitments.

By the end of the term I was all in, and I had a pretty shrewd suspicion that something was amiss. The first day of the vacation I had an appointment with one of my colleagues to discuss some college business after lunch, and though my chest was giving me intense pain, I foolishly kept my appointment. I could scarcely walk to his room, and when I sat down I had to pause to get my breath back. Somehow I kept going, and later walked slowly back to the library to pick up my car. I drove home and telephoned the doctor. He advised me to go direct to the hospital casualty department, where I was immediately admitted. As I had long suspected, my heart was the cause of the trouble. An angiogram confirmed the diagnosis of severe atheroma of the coronary arteries. At first the doctors were optimistic and suggested I would not need more than a few days' good rest, to be followed by treatment with drugs and general care. I was home in a few days, and was able to resume a reasonably normal life. Fortunately I had no teaching in the following term and was able to concentrate on writing and research, which I

5 PS Atiyah and RS Summers, *Form and Substance in Anglo-American Law: A Comparative Study of Legal Reasoning, Legal Theory, and Legal Institutions* (1987).

was able to do mostly at home. I was still able to give the Hamlyn Lectures at Leeds University that winter,[6] and I was even able to go to Duke Law School for a few weeks in the Spring.

But my condition was deteriorating all the time, and eventually the doctors advised a coronary bypass operation. After two further severe attacks in June, it was decided that there was no time to be lost, and I had the operation on 16 June 1987.

The operation was indeed successful, and I made a good recovery, but I never felt the same again. I decided to seek early retirement and eventually I was permitted to retire on medical grounds. For a while I continued to do a certain amount of work, preparing new editions of two of my books,[7] and giving the occasional lecture.[8] I still travelled quite extensively – my visit to Sweden was in 1988 and to Hong Kong in 1988–89. I gave a lecture in Minnesota in 1990 preceded by a splendid vacation in California (where we were literally shaken by a severe earthquake while visiting Yosemite) and Oregon (where we met up with Bob and Dorothy Summers).

But mostly my life has been quieter, though no less enjoyable. Indeed, I often think that, with ambition spent, I actually enjoy my life much more today than I ever did as a younger person with health and energy still unimpaired. My wife and I take great pleasure in the company of our four children, their wives and our grandchildren. We still spend several months a year at our home in France. And I have enjoyed reminiscing over the past and writing this memoir.

A few more honours and distinctions have come my way since I retired. One of the honours which has given me most satisfaction was

6 The book that the lectures yielded, PS Atiyah, *Pragmatism and Theory in English Law* (1987), was described as "a sparkling critique of the pragmatic tradition in English law": D Gibson, "Defending Logic From a Bum Rap: Pragmatism and Theory in English Law" (1987) 17 *Manitoba Law Journal* 227. In the first lecture, Atiyah argued that English lawyers are more pragmatic than their continental colleagues, who are more theoretically inclined. English lawyers, he said, have a "preference for precedent or pragmatism over principle" (at 31). The burden of the second lecture was to pay tribute to the strengths of the English legal system's pragmatism, and Atiyah discussed in this regard innovations such as the *Mareva* injunction and *Anton Piller* order. In the final lecture, Atiyah explored what he regarded as defects in English law's being "neglectful of the need for rationality in the law" (at 103).

7 In fact, in his retirement Atiyah published new editions of his *The Sale of Goods* (PS Atiyah, *The Sale of Goods*, 9th edn (1990)) and *Law and Modern Society* (PS Atiyah, *Law and Modern Society*, 2nd edn (1995)), as well as two further editions of his *Introduction to the Law of Contract* (PS Atiyah, *An Introduction to the Law of Contract*, 4th edn (1989); PS Atiyah, *An Introduction to the Law of Contract*, 5th edn (1995)).

8 This very significantly understates the further research that Atiyah undertook. In particular, he wrote Atiyah, *The Damages Lottery* (1997). See pp xx–xxi.

Figure 14.2 Michael, Patrick and Joseph Atiyah (l-r), Trinity College, Cambridge. Credit: Atiyah family.

the publication in 1991 of a collection of essays (called *Essays for Patrick Atiyah*)[9] by Oxford University Press, written by my former students and colleagues. The dinner at which a superbly bound leather version of the book was presented to me was rather like a *This is Your Life* programme, in that the authors were all friends and colleagues who I had encountered at various stages of my career – William Twining from Khartoum, John Dwyer from Australia, Jan Hellner from Stockholm, my friend and co-author Bob Summers from America, as well as Paul Carrington from Duke (though he was unable to be present at the dinner) and several colleagues, of course, from Oxford itself besides the two editors, Peter Cane and (his wife) Jane Stapleton.

A day or two after this presentation dinner we were dining with the new Master of Trinity at Cambridge.[10] Sir Michael expressed considerable surprise when he heard about the *Festschrift*. "When I was a Delegate at the Oxford University Press", he insisted, quite unconscious of the implication

9 P Cane and J Stapleton (eds), *Essays for Patrick Atiyah* (1991).

10 This was a reference to his elder brother, who had been elected Master of Trinity College, Cambridge in 1990.

of his words, "we made a firm decision only to publish *Festschrifts* for academics of quite exceptional distinction".[11] Thus was I firmly put in my place – but it also led me to choose the title for this autobiography for which I had previously been at a loss.

11 It is entirely possible that Patrick misunderstood the remark, which Michael seemingly intended as a compliment. In an obituary that he wrote regarding Patrick, Michael noted that "[h]is international standing is clear from the *Festschrift* produced in 1991 with contributions from 15 scholars around the world . . .": M Atiyah, "Patrick Selim ATIYAH QC (Hon) FBA" *New College Record 2018* (2019) 89, 90.

PS Atiyah's Published Works

BOOKS

PS Atiyah, *The Sale of Goods* (1957).
PS Atiyah, *An Introduction to the Law of Contract* (1961).
PS Atiyah, *The Sale of Goods*, 2nd edn (1963).
PS Atiyah, *The Sale of Goods*, 3rd edn (1966).
PS Atiyah, *Negligence and Economic Loss* (1967).
PS Atiyah, *Vicarious Liability in the Law of Torts* (1967).
PS Atiyah, *Accidents, Compensation and the Law* (1970).
PS Atiyah, *An Introduction to the Law of Contract*, 2nd edn (1971).
PS Atiyah, *Consideration in Contracts: A Fundamental Restatement* (1971).
PS Atiyah, *The Sale of Goods*, 4th edn (1971).
PS Atiyah, *Accidents, Compensation and the Law*, 2nd edn (1975).
PS Atiyah, *The Sale of Goods*, 5th edn (1975).
PS Atiyah, *From Principles to Pragmatism: Changes in the Function of Judicial Process and the Law* (1978).
PS Atiyah, *The Rise and Fall of the Freedom of Contract* (1979).
PS Atiyah, *Accidents, Compensation and the Law*, 3rd edn (1980).
PS Atiyah, *The Sale of Goods*, 6th edn (1980).
PS Atiyah, *An Introduction to the Law of Contract*, 3rd edn (1981).
PS Atiyah, *Promises, Morals, and Law* (1982).
PS Atiyah, *Law and Modern Society* (1983).
PS Atiyah, *The Sale of Goods*, 7th edn (1985).
PS Atiyah, *Essays on Contract* (1986).
PS Atiyah, *Pragmatism and Theory in English Law* (1987).
PS Atiyah and RS Summers, *Form and Substance in Anglo-American Law: A Comparative Study of Legal Reasoning, Legal Theory, and Legal Institutions* (1987).
PS Atiyah, *An Introduction to the Law of Contract*, 4th edn (1989).
PS Atiyah, *Freedom of Contract and the New Right* (1989).
PS Atiyah, *Essays on Contract*, rev edn (1990).
PS Atiyah, *The Sale of Goods*, 8th edn (1990).
PS Atiyah, *An Introduction to the Law of Contract*, 5th edn (1995).

PS Atiyah, *Law and Modern Society*, 2nd edn (1995).
PS Atiyah, *The Damages Lottery* (1997).
PS Atiyah, *Judgments in England* (1998)

ARTICLES

PS Atiyah, "A Re-Examination of the Jus Tertii in Conversion" (1955) 18 MLR 98.

PS Atiyah, "A New Sale of Goods Bill" [1957] *Sudan Law Journal and Reports* 107.

PS Atiyah, "*Couturier v Hastie* and the Sale of Non-Existent Goods" (1957) 73 LQR 340.

PS Atiyah, "Equitable Relief in Contracts of Hire Purchase" (1958) 5 *Business Law Review* 71.

PS Atiyah, "Injustices and Anomalies in the Law of Hire Purchase" (1958) 5 *Business Law Review* 24.

PS Atiyah, "Legal Education in the Sudan" (1958) 4 *Society of Public Teachers of Law* 137.

PS Atiyah, "Public Benefit in Charities" (1958) 21 MLR 138.

PS Atiyah, "Re Gillingham Bus Disaster Fund" (1958) 74 LQR 489.

PS Atiyah, "Some Problems of Family Law in the Sudan Republic" (1958) 39 *Sudan Notes and Records* 88.

PS Atiyah, "The Infants' Relief Act 1874 – A Reply" (1958) 74 LQR 97.

PS Atiyah, "Recission of a Contract of Sale of Goods" (1959) 22 MLR 76.

PS Atiyah, "The Liability of Infants in Fraud and Restitution" (1959) 22 MLR 273.

PS Atiyah, "Commercial Law in Ghana" (1960) *Journal of Business Law* 430.

PS Atiyah and FAR Bennion, "Mistake in the Construction of Contracts" (1961) 24 MLR 421.

PS Atiyah, "Causation, Contributory Negligence and *Volenti Non Fit Injuria*" (1965) 43 *Canadian Bar Review* 609.

PS Atiyah, "Loss of Buyer's Right to Reject in Contracts of Sale" (1965) 81 LQR 487.

PS Atiyah, "The Transfer of Title by Non-Owners" (1965) *Journal of Business Law* 130.

PS Atiyah, "Thoughts on Company Law Philosophy" (1965) 9 *The Lawyer* 15.

PS Atiyah, "Trespassers on Railway Lines – A Further Note" (1965) 81 LQR 186.

PS Atiyah, "Company Law and Partnership" (1966) *Annual Survey of Commonwealth Law* 443.

PS Atiyah, "Law Reform Committee: Twelfth Report" (1966) 29 MLR 541.

PS Atiyah, "National Insurance Act 1966" (1966) 29 MLR 537.

PS Atiyah, "Company Law and Partnership" (1967) *Annual Survey of Commonwealth Law* 461.

PS Atiyah, "Negligence and Economic Loss" (1967) 83 LQR 248.

PS Atiyah and G Treitel, "Misrepresentation Act 1967" (1967) 30 MLR 369.

PS Atiyah, "Company Law and Partnership" (1968) *Annual Survey of Commonwealth Law* 529.

PS Atiyah, "Conceptualism Triumphant in the Court of Appeal" (1968) 31 MLR 332.

PS Atiyah, "Judicial Techniques and the English Law of Contract" (1968) 2 *Ottawa Law Review* 337.

PS Atiyah, "British Columbia Royal Commission on Automobile Insurance" (1969) 32 MLR 547.

PS Atiyah, "Compensation for Personal Injuries" (1969) 119 *New Law Journal* 653.

PS Atiyah, "Collateral Benefits Again" (1971) 34 MLR 397.

PS Atiyah, "Compensating the Accident Victim" (1971) 43 *The Australian Quarterly* 16.

PS Atiyah, "Compensation for the Injured" (1971) 34 MLR 432.

PS Atiyah, "Loss of Earnings or Earning Capacity?" (1971) 45 *Australian Law Journal* 228.

PS Atiyah, "Misrepresentation, Warranty and Estoppel" (1971) 9 *Alberta Law Review* 347.

PS Atiyah, "Bills of Lading and Privity of Contract" (1972) 46 *Australian Law Journal* 212.

PS Atiyah, "Res Ipsa Loquitur in England and Australia" (1972) 35 MLR 337.

PS Atiyah, "Automobile Insurance . . . For Whose Benefit?" (1973) 7 *Sydney Law Review* 146.

PS Atiyah, "Accident Prevention and Variable Premium Rates for Work-Connected Accidents" – I (1975) 4 *Industrial Law Journal* 1.

PS Atiyah, "Accident Prevention and Variable Premium Rates for Work-Connected Accidents" – II (1975) 4 *Industrial Law Journal* 89.

PS Atiyah, "Contracts, Promises and the Law of Obligations" (1978) 94 LQR 194.

PS Atiyah, "Compensation Orders and Civil Liability" (1979) *Criminal Law Review* 504.

PS Atiyah, "Consumer Protection – Time to Take Stock" (1979) 1 *Liverpool Law Review* 20.

PS Atiyah, "Promises and the Law of Contract" (1979) 88 *Mind* 410.

PS Atiyah, "From Principles to Pragmatism: Changes in the Function of the Judicial Process and the Law" (1980) 65 *Iowa Law Review* 1249.

PS Atiyah, "Judges and Policy" (1980) 15 *Israel Law Review* 346.

PS Atiyah, "Liability for Railway Nuisance in the English Common Law: A Historical Footnote" (1980) 23 *Journal of Law and Economics* 191.

PS Atiyah, "No Fault Compensation: A Question That Will Not Go Away" (1980) 54 *Tulane Law Review* 271.

PS Atiyah, "No-Fault Compensation: A Question That Will Not Go Away" (1980) 694 *Insurance Law Review* 625.

PS Atiyah, "The Theoretical Basis of Contract Law – An English Perspective" (1981) 1 *International Review of Law and Economics* 183.

PS Atiyah, "Lawyers and Rules: Some Anglo-American Comparisons" (1983) 37 *Southwestern Law Journal* 545.

PS Atiyah, "The Legacy of Holmes through English Eyes" (1983) 63 *Boston University Law Review* 341.

PS Atiyah, "Common Law and Statute" (1985) 48 MLR 1.

PS Atiyah, "Contract and Fair Exchange" (1985) 35 *University of Toronto Law Journal* 1.

PS Atiyah, "Economic Loss in the United States" (1985) 5 OJLS 485.

PS Atiyah, "The 'Neutrality' of Contract Law" (1985–86) 35 *King's Counsel* 7.

PS Atiyah, "Medical Malpractice and the Contract/Tort Boundary" (1986) 49 *Law and Contemporary Problems* 287.

PS Atiyah, "The Hannah Blumenthal and Classical Contract Law" (1986) 102 LQR 363.

PS Atiyah, "American Tort Law in Crisis" (1987) 7 OJLS 279.

PS Atiyah, "The Emergence and Rise of Medical Law and Ethics" (1987) 50 MLR 241.

PS Atiyah, "Tort Law and the Alternatives: Some Anglo-American Comparisons" (1987) 6 *Duke Law Journal* 1002.

PS Atiyah, "Shorter Notices" (1990) 105 *English Historical Review* 1071.

PS Atiyah, "Justice and Predictability in the Common Law" (1992) 15 *University of New South Wales Law Journal* 448.

PS Atiyah, "The Right to Break Bad Laws" (1993) 143 *New Law Journal* 66.

PS Atiyah, "Lord Denning's Contribution to Contract Law" (1999) 14 *Denning Law Journal* 1.

CHAPTERS

PS Atiyah, "Misrepresentation", "Personal Incapacity", "Corporations and Unincorporated Associations", "Assignments" and "Death and Bankruptcy" in *Chitty on Contracts*, 23rd edn, vol 1 (1968).

PS Atiyah, "Loan and Interest", "Suretyship" in *Chitty on Contracts*, 23rd edn, vol 2 (1968).

PS Atiyah, "Mistake", "Misrepresentation", "Duress and Undue Influence", "Personal Incapacity", "Corporations and Unincorporated Associations", "Joint Obligations", "Death and Bankruptcy" in *Chitty on Contracts*, 24th edn, vol 1 (1977).

PS Atiyah, "Suretyship" in *Chitty on Contracts*, 24th edn, vol 2 (1977).

PS Atiyah, "What Now?" in DK Allen et al (eds), *Accident Compensation After Pearson* (1979).

PS Atiyah, "Further Random Reflections on the Ontario Proposals and Some Comments on Professor Ziegel's Paper" in JS Ziegel (ed), *Workshop on Commercial and Consumer Law* (1981).

PS Atiyah, "Recent Judicial Development in Private Law" in DM da Costa (ed), *The Cambridge Lectures: Selected Papers based upon Lectures Delivered at the Cambridge Conference of the Canadian Institute for Advanced Legal Studies* (1981).

PS Atiyah, "Reflections on some Differences in the Common-Law Tradition Between the Commonwealth and the United States" in JS Ziegel (ed), *Workshop on Commercial and Consumer Law* (1981).

PS Atiyah, "A Legal Perspective on Recent Contributions to the Valuation of Life" in MW Jones-Lee (ed), *The Value of Life and Safety: Proceedings of a Conference Held by the Geneva Association* (1982).

PS Atiyah, "Mistake", "Misrepresentation", "Duress and Undue Influence", "Personal Incapacity" and "Joint Obligations" in *Chitty on Contracts*, 25th edn, vol 1 (1983).

PS Atiyah, "Suretyship" in *Chitty on Contracts*, 25th edn, vol 2 (1983).

PS Atiyah, "Contract and Tort" in JL Jowell and JPWB McAuslan (eds), *Lord Denning: The Judge and the Law* (1984).

PS Atiyah, "Form and Substance in Legal Reasoning: The Case of Contract" in N MacCormick and P Birks (eds), *The Legal Mind: Essays for Tony Honoré* (1986).

PS Atiyah, "Judicial-Legislative Relations in England" in RA Katzmann (ed), *Judges and Legislators: Toward Institutional Comity* (1988).

PS Atiyah, "Judgments in England" in *La sentenza in Europa: Metodo, Tecnica e Stile: Atti del Convegno Internazionale per L'inaugurazione Della Nuova Sede Della Facolta, Ferrara* (1988).

PS Atiyah, "The Binding Nature of Contractual Obligations" in D Harris and D Tallon (eds), *Contract Law Today: Anglo-French Comparisons* (1989).

PS Atiyah, "An Autobiographical Fragment" in GP Wilson (ed), *Frontiers of Legal Scholarship* (1995).

PS Atiyah, "Personal Injuries in The Twenty-First Century: Thinking the Unthinkable" in P Birks (ed), *Wrongs and Remedies in the Twenty-First Century* (1996).

PS Atiyah, "Chadwick, Edwin (1800–1890)" in *The New Palgrave Dictionary of Economics*, 3rd edn (2018).

PS Atiyah, "Common Law" in *The New Palgrave Dictionary of Economics*, 3rd edn (2018).

NOTES

PS Atiyah, "The Relation between the Provocation and the Resentment" (1954) 17 MLR 459.

PS Atiyah, "Charitable Trusts (Validation) Act 1954" (1955) 18 MLR 152.

PS Atiyah, "Maintenance and Common Interest" (1955) 18 MLR 292.

PS Atiyah, "The Aged, Impotent and Poor" (1955) 18 MLR 76.

PS Atiyah, "*Abdel Gadir El Baloula v El Saggay Agricultural Scheme*" [1956] *Sudan Law Journal and Reports* 95.

PS Atiyah, "*Hassan Khalil Suleiman v El A'Gig Ali and Christos Simos v Mohd. Ali Ahmed*" [1956] *Sudan Law Journal and Reports* 94.

PS Atiyah, "*Roughdi Boutros v Christos Simos*" [1956] *Sudan Law Journal and Reports* 93.

PS Atiyah, "*Sid Ahmed Mohamed v Sudan Mercantile Co*" [1956] *Sudan Law Journal and Reports* 55.

PS Atiyah, "*Sudan Government v Bakheit Adam Mohammed* and the recovery of lost and stolen property ordinance, 1924" [1956] *Sudan Law Journal and Reports* 47.

PS Atiyah, "*Sudan Government v Hirachand Jeraj Shah*" [1956] *Sudan Law Journal and Reports* 97.

PS Atiyah, "The Right to Reject Goods for Breach of Condition" (1956) 19 MLR 315.

PS Atiyah, "*Baker v Willoughby*: An Addendum" (1969) 85 LQR 475.

PS Atiyah, "Restraint of Trade – Contract – Restrainable by Injunction at Suit of Third Party" (1972) 46 *Australian Law Journal* 235.

PS Atiyah, "*Watt v Rama*. Negligence, Unborn Infants and the Duty of Care" (1972) 10 *University of Western Australia Law Review* 159.

PS Atiyah, "Consideration and Estoppel: The Thawing of the Ice" (1975) 38 MLR 65.

PS Atiyah. "Conceptual Construction" (1976) 39 MLR 335.

PS Atiyah, "When is an Enforceable Agreement Not a Contract? Answer: When it is an Equity" (1976) 92 LQR 174.

PS Atiyah, "Economic Duress and the 'Overborne Will' Theory" (1982) 98 LQR 197.

PS Atiyah, "Duress and the Overborne Will Again" (1983) 99 LQR 353.

BOOK REVIEWS

PS Atiyah, "Book review: *Personal Property* by JC Vaines" (1955) 18 MLR 523.

PS Atiyah, "Book review: *Hire Purchase Law and Practice* by RM Goode" (1962) 7 *Journal of the Society of Public Teachers of Law (NZ)* 95.

PS Atiyah, "Book review: *The Law of Quasi-Contract* by S J Stoljar" (1966) 29 MLR 347.

PS Atiyah, "Book review: *Diplomatic Conference on the Unification of Law Governing the International Sale of Goods, The Hague 2–25 April 1964*" (1967) 16 *International and Comparative Law Quarterly* 839.

PS Atiyah, "Book review: *Studies in Canadian Tort Law* by A Linden" (1969) 10 *Journal of the Society of Public Teachers of Law* 232.

PS Atiyah, "Book review: *The Costs of Accidents* by G Calabresi" (1970) 44 *Australian Law Journal* 297.

PS Atiyah, "Book review: *Automobile Insurance . . . For Whose Benefit?* By State of New York Insurance Department" (1973) 7 *Sydney Law Review* 146.

PS Atiyah, "Book review: *Consideration Reconsidered* by KCT Sutton" (1976) 92 LQR 625.

PS Atiyah, "Book review: *Ending Insult to Injury* by J O'Connell" (1976) 45 *University of Cincinnati Law Review* 340.

PS Atiyah, "Book review: *Products Liability* by SM Waddams" (1976) 26 *University of Toronto Law Journal* 118.

PS Atiyah, "Book review: *The Death of Contract* by G Gilmore" (1977) 71 *American Political Science Review* 636.

PS Atiyah, "Book review: *Legal Reasoning and Legal Theory* by N MacCormick" (1979) 42 MLR 471.

PS Atiyah, "Book review: *The Law of Restitution,* 2nd edn by R Goff and G Jones" (1979) 42 MLR 727.

PS Atiyah, "Book review: *Anson's Law of Contract*, 25th edn by AG Guest" (1981) 1 LS 100.

PS Atiyah, "Book review: *Contract as Promise: A Theory of Contractual Obligation* by C Fried" (1981) 95 *Harvard Law Review* 509.

PS Atiyah, "Book review: *Studies in Contract Law* (ed), BJ Reiter and J Swan" (1981) 26 *McGill Law Journal* 408.

PS Atiyah, "Book review: *Contract as Promise: A Theory of Contractual Obligation* by C Fried" (1983) 81 *Michigan Law Review* 904.

PS Atiyah, "Book review: *Law and Inflation* by K Rosenn" (1983) 132 *University of Pennsylvania Law Review* 187.

PS Atiyah, "Book review: *The Principles of Social Order* by LL Fuller" [1983] *Duke Law Journal* 669.

PS Atiyah, "Comments on 'The Modern Role of Contract' by S Waddams" (1983) 8 *Canadian Business Law Journal* 10.

PS Atiyah, "Book review: *Policy Arguments in Judicial Decisions* by J Bell" (1985) 33 *American Journal of Comparative Law* 342.

CORRESPONDENCE

PS Atiyah (1955) 18 MLR 595.

PS Atiyah (1987) 50 MLR 267.

REPORTS

PS Atiyah, *A Review of Insurance in Relation to Road Safety* (1973).

Atiyah Family Tree

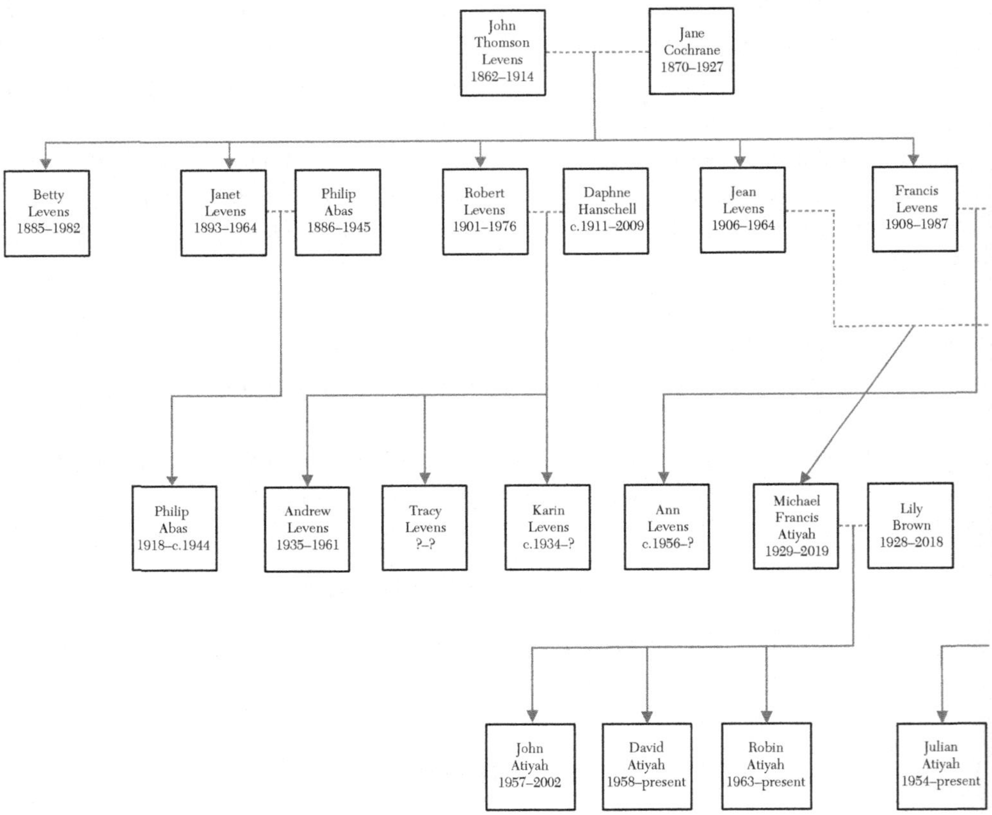

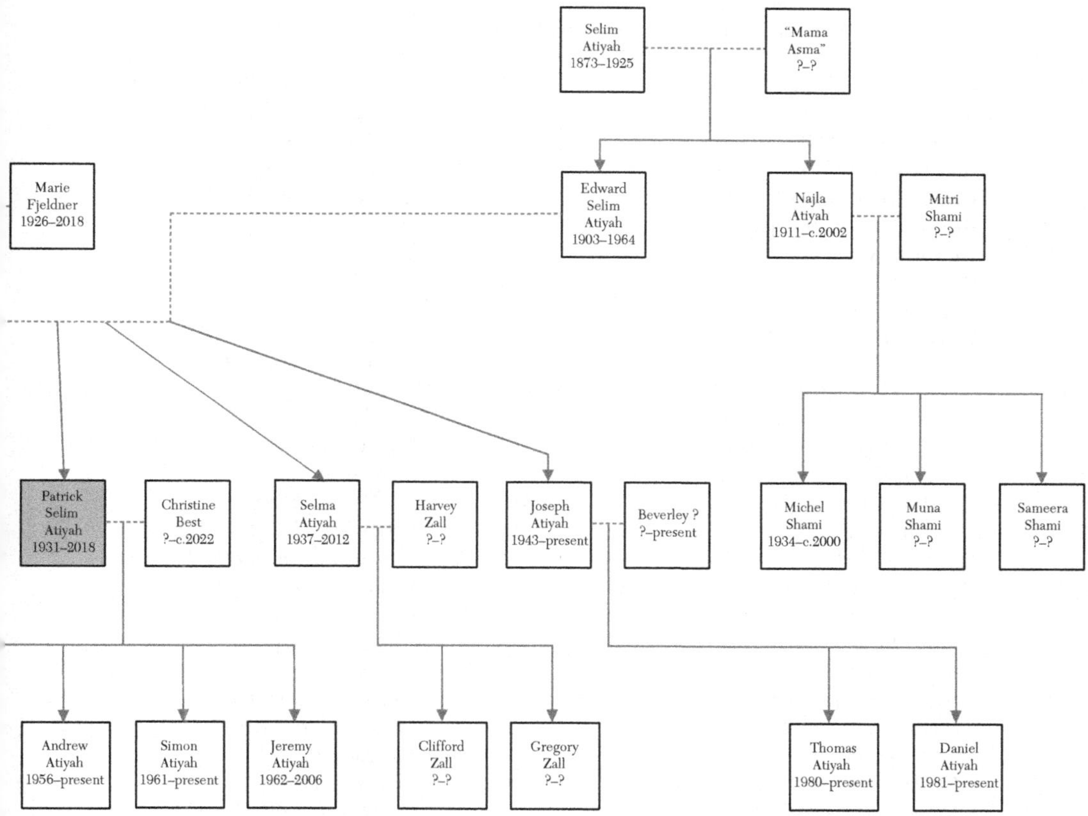

Selim Atiyah 1873–1925
"Mama Asma" ?–?
Marie Fjeldner 1926–2018
Edward Selim Atiyah 1903–1964
Najla Atiyah 1911–c.2002
Mitri Shami ?–?
Patrick Selim Atiyah 1931–2018
Christine Best ?–c.2022
Selma Atiyah 1937–2012
Harvey Zall ?–?
Joseph Atiyah 1943–present
Beverley ? ?–present
Michel Shami 1934–c.2000
Muna Shami ?–?
Sameera Shami ?–?
Andrew Atiyah 1956–present
Simon Atiyah 1961–present
Jeremy Atiyah 1962–2006
Clifford Zall ?–?
Gregory Zall ?–?
Thomas Atiyah 1980–present
Daniel Atiyah 1981–present

Index

Illustrations are indicated by page numbers in *italics*.
Notes are indicated by page number and the letter 'n' (e.g. 80n).

EU Authorised Representative:
Easy Access System Europe Mustamäe tee 50, 10621 Tallinn, Estonia
gpsr.requests@easproject.com

Printed and bound by CPI Group (UK) Ltd, Croydon, CR0 4YY
14/09/2026
02216780-0005